Trade Policy Reforms in Latin America

Trade Policy Reforms in Latin America

Multilateral Rules and Domestic Institutions

Edited by

Miguel F. Lengyel
Facultad Latinoamericana de Ciencias Sociales
Argentina

and

Vivianne Ventura-Dias
United Nations Economic Commission for Latin America
and the Caribbean Chile

palgrave
macmillan

First published 2004 by
PALGRAVE MACMILLAN
Houndmills, Basingstoke, Hampshire RG21 6XS and
175 Fifth Avenue, New York, N.Y. 10010
Companies and representatives throughout the world

PALGRAVE MACMILLAN is the global academic imprint of the Palgrave Macmillan division of St. Martin's Press, LLC and of Palgrave Macmillan Ltd. Macmillan® is a registered trademark in the United States, United Kingdom and other countries. Palgrave is a registered trademark in the European Union and other countries.

ISBN 0–333–98724–1

This book is printed on paper suitable for recycling and made from fully managed and sustained forest sources.

A catalogue record for this book is available from the British Library.

Library of Congress Cataloging-in-Publication Data
Trade policy reforms in Latin America : multilateral rules and domestic institutions / edited by Miguel F. Lengyel and Vivianne Ventura-Dias.
p. cm.
Includes bibliographical references (p.) and index.
ISBN 0–333–98724–1 (cloth)
1. Latin America—Commercial policy. 2. Free trade—Latin America.
I. Lengyel, Miguel. II. Ventura-Dias, Vivianne.

HF1480.5.T72 2003
382′.3′098—dc21 2003051974

10 9 8 7 6 5 4 3 2 1
13 12 11 10 09 08 07 06 05 04

Printed and bound in Great Britain by
Antony Rowe Ltd, Chippenham and Eastbourne

Contents

List of Tables and Figures

Tables

Figures

Acknowledgements

The country studies that integrate this book started as a joint enterprise of the Latin American Trade Network (LATN), the Economic Commission for Latin America and the Caribbean (ECLAC), and the United Nations Conference on Trade and Development (UNCTAD), two United Nations agencies. Ambassador Rubens Ricupero, Secretary-General of UNCTAD, provided the inspiration for the first studies. The project was engendered in several meetings conducted in 1997. The first was organized by UNCTAD, in March, in Geneva, with the purpose of critically evaluating the results of the Uruguay Round from a development perspective. Soon after, in April, a brainstorming session on 'Emerging Issues in International Trade Relations' was organized in Buenos Aires, by the Area of International Relations of FLACSO (Latin American Faculty of Social Sciences)-Argentina with the support of the Canadian International Development Research Centre (IDRC). There, not just the national studies but the LATN project began to take shape. Finally, in July, ECLAC convened a regional seminar on trade policy, in Santiago, to discuss the interplay between unilateral and negotiated trade liberalization in Latin America.

The terms of reference for the first national studies (Argentina, Brazil, Chile and Uruguay) were drafted by ECLAC and UNCTAD at the end of 1997, and they addressed two sets of questions: (i) the adjustment of Latin American economies, trade policies and institutions to the new obligations derived from the Uruguay Round Agreements (URAs); and (ii) the process of formulating and advancing a pro-active trade agenda that could redress the asymmetries of rights and obligations in the WTO.[1] The four country studies were included in the first cycle of studies developed by LATN with the support of IDRC. The project was later expanded to include Colombia, Mexico, Peru and Venezuela. Therefore, the focus of research was middle-income Latin American exporters.

A preliminary version of the first four studies was presented in August 1998 to Latin American policy-makers and academics in Santiago, and later, in September, to trade analysts and development agencies in a follow-up of the UNCTAD meeting in Geneva. Together with the other studies, they were subsequently addressed in the first coordinating meeting of LATN in Geneva, in which substantive issues of the trade agenda were also discussed through presentations made by the network members. Two other meetings of LATN took place in Buenos Aires (1999) and Washington (2000) for which the studies were revised and updated. The methodology of work that the LATN project adopted was extremely enriching by allowing cross-fertilization between country analysis and issue-oriented studies. While the former constitute the chapters of this book, the issue-analysis was the point of entry of the companion edited by Diana Tussie, *Trade Negotiations in Latin America: Problems and Prospects*.

As any collective academic endeavor, this book is the product of the active involvement of many people in the various stages of the intellectual process through which conceptual approaches and methodology are generated, in particular the members of LATN and our colleagues at FLACSO/Argentina and ECLAC/Chile. We are especially grateful to Diana Tussie for constantly keeping us focused on the many tasks that have been necessary in creating a book from these country studies, notwithstanding our daily duties. We also want to acknowledge the contribution of Brita Siepker, Roberto Muñoz and Judith Evans in the preliminary stages of the translation and editing of some of the chapters.

A special word of thanks goes to our spouses, who accepted with patience and a good sense of humor that the preparation of this book would intrude into our private lives.

MIGUEL F. LENGYEL
VIVIANNE VENTURA-DIAS

Note

1. The terms of reference were drafted by Vivianne Ventura Dias (ECLAC) in consultation with Harmon Thomas (UNCTAD).

List of Abbreviations

AA	Agriculture Agreement of the WTO
ACAP	Andean Common Automotive Policy
ACN	Andean Community of Nations
AD	Anti-dumping
ADEX	Peruvian Association of Exporters
AFTA	Andean Free Trade Agreement
ALADI	Asociación Latinoamericana de Integración (Latin American Integration Association)
ALTEX	Mexican Program for Export-Intensive Industries
AMIA	Mexican Association of Automotive Manufacturers
AMS	Aggregate Measure of Support
ANIT	Mexican National Association of the Transformation Industry
APEC	Asian Pacific Economic Cooperation
APEX	Agency for Export Promotion
ASEAN	Association of South East Asian Nations
ASCM	Agreement on Subsidies and Countervailing Measures of the WTO
ASEXMA	Chilean Association of Manufacturing Exporters
ATC	Agreement on Textiles and Clothing of the WTO
ATPA	Andean Trade Preference Act
BANCOMEXT	Mexican National Foreign Trade Bank
BNDES	Brazilian National Bank of Economic and Social Development
CAC	Codex Alimentarius Commission
CACM	Central American Common Market
CANACINTRA	Mexican National Industrial Transformation Chamber
CANAME	Mexican National Chamber of Electric Manufactures
CANIETI	Mexican National Chamber of the Electronics, Telecommunications and Computer Industries
CARICOM	Caribbean Common Market
CASS	Venezuelan Anti-dumping and Subsidies Commission
CCE	Mexican Business Coordinating Council
CCS	Chilean Chamber of Commerce of Santiago
CERT	Certificate of Tax Reimbursement
CES	Chilean Committee of Exporters in Services

CET	Common External Tariff
CFC	Mexican Federal Competition Commission
CKD	Completely Knocked Down
CNI	Brazilian National Manufacturing Association
COECE	Mexican Foreign Trade Business Organizations Coordinating Council
COMEX	Peruvian Society of Foreign Trade
COMPEX	Mexican Mixed Commission for Export Promotion
CONASUPO	Mexican National Subsidized Staple Products Company
CONCAMIN	Mexican Industrial Chambers Confederation
CORFO	Chilean Industrial Promotion Agency
CPC	Chilean Confederation of Production and Commerce
CTM	Mexican Workers Confederation
CUT	Brazilian Unique Central of Workers
CVD	Countervailing Duty
DIRECON	Chilean General Directorate of International Economic Relations
DSB	Dispute Settlement Body
DSU	Dispute Settlement Understanding of the WTO
ECA	Economic Complementarity Agreement
ECLAC	Economic Commission for Latin America and the Caribbean
EFTA	European Free Trade Association
EPZ	Export Processing Zone
ERP	Effective Rates of Protection
EU	European Union
FDI	Foreign Direct Investment
FOBAPROA	Mexican Savings Protection Fund
FTA	Free Trade Agreement
FTAA	Free Trade Area of the Americas
G-3	Group of Three (Mexico, Colombia and Venezuela)
GATS	General Agreement on Trade in Services
GATT	General Agreement on Tariffs and Trade
GDP	Gross Domestic Product
GSP	Generalized System of Preferences
HACCP	Hazard Analysis Critical Control Points
IADB	Inter-American Development Bank
ILO	International Labor Organization
IMF	International Monetary Fund
INDECOPI	Peruvian Institute for the Defense of Competition and International Trade Negotiations

IPR	Intellectual Property Rights
ISI	Import-substituting Industrialization
ISO	International Standardization Organization
ITA	WTO Ministerial Declaration on Trade in Information Technology Products
ITC	International Trade Center
ITO	International Trade Organization
LAIA	Latin American Integration Association
LATN	Latin American Trade Network
LICONSA	Mexican CONASUPO Industrialized Milk
LDC	Less Developed Country
MEF	Peruvian Ministry of Economics and Finance
MEP	Minimum Export Price
MERCOEX	External Trade Council of Mercosur
MERCOSUR	Southern Cone Common Market
MFA	Multi-fiber Agreement of the WTO
MFN	Most-Favored Nation
MFR	Ministry of Foreign Relations
MIC	Venezuelan Ministry of Industry and Trade
MINCOMEX	Colombian Foreign Trade Ministry
MITINCI	Peruvian Ministry of Industry, Tourism, Integration and Comercio Internacional
NAFTA	North American Free Trade Agreement
NGO	Non-Governmental Organization
NTB	Non-Tariff Barrier
OECD	Organization for Economic Cooperation and Development
PECC	Pacific Economic Cooperation Council
PEMEX	Mexican Petroleum Company
PITEX	Mexican Temporary Imports Program
PRI	Mexican Institutional Revolutionary Party
PROCAMPO	Mexican Direct Support for the Countryside Program
PROCHILE	Chilean Export Promotion Directorate
PROMPEX	Peruvian Commission for the Promotion of Exports
PROSEC	Mexican Sectoral Promotion Programs
QR	Quantitative Restriction
RMALC	Mexican Trade Action Network
S&D	Special and Differential Treatment
SAFP	Andean Price Band System
SECOFI	Mexican Ministry of Trade and Industrial Development
SIEX	Special Import–Export Program

SITC	United Nations Code of Product Classification
SME	Small and Medium Enterprise
SNA	Chilean National Agricultural Society
SOFOFA	Chilean Society of Industrial Promotion
SONAMI	Chilean National Mining Society
SPS	Sanitary and Phytosanitary Measures
TELMEX	Mexican Telephone Company
TBT	Technical Barriers to Trade
TIC	ACN-US Bilateral Trade and Investment Council
TNC	Transnational Corporation
TPA	Trade Promotion Authority of the US Congress
TPR	Trade Policy Review of the WTO
TRIMs	Agreement on Trade-Related Investment Measures of the WTO
TRIPs	Agreement on Trade-Related Aspects of Intellectual Property Rights (WTO)
UNCTAD	United Nations Conference on Trade and Development
UNDP	United Nations Development Programme
UPOV	International Union for the Protection of New Vegetable
UR	Uruguay Round
URA	Uruguay Round Agreement
USTR	United States Trade Representative
VAT	Value-Added Tax
VER	Voluntary Export Restraint
WIPO	World Intellectual Property Organization
WTO	World Trade Organization

Notes on the Contributors

Gabriel Casaburi holds a PhD in Political Economy from Yale University. Gabriel is a Senior Researcher in the Institute of Argentina and Latin American Reality Studies (IERAL) at the Fundación Mediterránea. He is a professor at the University Torcuato Di Tella and FLACSO Argentina.

Juan José Echavarría holds a PhD in Economics from Oxford University. Juan José is Executive Director of Fedesarrollo (The Foundation for Higher Education and Development) and teaches macroeconomics and international trade at Oxford University, Universidad de los Andes, Universidad Nacional, Universidad Externado and Universidad Javeriana.

Alan Fairlie Reynoso holds a Master's degree in Economics from the Torcuato di Tella Institute in Buenos Aires. Alan is a professor of International Economics at the Pontificia Universidad Católica de Perú (PUCP).

Cristina Gamboa is a research assistant at Fedesarrollo (The Foundation for Higher Education and Development) in Bogotá.

Miguel F. Lengyel is a PhD candidate in Political Science at the Massachusetts Institute of Technology. Miguel is an Associate Researcher in the Program on International Economic Institutions at FLACSO Argentina, and Co-Director of the Latin American Trade Network (LATN). He teaches international trade at FLACSO Argentina and the Universidad de Buenos Aires.

Pedro da Motta Veiga holds a Doctorate in Economics from the School of Higher Studies in Social Sciences from the Paris University. Pedro is Director of EcoStrat Consultants and adviser to the National Confederation of Industries (CNI) from Brazil.

Antonio Ortiz Mena holds a PhD in Political Science from the University of California (San Diego). Antonio is a professor and researcher at the Center for Economic Research and Teaching (CIDE) from Mexico.

Cintia Quiliconi holds a master's degree in International Relations from FLACSO Argentina. Cintia is a researcher in the Program on International Economic Institutions at FLACSO Argentina and a researcher and project assistant to the Latin American Trade Network (LATN).

Verónica Silva holds a master's degree in International Relations from the Universidad de Chile. Verónica is Economic Affairs Officer at the International Trade and Integration Division of the UN Economic Commission for Latin America and the Caribbean (ECLAC) in Santiago, Chile.

Diana Tussie received a PhD in International Relations and Economics from the London School of Economics. Diana is Director of the Latin American Trade Network (LATN) and Director of the Research Program on International Economic Institutions of FLACSO Argentina.

Marcel Vaillant is a PhD candidate in Economics at the University of Antwerpen (UFSIA) in Belgium. Marcel is a researcher and professor in the Department of Economics of the University of Uruguay.

Vivianne Ventura-Dias holds a PhD in Agricultural and Natural Resource Economics from the University of California (Berkeley). Vivianne is Director of the International Trade and Integration Division of the UN Economic Commission for Latin America and the Caribbean (ECLAC) in Santiago, Chile.

1

Introduction: Juggling with WTO Rules in Latin America

Vivianne Ventura-Dias

Introduction

Latin American countries, as small exporters not able to affect their terms of trade, should open their markets regardless of what others states do. That they have rarely done so have puzzled trade economists. In the 1980s, when finally Latin American governments adopted a trade regime based on low average tariffs, economists were still questioning why had them for so long stubbornly eluded the full benefits of free trade. Trade policy analysts have concluded, however, that the vast gaps between the normative prescriptions of the basic model of trade theory and the reality of domestic and international trade policies pointed to the inadequacy of these market-based and rules-absent trade models for describing the economic policy process. Markets do not operate in a vacuum of rules and power. Equally, markets and governments are inescapable and mutually supportive components of the economic reality, albeit they are both imperfect systems.[1] As the literature on institutions recognizes, all participants in the trade policy-making process face several types of transaction costs in the form of contracting problems, asymmetric information, vulnerability to opportunism, and the need for credible commitments to policy rules.[2] Participants in the economic policy-making process adopt strategic behavior in a context of interdependent decisions to deal with these costs Schelling, 1960; Dixit, 1996). The inclusion of transaction costs in the conceptual framework integrated politics into the economic analysis of trade policy.

It was through the interplay of power and rules that governments accepted to reverse the protectionist behavior that had become prevalent in the interwar period. Enlightened mercantilism and fair trade presided over the liberalization of trade under the General Agreement on Tariffs and Trade (GATT). Distributive conflicts among individual participants were restrained by a common interest in reaching mutually advantageous results. Besides, the skewed power distribution among states, which was reflected in the production and trade specialization of the post-war period, limited trade liberalization mostly to goods traded among industrial countries, and to non-agricultural goods, with additional exceptions affecting trade in textiles and apparel (Tussie, 1987). Developing countries were not to be blamed for showing little interest in the multilateral trading system in the first years of the GATT existence. They had few positive incentives to participate. Latin American export reports, in particular, faced no market access problems since – with exception of temperate agricultural products – they were concentrated in commodities that did not compete directly with domestic products in importing markets.[3]

The convergence of production and trade structures between countries that occurred in the 1970s increased their interdependence and challenged the effectiveness of established institutions and rules. The trade organization that emerged from the last round of trade negotiations of the GATT was endowed with a broad mandate that expanded the reach of trade policy to include any trade-related measure that might inhibit the contestability of domestic markets by foreign enterprises. Movements of goods, services, capital, and knowledge assets became closely associated as complementary forms through which enterprises may contest a market (Hoekman, 1995).[4] At the same time, GATT membership was also increasing in number and in diversity, reaching more than 130 countries when the World Trade Organization (WTO) became operational in January 1995. The result has been a trend away from the accommodating nature of the GATT toward increasing legalization of the WTO. In other words, it has been a move towards imposing international legal constraints on governments (Goldstein *et al.*, 2000). A greater precision of the GATT rules, binding obligations on all states, with few exceptions, and an effective mechanism for dispute settlement raise the costs of non-compliance and reduce the chances of opportunistic behavior (Goldstein and Martin, 2000). On the other hand, tightly binding international rules concurrently with the uncertainty of volatile international markets impose a dilemma to governments. They may face the choice between meeting multilateral obligations or providing effective solutions to pressing domestic demands. Therefore, tightly binding obligations could repeat the mistakes of the period between the two World wars that the founding fathers of the stillborn International Trade Organization (ITO) were trying to avoid (Brown, 1950).

As the Uruguay Round unfolded, development analysts became deeply concerned with the burden of the new rules to the formulation and execution of developing countries' economic policies. This book is the result of a research project that emerged out of questions related to the institutional capacity of Latin American countries to adjust to the new trading rules in a context of great interdependence and reduced national autonomy. The set of country studies provides insights into the various ways through which Latin American governments have coped with the new international context of power and rules while attending to matters of national interest. Over the past decade, economic agents, public policy-makers, and the civil society in these countries have been assimilating the impact of new international obligations stemming from multilateral trade agreements, but also from a web of bilateral and subregional preferential liberalization initiatives that were implemented in Latin America. In fact, regional liberalization agreements such as the North American Free Trade Agreement (NAFTA) and the Southern Common Market (Mercosur) had stronger and more concrete consequences on associate countries than the remote WTO obligations (see Ortiz Mena, Chapter 3; Tussie *et al.*, Chapter 4; Motta Veiga and Ventura-Dias, Chapter 5 and Vaillant and Ventura-Dias, Chapter 6). At the end of 1994, led by the United States and in parallel to the implementation of the WTO, Canada, Latin American and Caribbean countries, except Cuba, and Canada, launched the preparatory work for the creation of a Free Trade Area of the Americas (FTAA). All these institutional changes were a drop in the sea of deep structural transformations in Latin American countries to which national economies, domestic enterprises, public agencies, and society had to accommodate their practices.

Accordingly, the subject of the book is the interaction between the domestic institutions that influence the formulation and execution of trade policy in Latin America and the political economy of international relations. The traditional literature on international relations refers to the interface between international bargaining and domestic politics as a two-level game. At the national level, domestic groups express their views, and try to persuade governments to adopt favorable policies. Central executives have an important role in mediating domestic and international pressures. At the international level, national governments seek to maximize their own ability to satisfy domestic pressures, and try to reduce the detrimental effects of foreign developments (Putnam, 1988;

Evans *et al.*, 1993). At the domestic level, formal institutions enable national preference formation, and the behavior of decision-makers can be sanctioned by the civil society through the electoral process. The dual-game is a useful 'metaphor' for the bargaining of governments in two negotiating tables, even though the characteristics of Latin American institutions make it more difficult to convert the metaphor in formal models. The subordinated role of Latin American countries in the international system together with weak or highly ineffective political and legal institutions, and an opaque economic decision-making process suggest that more information should be provided on the domestic trade policy-making process in Latin America before a model of reciprocal causation could be devised.

Likewise, the studies viewed the obligations under the Uruguay Round Agreements (URAs) as exogenous data to which domestic trade policies, legislation, decision-making process, regulations, etc. had to adjust. Project participants started with a common perception that during the UR negotiations Latin American countries were not adequately trained, and the defensive negotiating agenda poorly prepared them for the outcome of the negotiations. Despite the diversity of development situations, selected Latin American countries were under the same pressures and challenges posed by common external problems, the rules of the WTO and the definition of the bargaining strategy for the new round of trade negotiations at the end of the 1990s. The purpose of the studies was, therefore, to describe the adjustment efforts by public institutions and non-governmental actors, and also to show that notwithstanding the new strict international rules there remained several degrees of freedom for domestic state action, that were to same extent used.

In effect, greater pragmatism prevailed in the way trade liberalization was carried out than implied by trade reform literature. Governments retained considerable space for discretionary actions. The new wave of regionalism that emerged together with the deepening of multilateral rules is a good illustration of how governments tried to manage the overpowering pressure for greater openness of domestic markets and for convergence of rules and institutions. The adoption of other governance structures to organize and enforce trade liberalization agreements was facilitated by the endorsement of a multi-track trade policy by the US, and by the deepening of the European regional integration process. In addition, there was a pervasive use of trade remedies as a new contingent protection mechanism (see Tussie *et al.*, Chapter 4).

The country studies stress some central aspects of national preference formation in post-authoritarian regimes. The political economy literature based on interest group models has focused on distributional coalitions formed by three major interest-motivated groups, consumers, and exporting and import-competing producers.[5] Producers more than consumers can avoid collective action problems, since the former may provide incentives leading individual members to overcome the Prisoner's Dilemma and behave as a consistent interest group with common interests. These categories are useful to describe how individuals and groups cooperate in promoting or resisting trade liberalization when trade is limited to trade in goods and tariff is the basic protection instrument. It does not adequately interpret the new context of trade policy that includes mostly regulatory standards, transborder actors' interests and the establishment of institutions to protect and enforce property rights. Coalitions of domestic interests are many times initiated and promoted by non-elected public bureaucracies that play an important autonomous role (see Motta Veiga and Ventura-Dias, Chapter 5 and Ortiz Mena, Chapter 3). Due to the nature of the Latin American state, public officials have more latitude to follow their own policy preferences without social pressures for accountability that are customary in modern democracies. The studies show, however, that there has been more transparency and information diffusion in the recent years. Other actors, such as Congress, organized labor, and civil society are just beginning to acquire more prominence, although their access to information and training differ greatly among countries (see Silva, Chapter 2, and Motta Veiga and Ventura-Dias, Chapter 5).

The studies indicated that in some cases, the construction of more fluid channels between public officials and non-governmental actors was concomitant with the democratization process, with broad impact on trade policy-making and trade negotiations (see Tussie *et al.*, Chapter 4). In many ways, economic policies and the process of economic policy-making were changing while democratic institutions were gradually being recreated (see Ortiz Mena, Chapter 3). In different measures, producers, consumers, workers, and other social groups have been learning across countries to articulate, express and defend their own perceptions of how international trade and international trading rules affect their lives (see Motta Veiga and Ventura-Dias, Chapter 5). The country studies document the learning process that occurred in Latin America, from the end of the Uruguay Round to the drafting of a proactive negotiating agenda that eventually became the core agenda of the Doha Round of Trade Negotiations (see Motta Veiga and Ventura-Dias, Chapter 5; Silva, Chapter 2 and Vaillant and Ventura-Dias, Chapter 6).

The chapter is organized as follows. After this brief introduction, the following section sets the context of power and rules of the multilateral trading system that became important exogenous variables to the design and implementation of Latin American trade policy. First, a sketchy description of the evolution of the GATT–WTO system of trading rules and procedures is presented to characterize the continuities and discontinuities between the more tolerant GATT system and the more compelling WTO legal system. International systems face collective action dilemmas of increasing the compliance to a set of rules that necessarily reduces the autonomy of action of national governments. Dominant economies have molded international norms with the degrees of freedom that they required to respond to domestic political imperatives. Small exporters' requests for preferential treatment were tolerated in the GATT but were not converted into binding commitments by industrial countries. Following the failed Seattle WTO Ministerial Conference of 1999, Latin American countries, as part of several coalitions in the WTO, have actively promoted the inclusion of the development dimension in the Doha trade agenda through concrete binding obligations. Yet, no concrete results were so far obtained due to the intransigence of industrial countries.

The penultimate section interprets some of the findings of the country studies regarding the political economy of Latin American trade policy. In many ways, ideas, interests and institution interacted to determine the particular way that trade reform took place in the countries analyzed. The prevailing liberal ideas of the late 1980s and early 1990s partially explain why governments accepted to tie their hands signing agreements that would severely constrain their future choice on trade policies. Nevertheless, political institutions and private interests led the process of trade reforms implementation with a surprising degree of pragmatism. The studies emphasized the importance of domestic bureaucracies in the trade policy process, and their active role in mediating and coordinating the coalitions of producers. At the same time, they indicated that the overlapping negotiations in which countries are involved have influenced the ways in which public and private actors and institutions interact domestically to define national interests and a national trade agenda. Additionally, the studies suggested that the proliferation of bilateral and plurilateral agreements in Latin America can be explained by the lack of measurable benefits from multilateralism when compared to the costs of constrained governmental autonomy. The chapter concludes with some final considerations.

Rules and power in the liberalization of world trade: collective action and national autonomy

The system of principles, rules and practices that govern the multilateral trading system has been in operation for more than 50 years. It started with the GATT in January 1948, and from January 1995, continued with the WTO. The continuity is however, more apparent than real. The Uruguay Round of multilateral trade negotiations replaced the neutrality of the GATT with a greater demand for *ex-ante* policy convergence regardless of the economic and institutional characteristics of trading countries. A salient feature of the GATT system was its emphasis on tariffs as the major instrument of trade policy along with commitments by contracting parties that non-tariff barriers such as technical or health standards, customs rules or procedures would not be used to nullify tariff concessions (Tussie, 1993). Governments were aware of the influence of non-tariff instruments of public policies directly on market access conditions, and indirectly on the volume and composition of trade.[6] The post-war political situation restricted international trading rules to the exchange of tariff reduction concessions.

In fact, it was due to its policy-neutrality and narrow scope that the GATT was materialized.[7] The Havana Charter of 1948, the formal constitution of the International Trade Organization, met with active opposition of the United States Congress, and in 1951, the President decided not to seek for the Congress ratification. Its objectives were considered too broad and in violation of the national sovereignty, even though the Agreement and the Charter reproduced, in spirit, and sometimes, in the letter, most of the general articles of the United States trade agreements program (Brown, 1950).[8]

The Havana Charter was conceived as a code of behavior in the conduct of international relations that recognized differences in the stage of economic development, in social organization and in economic regimes. Negotiators believed that their primary objective was the re-establishment of a multilateral nondiscriminatory trading system. The majority of Charter drafters, however, placed greater importance to the relationship between international rules and domestic priorities than to the trading system *per se*. Government representatives wanted to make sure that multilateral rules would not divert national governments from pursuing major national objectives, such as: (1) internal economic and social stability, including full and productive employment, and agricultural stabilization; (2) planned economic development and reconstruction; and (3) national security. Hence, the aim of negotiations was to show that the international objectives imposed by the Charter and the national objectives safeguarded by the Charter were not in contradiction.[9] In other words, the Charter was attentive to special national conditions that would call for flexible international rules. Protection should be afforded only by duties, taxes and charges, but other methods of influencing or regulating international trade such as export subsidies, quantitative restrictions, and commodity agreements were also tolerated, under pre-defined circumstances. Quantitative restrictions for protective purposes and regional preferential arrangements could be permitted if they were essential to the industrial development in developing countries, if they did not seriously injure other countries (Brown, 1950).

The tolerance for the priority of domestic objectives over multilateral rules that was embedded in the Havana Charter did not get any sympathy in the US. The Charter was rejected by US businessmen and their representatives in the Congress on the grounds that it did not go far enough in removing trade barriers, was permissive to economic nationalism and committed 'all members of the ITO to state planning for full employment' (Ostry, 1997, p. 66). The GATT was narrower in scope, and contained international obligation in terms of reciprocal reductions of trade barriers that were acceptable to US decision-makers.

The history of the GATT indicates that dominant countries had a clear perception of their domestic imperatives. To cater to these needs they requested freedom from international obligations. The balance between domestic policy objectives and international obligations was given by exceptions and escapes from negotiated liberalization commitments. The most important exceptions that are still affecting the credibility of industrial countries referred to the treatment of agriculture and to the system of bilateral quotas in textiles and clothing, known as Multi-Fiber Arrangement. The Arrangement started in 1957 to restrict Japanese exports of cotton textiles to the US for five years. It was later expanded to include other countries and other fibers; in practice, the agreement will hold until 31 December 2004. In other words, strong states did not renounce potentially valuable flexibility for attending domestic interests (Dixit, 1996; Goldstein and Gowa, 2002).

As mentioned before, developing countries had few incentives to actively participate in the GATT, since their products of interest were either removed from the disciplines of the trading system or had no problems of access. Of the eight countries studied, only Brazil and Chile were among the 23 countries that signed the GATT in 1947. Peru and

Uruguay joined the GATT a few years later, whereas Argentina waited almost two decades to join the GATT, getting into it in 1967, at the end of the Kennedy Round. Colombia joined it in 1981 but Mexico and Venezuela were not sufficiently convinced until the launching of the Uruguay Round in the middle of the 1980s.

In the first two decades of operation of the GATT, the environment of world trade considerably changed, with the technological catching-up of European and Japanese economies as well as the narrowing of the income gap between those economies and the US (Abramovitz, 1986). Moreover, through direct governmental intervention in their economies, several Latin American countries transformed themselves from commodity-producers into successful manufacturing exporters (see Ortiz Mena, Chapter 3 and Motta Veiga and Ventura-Dias, Chapter 5). In addition, as the GATT evolved, it became clear that non-tariff measures had been selected as the most expeditious way to control imports. The growing membership of the GATT was making extensive use of administrative measures applied at the border as well as fiscal and credit instruments to support domestic industries. Already the Kennedy Round (1963–67) included two areas of non-tariff measures: a code on antidumping and a system of customs valuation (Windham, 1986).[10] In the 1970s, the spread of several non-transparent protectionist arrangements in industrial countries exposed 'the tenuous nature of the [GATT] consensus concerning the respective roles of domestic policy and international rules' (Ostry, 1997, p. 74).[11]

The greater number and heterogeneity of participants in GATT negotiations, from the original 23 to 89 during the Tokyo Round (1973–79), increased the transaction costs of multilateral trade negotiations, since the divergent interests of new members exposed the vulnerability of the international contract. Many of the new signatories and participants in the GATT were developing nations whose development needs conflicted with the trading interests of the industrial nations that created the GATT. Furthermore, the multilateral system was gradually transformed 'from broad statements of principles, drafted by members of a small club who understood that what was left unwritten was as important as the written words, to detailed legalisms' (Ostry, 1997).[12] A defining characteristic of the multilateral trading system since the Tokyo Round has been the increasing 'legalization' of trade policy and the move from trade liberalization to trade policy regulation (Grey 1982 as in Ostry, 1997).

This gradual legalization of the multilateral trading system was the response of the system of rules to the greater number of participants at various stages of economic and institutional development. It was also the reaction of interstate cooperation to the changing nature of world trade, in which flows of services, technology, capital, and knowledge became equal or more important than those of goods, and trade between related partners through multinational corporations was widespread. The long-lasting Uruguay Round vastly increased the scope of the original GATT system. New negotiating topics such as trade in services and trade-related investment measures have significant regulatory components (see Abuggatás and Stephenson, 2003; Chudnovsky and López, 2003). With the implementation of the Agreement on Trade-Related Aspects of Intellectual Property Rights (TRIPS), the protection of intellectual property rights was included among the obligations of trade policy of WTO member states. New agreements on technical barriers to trade and on sanitary and phytosanitary measures also expanded the obligations in the WTO regarding regulatory standards thereby extending the policy convergence requirements.

The WTO was equipped with a more effective Dispute Settlement Body, with a system of notifications on policy changes, and a Trade Policy Review mechanism that greatly increased the transparence of domestic trade policy therefore reducing the costs of monitoring the compliance of international obligations (Weston and Delich, 2003). At the same time, the WTO is an organization of almost universal membership, in which the number of rich countries has not changed but that of non-rich countries tripled and makes nowadays almost 90 per cent of its membership. Although WTO voting system assigns one vote to any country regardless of its economic size, the decisions are taken by consensus, and the power of those 10–17 countries that concentrate almost 60 per cent of world trade is not ignored.

The skewed world distribution of power and wealth has been therefore translated into an asymmetric recognition of respect for domestic interests in individual countries. The special and differential treatment (S&D), that had been bargained for by developing countries as an exception to the Most-Favored-Nation (MFN) clause in the Tokyo Round (1973–79), was reduced in breadth just to longer periods to implement the agreements. As part of the UR negotiations, the principle of nondiscrimination and reciprocity in trade concessions was extended to all WTO members, regardless of their level of economic and institutional development. Latin American countries, as middle-income developing countries, assumed binding obligations to eliminate several policy instruments including production subsidies, national content requirements, and other export promotion instruments without getting much in return.

Textiles and apparel will not be fully integrated into WTO disciplines until the last minute of the last day of 2004. The liberalization of agriculture is now the major topic of the Doha round, but negotiations are virtually stalled since the failed Seattle Ministerial Conference (Diaz Henderson, 2003).

Industrial countries profited from URAs thanks to longer periods for the adjustment of their agriculture and traditional industries to new competitive conditions in domestic markets, as well as to the inclusion of new rules in areas in which they had a considerable advantage, such as trade in services, knowledge asset creation, and multinational corporation operations. Developing countries were forced to accept a *de facto* graduation concerning their development needs. In the GATT/WTO there is no precise definition of what makes a country a developing country. It is a voluntary self-assessment. After the UR, only countries defined as least-developed countries (LDCs) would qualify for preferential treatment.[13] In other words, the Uruguay Round reduced the reach for affirmative action in market access and trading opportunities.

Gradually, developing countries began to feel the costs of complying with their multilateral obligations as other countries challenged their policies in the Dispute Settlement Body (DSB). It became clear that Latin American countries had lost their preferential condition as developing countries, when the DSB did not admit development needs and development situations as sound justifications for infringing URA obligations. For instance, Brazilian diplomats were amazed by the DSB refusal in admitting that Brazil, as a developing country, faced a spread over the market interest rate that was significantly higher than that of Canada (see Bombardier against Embraer in Motta Veiga and Ventura-Dias, Chapter 5). In contrast, when the DSB found that the rights of developing countries were impaired by other countries' policies, their capacity to enforce those rights was hampered by the fact that they were small economies. They had the right to retaliate but no effective power of exercising the right (Weston and Delich, 2003). In other words, the legal system of WTO endows all countries with equal rights and duties irrespective of size and power, but in reality, the right to retaliate is commensurate with the economic size of each country.[14] When these costs are set against the meager market access benefits derived from the URAs, the net results seem disproportionately low. Developing countries were also weary of not having the multilateral protection of a system of rules that they expected. Several Latin American countries became targets of antidumping actions by the US, while the WTO did not prevent US from harassing them on inadequate intellectual property protection (see Silva, Chapter 2; Tussie *et al.*, Chapter 4; Motta Veiga and Ventura-Dias, Chapter 5 and Lengyel, Chapter 9).

It should be remarked that a more effective participation of developing countries in the WTO was promoted by the continuing improvement in information dissemination. Besides the reduction in enforcement and monitoring costs, the greater transparence of norms and procedures in WTO, helped by the technology of information and communication, has contributed to the simplification, codification and diffusion of otherwise complex technical knowledge. Although some authors fear that opponents to trade liberalization will be therefore better organized, the reduction in information asymmetry has facilitated the participation of small countries (Goldstein and Martin, 2000). Diplomats from developing countries became skillful *connoisseurs* of URAs as proved by the technical sophistication of proposals put forward individually or in small coalitions in continuous negotiations in the WTO. Improvements in information access have also helped developing countries to make a more precise assessment of gains and losses.

It is important to emphasize that full cooperation for trade liberalization requires that distributive conflicts among participants do not interfere with the common interest in trade expansion through agreed rules and disciplines. Albeit unevenly distributed, trade liberalization should provide measurable benefits to all if voluntary cooperation of powerful and weak countries is expected. There are no indications that governments are willing to either reverse their commitment to trade liberalization or to abdicate of their right to respond to essential national objectives. The preference that Latin American governments have expressed for bilateral and subregional preferential trade liberalization, underscores their demand for an extensive control over the pace, sequencing, and direction of the opening process.

Ideas, interest and institutions in the political economy of Latin American trade policy

Trade policy can be perceived as the outcome of: (i) conflicting interests of individuals and groups of individuals that have their own perception of how their welfare will be affected by trade policies and try to influence the actions of immediate policy-makers; (ii) ideas or policy preferences of different private and public actors given their own individual interests; and (iii) institutions, which are sets of rules and incentives that provide solutions to coordination problems, and thereby promote collective action. Private and public actors operate in a context of incomplete information, bounded rationality, uncertainty, and vulnerability to opportunism when individual actors face feasible alternative options. Institutions can also be defined as mechanisms designed to cope with specific transaction costs, broadly defined as information, negotiation, and enforcement costs (Keohane, 1984; Yarbrough and Yarbrough, 1992; Dixit, 1996).[15]

The literature on transaction costs has underlined the inability of policy-makers to foresee all possible contingencies that will affect a course of action; the complexity of defining specific rules even for the few contingencies that can be foreseen, and the difficulty of directly observing and verifying contingencies in a way that pre-defined procedures could be implemented. Therefore, in this highly uncertain environment, rules are partially written as the events unfold, while policy acts have long-lasting effects. In effect, a high degree of inertia guides the selection of instruments that may serve unanticipated purposes. There is a *hysteresis* of policy acts, this is to say that policy and institutions that are created for one specific situation end up having a life of its own.[16] A good example is the above mentioned 1957 agreement to limit Japanese cotton exports to the US that was later transformed into the Multi-fiber Agreement and lasted well beyond the temporary period of five years (Dixit, 1996). The Uruguayan Law of Exchange Rate and Monetary Reform of 1959 is another good example. Originally intended to eliminate a system of multiple exchange rates, the law allowed several Uruguayan governments to impose administrative barriers including partial or complete prohibition of specific imports, to be used later in the 1970s as the backbone to an outward model of growth.(see Vaillant and Ventura-Dias, Chapter 6). Economic policy-making is therefore a path-dependent process in which solutions for the present situation are constructed based on rules and procedures inherited from the past, and the refurbished outcome may yet outlast its newly defined purposes.

When applied to Latin America, the economic policy-making process has additional elements of uncertainty that result from the relative mobility of political and private actors, and the lack of continuity in politics and policies in a highly volatile political context (see Motta Veiga and Ventura-Dias, Chapter 5). In other words, preferences are not stable. Disappointments with the results of public policies and instruments may lead to a painful reassessment of preferences and priorities. In Latin America, preferences for liberal policies came as a reaction to a decade of protectionist distortions that followed the debt crisis. However, the lack of concrete results from liberal reforms led policy-makers, academics and entrepreneurs to revaluate the costs and benefits of those policies. While there is no observable trend toward reverting the gains from stable monetary and fiscal policies as well as from market openness, in most of the countries studied policy-makers felt that the costs of adjustments were high and pervasive. Therefore, with few exceptions, governments sought after greater reciprocity in market access through bilateral and minilateral (plurilateral) preferential trade agreements (see Silva, Chapter 2; Ortiz Mena, Chapter 3), and also through the strengthening of existing regional integration schemes (see Echavarria and Gamboa, Chapter 7).

The action of individuals actors to persuade policy-makers to adopt policies of their preferences has been analysed by the political economy literature. The demands for protection by pressure groups can be convergent with preferences and interests of policy-makers. Likewise, the ability of policy-makers can be enhanced by domestic institutions. The country studies contribute to understanding the process through which individual interests are translated into national interests as the guiding principle of trade negotiations. The aggregation of policy preferences of all groups that have a voice in the political and administrative system of each country may not add to a coherent project. In general, globally competitive exporters of commodities will demand governmental action aiming at greater and better market access in industrial countries, through bilateral and multilateral bargaining. Import-sensitive sectors will look for protection or otherwise a gradual implementation of market opening obligations. Less globally competitive industries will prefer trade agreements of a narrower scope in which their improved bargaining power could ensure better access conditions for their products.

The micro management of international competition: multiple arrangements for market access

The studies showed that although correct the premises that developing countries have weak institutions and that they had difficulties in adjusting to the new environment, analysts had failed to perceive all the other movements that were co-evolving with changes in the multilateral trading system. In the 12 years that elapsed from the GATT Ministerial meeting held in Geneva in 1982 to the formal signature of the Marrakech Final Act in March 1994, Latin American societies went through a difficult process of adjustment to the new financial and economic conditions of the international economy. Albeit countries varied in their domestic political and institutional settings and the policies were implemented at a different pace, they all moved from a development strategy based on discriminatory trade policies to different kinds of liberal trade and investment regimes. By the time the negotiations of the Uruguay Round were completed, Latin American countries had all embarked in a vast process of privatization, deregulation and liberalization of their markets that focused the attention of public and private actors. In many cases, out of a weak bargaining power, and in a few others, out of liberal ideas, the trade regime changed radically. The common trend in the region of adjusting to a new economic and political international context preceded the conclusion of the Uruguay Round. Conversely, the debt problem crisis and the restructuring of the international economy considerably reduced the bargaining power of major countries in multilateral negotiations (see Glover and Tussie, 1993). Countries at higher levels of development such as Argentina, Brazil, and Mexico were under heavy pressure from their industrialized partners to fully assume their responsibilities towards the rest of the international community. The policy-making process as much as the bargaining power of these countries were directly affected by major events outside Geneva. In particular, the financial crisis increased the influence of international institutions such as the World Bank and the International Monetary Fund on policy-making in debtor countries, and made room for policy-based loans that had a direct impact on the characteristics of Latin American trade regimes.

A broad set of macroeconomic reforms redefined trade protection mechanisms with the virtual elimination of non-tariff barriers, the adoption of low average tariffs and a greater uniformity of tariff structures. In parallel, and consistent with the liberalization trend, nearly all Latin American and Caribbean countries became members of the GATT, and later of the WTO, abiding by the rights and obligations derived from the URAs. Ultimately, the reform process seemed to have replaced the discretionary economic policy-making of the import-substitution trade regime with the rule of law of a liberal regime. At closer attention, however, a great pragmatism prevailed in the way the reforms were carried out. In effect, governments retained more discretionary power to micromanage the process than was originally thought. The new wave of regionalism that emerged together with the widespread use of contingent defense mechanisms (antidumping and safeguards acations) is a good illustration of how governments tried to manage the overpowering pressure for greater openness of domestic markets as well as for convergence of rules and institutions. It was not until late in the 1990s that Latin American minds became more focused on multilateral rules and obligations. Hence, in retrospect, the concerns expressed by trade analysts that the URAs would drastically reduce the space for policy design and implementation in developing countries were miscalculated in time. This is not to say that the space for development policies had not been severely reduced but, after reviewing country experiences, it seems that the role of the URAs in that reduction was not as important as originally thought.

Most countries had to adjust their economies and institutions to the patterns of international liquidity and to the conditionality imposed by creditor countries and multilateral institutions following the debt crisis of the 1980s. Macroeconomic adjustments were quite dramatic forcing governments to reduce expenditures while increasing fiscal and export revenues. Governments were forced to abandon fiscal and credit instruments to promote local industries and export diversification even before some of the new rules on export subsidies were enforced in the WTO (see Motta Veiga and Ventura-Dias, Chapter 5 and Echavarria and Gamboa, Chapter 7). Although in the 1990s, the region recovered its attractiveness for private capital flows, the nature of those capital flows, the inherent fragility of stabilization plans implemented by Latin American countries anchored on a fixed exchange rate, and the overall interdependence of markets restrained governments from applying expansive fiscal policies (see Tussie *et al.*, Chapter 4 and Motta Veiga and Ventura-Dias, Chapter 5).

Hence, at the micro level, enterprises of all sizes had to learn how to survive and operate in open trade regimes and become competitive in international markets, well before the end of the Uruguay Round. Unilateral liberalization preceded formal tariff concessions and tariff bindings in the GATT. It is true that for the first time, tariff schedules included almost the totality of their tariff items. Yet, the ceiling of their tariff bindings, as in the majority of all developing countries, was considerably higher than the tariff level reached at the end of the process of unilateral tariff reduction (see Motta Veiga and Ventura-Dias, Chapter 5 and Lengyel, Chapter 9).

Finally, as mentioned, in parallel to the extension and deepening of those multilateral commitments, governments decided that the multilateral liberalization process would be preceded by bilateral and subregional preferential agreements. Sometimes those agreements, as it was the case with the NAFTA contained broader agendas and higher levels of commitments than those included in the URAs. Furthermore, Mexico became a hub of several bilateral and minilateral free trade agreements with similarly broad trade and investment disciplines (see Ortiz Mena, Chapter 3). Such is the case of the Group of Three (G-3) associating Colombia and Venezuela to Mexico (see Echavarria and Gamboa, Chapter 7). Over the 1990s, Latin America became increasingly important for the export strategy of other Latin American countries. At the end of the century, there was a perceptible difference in the composition of trade in Latin America: the United States became a major trading partner for Mexico and Central American countries whereas the more distant Southern Cone countries were exporting a great share of their goods and services to neighboring countries.

The impact of subregional developments on entrepreneurial behavior should not be overlooked. For instance, positive and negative results of tariff negotiations within the Mercosur were visible results to private entrepreneurs in member countries that contrasted with negligible concessions in market access that their governments had obtained in the Uruguay Round. Additionally, the on-going process aiming at the creation of a Western Hemisphere Free Trade Area has drawn more attention in the region than the potential launching of new (or the deepening of old) negotiations at WTO. In fact, it was not until the massive protests in the failed Seattle Ministerial that WTO became a subject of media interest in Latin America (see Tussie *et al.*, Chapter 4, and Motta Veiga and Ventura-Dias, Chapter 5).

The interplay between private and public interests: the learning process

The interaction of private and public actors in the formulation and implementation of Latin American trade policy has been very little documented, even though there is a vast literature on trade reforms.[17] In many cases, the influence of specific interest groups on trade policies is inferred from the results in terms of inter-industry differences in tariff protection. Pieces of legislation permit to relate a given policy to elected and non-elected public officials, and to specific institutions that were in charge of the trade policy-making process. Nevertheless, despite the identification of the beneficiaries of those policies, it remains a conjecture as to whether they resulted from the direct intervention of organized private interests because private actors make use of informal channels of influence (Lengyel, Chapter 9). The powerful role of state bureaucracies in Latin American economic policy-making, during the long period of state-led growth, created intimate linkages between public officials and private entrepreneurs. The final decision of the policy-making process, however, rested with state bureaucrats.

In most countries, the design and implementation of trade policies are prerogatives of the Executive.

The studies describe a diversity of institutional situations in the eight countries that are reflected in the way trade policies were formulated and implemented. Trade liberalization was shaped by the production and trade structure of individual countries, as well as by the characteristics of their integration to the world economy. In one extreme, Chile, Mexico and Uruguay have moved further in the adoption of more open trade policies, although Uruguay has had less consistent policies than Chile. The intensification of the Mexican process of trade liberalization occurred together with a greater integration with the US economy, at first through bilateral and sectoral agreements and later through the NAFTA. Chile chose to keep a low flat tariff while adopting a multi-track market access strategy, multiplying free trade agreements with all trading partners. Therefore, although Chilean exports follow a natural resource-based comparative advantage, the destination markets are quite diversified. Mexico, through international production sharing schemes, has been able to diversify into highly elaborated products, albeit mostly labor-intensive manufacturing operations are performed in the country. Trade and investment are concentrated in the United States that accounts for more than 86% of Mexican exports and imports. Uruguay has preferred to deepen its integration with the other countries of Mercosur due to its geographical situation, and the historical integration of the Uruguayan economy with that of Argentina and Brazil (see Silva, Chapter 2; Ortiz Mena; Chapter 3; and Vaillant and Ventura-Dias, Chapter 6). Colombia, Peru and Venezuela are more or less in the middle of trade liberalization preferences, but, again, each one of these countries encapsulates specific economic and political institutions and processes, that have determined the precise characteristics of their integration in the world economy. The three economies are natural-resource exporters, with oil accounting for a significant fraction of their revenues. Trade relations between Colombia and Venezuela represented the core of the renewed Andean Community of Nations through which the two countries sought to diversify their production and trade (see Echavarria and Gamboa, Chapter 7 and Fairlie Reynoso, Chapter 8).

At the other extreme, Brazil, the country with the most diversified and sophisticated economy, has pragmatically rationalized border protection, reduced the average tariff levels, eliminated most of its non-tariff barriers and made its export promotion schemes conform to WTO rules (but not before having to do so by WTO rulings). However, trade policies were employed by Brazilian technocrats as instruments to promote competition in domestic markets thereby contributing to price stabilization plans. Since middle 1980s, there has been continuity in Brazilian policies aiming at greater integration with Argentina first, and later with the other countries of the Southern Cone, through the construction of the Mercosur. Both Argentine and Brazilian exports suffered the consequences of a overvalued exchange rate. Brazil moved into a flexible rate, in 1999, whereas Argentina did so at the end of 2001, in difficult circumstances (see Tussie *et al.*, Chapter 4, and Motta Veiga and Ventura-Dias, Chapter 5).

In these eight countries, private and public interests have been expressed in specific policy preferences through formal and informal institutions. In all countries, the all-encompassing categories of exporting and import-sensitive producers summarize major intersectoral distributive tensions. However, as the economy becomes more complex, interests of individual actors are also defined more finely. Hence, producers should also be differentiated according to their reliance on imported or domestic inputs (see Tussie *et al.*, Chapter 4). Size and ownership of capital are other important variables, particularly in economies in which the process of privatization of public assets and the de-regulation of markets that went together with the process of trade liberalization resulted in great de-nationalization of assets.

Mexico innovated in the inclusion of business in the negotiations of the NAFTA, institutionalizing the 'room next door', which was later followed by Colombia and more recently by Chile. The intimate collaboration of government and business in the formulation of a bargaining agenda in trade negotiations was a successful example of the transition from conflictive to collaborative relations between the private and public sector in Mexico. It was possible after the creation of a single association that unified Mexican private enterprises interests, that was promoted by the Mexican Administration in 1988, initially with the intention of encouraging the diversification and growth of exports. When the private sector was later invited to participate in the NAFTA negotiations, the association was reorganized based on the Private Sector Advisory System created by the Trade Act of 1974 to assist the US Trade Representative (Alba, 1996; see Ortiz Mena, Chapter 3). In Colombia, in the past ten years, although in a less systematic manner, the Ministry of Foreign Trade has been engaged in an intense round of negotiations with the business sector. Representatives of business groups accompany the official delegations in trade negotiations and await the official request for consultation. At the end of each day, the government's technical team meets with business sector representatives and updates them on the negotiations (Langeback, 2002). The same 'room next door' consultation mechanism was used in the negotiations aiming at a free trade agreement (FTA) between Chile and the US. The private sector was also directly involved in the negotiations for the Political, Economic and Cooperation Agreement between Chile and the European Union (see Silva, Chapter 2).

In Brazil, throughout the Uruguay Round, the Ministry of Foreign Affairs promoted periodic consultations with representatives of private interests to get their views on major issues that were part of the trade agenda. However, nothing was then more remote to Brazilian entrepreneurs than multilateral trade negotiations, and there was no feedback from trade negotiators on their bargaining strategies. In the early 1990s, business representatives were completely neglected during Mercosur negotiations, and a compulsory trade liberalization schedule of tariff reductions every six months was defined to prevent business influencing the results. Nevertheless, at that moment, Brazilian entrepreneurs were sufficiently concerned with the new context of domestic competition to contact their peers in Argentina and jointly to find ways and means to take part in the negotiations. When the US indicated its willingness to extend a NAFTA-type of agreement to the rest of the America (excepting Cuba) Brazilian business associations as well as associations in other Mercosur countries were better prepared to participate in the debate (see Motta Veiga and Ventura-Dias, Chapter 5).

Hence, the creation of the Mercosur has been associated with an enriching learning process with spillover and accumulative effects that member countries can use in other negotiating forums. Likewise, public and private agents in Chile and Mexico, that are hubs of an impressive network of trade agreements, have accumulated a solid knowledge of trade and trade-related components of international negotiations.

Final considerations

The adjustment of public and private sectors to the new environment of trade and investment in the background of Uruguay Round negotiations took place before the effects of the URAs could be felt. Accordingly, until the end of the 1990s, few economic and policy adjustments were perceived as brought about by the new trading system of the WTO. Individual countries selected pragmatically how to carry out trade liberalization in ways that could be supportive to their production and trade structures, and that were consistent with their stage of economic integration. 'Minilateral' trade liberalization through NAFTA, Mercosur, the Andean Community, or bilateral FTAs accommodated the need for greater control of the pace and length of the process. Countries became fully engaged in the complex negotiations aiming at the creation of the FTAA, even those that feel they are better served by multilateral rather than by hemispheric rules.

By the end of the 1990s, however, trade policy instruments began to be challenged in WTO committees and dispute settlement mechanism: price bands and simplified drawback schemes in Chile, price reference in Uruguay, export credit (PROEX) in Brazil, tobacco subsidy in Argentina, among others. In individual countries, public officials became increasingly aware of the restrictions imposed by their commitments in the WTO as much as of the difficulties to fully implement URAs' obligations. After the failed Seattle Ministerial Conference, WTO was definitely included, together with the FTAA, in business concerns and in Latin American public debate. In many ways, it is clear that a multi-track market access strategy includes multilateral rules, norms and procedures as the broad framework of reference. FTAs with the US, however, contain rules for topics such as investment, government procurement, trade and environment for which multilateral rules have not yet been negotiated.

Latin American negotiators used their technical knowledge on WTO rules for the preparation of the positive agenda proposed by developing countries at the Seattle Conference, that later became the development agenda in the new round launched in Doha, Qatar, in November 2001. The Doha mandate acknowledged the difficulties that developing countries have to fulfill their obligations under the URAs. These difficulties go beyond lack of technical capability to implement the agreements. The questions have been debated as part of two negotiating sets: (1) implementation issues and (2) special and differentiated treatment. Both sets summarize the tensions between the legalization of multilateral rules and the national autonomy for formulating and executing development policies. Developing countries in general, and Latin American, in particular, are trying to negotiate a more balanced treatment of domestic objectives.

There is an asymmetric treatment of national interests in multilateral rules that should be recognized. Industrial countries want to protect sectors such as agriculture, textile and natural resource processing, in which their industries lost competitiveness to those in developing countries. On the other hand, middle-income developing countries, such as Latin Americans demand greater flexibility in rules and disciplines to allow them to diversify exports toward goods and services of higher knowledge content.

In addition, rich countries received a more favorable treatment to the adjustment of their sunset industries to the new competitive structure of international markets than countries of lower economic and institutional conditions. The multilateral trading system must include binding commitments that explicitly address development needs rather than forcing Latin American governments to stretch the maneuvering space in order to respond to domestic interests.

Notes

1. As Dixit (1996, p. 5) asserted: '... perfect markets and perfect governments do an equally good job of achieving economic efficiency.'
2. Trade theory also excludes all the adjustment costs that occur when a country increases its integration to the world economy. They are, among others, the inter-industry distribution of domestic costs and benefits of trade liberalization, the capacity of employment creation relative to employment destruction, the birth and death of small and medium sized enterprises, etc.
3. The majority of developing countries were not independent in the first decades of the post-War period.
4. Hoekman (1995, p. iii) defines trade policy as 'all policies that imply discrimination against foreign products/ producers, or between foreign sources of supply. It pertains to goods (tangible products), services (intangible products), and knowledge (intellectual property). Consequently, trade policy more broadly defined extends also to government procurement practices, the development and enforcement of product standards, or the regulations affecting inward and outward foreign direct investment (FDI). FDI is often the preferred route for foreign firms to contest a market, and is often the most effective way for the host nation to obtain new technologies, enhance the security of access to export markets, or increase the efficiency of the service sector.'
5. The full reach of the impact of the URAs called other coalitions into play that are concerned with the division of gains of trade liberalization but that do not speak on their own name and will not benefit directly from any redistribution of gains. The highly visible non-governmental organizations (NGOs) were called *transformational coalitions* by Ostry, 2002.
6. The trade agreement signed between Mexico and the United States in 1942 included several non-tariff items.
7. According to Dixit (1996, p. 125), the GATT 'was shaped by many unanticipated events, it evolved in ways quite different from those foreseen, and it has a record of important successes as well as failures in its mission.'
8. The GATT did not require formal ratification by the United States Congress because it fell under the mandate of the Reciprocal Trade Agreements Act of 1934.
9. One of the principles of the Havana Charter was: 'National efforts to promote and maintain full and productive employment are of international concern, and affect trading relationships in ways that should be taken fully into account in the development of commercial policy. They should be supplemented and at times safeguarded by international co-operative effort' (Brown, 1950; p. 170).

10. Both the antidumping code and the system of custom valuation were repudiated by the United States Congress because they were not covered by the negotiating mandate from Congress (Windham, 1986, p. 69).
11. Ostry argued against Ruggie's (1982) suggestion (that she called 'mythology') that the GATT system represented a transatlantic vision of 'embedded liberalism' or 'a shared view about the nature and role of government in a mixed economy and that the relationship between domestic and international policy objectives' (1997, p. 94).
12. See also the special issue of *International Organisation*, 2000.
13. In Latin America and the Caribbean, only Haiti, measured by income per capita, falls in the category of LDC.
14. The effectiveness of retaliation in WTO is part of the current debate in the Doha round of negotiations.
15. Institutions can also be seen as instruments for power sharing since they may provide a voice to social groups and private citizens to engage in public action, and to express their agreements or disagreements with prevailing interests (Hirschman, 1970).
16. Dixit (1996) called it a QWERTY politics in allusion to the typewriter keyboard that became a parameter for typewriters and digital machines without any functional reason (David, 1985).
17. See Edwards (1995); Edwards and Lederman (1998) and Ostry (2002).

Part I

Trade Liberalization and Preferential Market Access

2
Chile: A Multi-Track Market Access Strategy

Verónica Silva

Introduction

Chile is often cited as a successful case of an export-led economy in Latin America. The process of liberal reforms began with the military government in 1973 and continued throughout the following decades except during the financial crisis of 1982. After the democratization in 1990, the coalition of center-left parties (*Concertación*), which has ruled the country ever since, combined a low flat tariff structure with negotiations aiming at greater market access through bilateral free trade agreements. The strategy of 'open regionalism' was motivated by the need to diversify Chilean exports in terms of both product mix and final destination, and to attract new investments. At the end of the decade, the high concentration of Chilean exports in primary products, notwithstanding the continuing diversification progress since the second half of the 1980s, was associated with a decreasing rhythm of growth of the economy. The diversifying effort until the middle 1990s, also called the 'second exporting stage', faces an entirely different international context than the first period of export expansion. Fierce competition in international markets and the ongoing revolution in information and communication technologies pose disquieting challenges for Chilean policy-makers and entrepreneurs.

Three coalition governments have imparted continuity and consistency to public policy in Chile. It is remarkable the social consensus that was built around the export orientation of the economy in a society still divided on ideological grounds. Although much has yet to be done in terms of incorporating the civil society in the consultation process, and in particular trade union concerns, the Chilean government has greatly enhanced the transparence of trade negotiations and of the policy-making process. Innovative means of consulting with the private sector and having their views expressed in crucial bargaining moments have also been created. As bilateral negotiations moved away from Latin American countries to include Canada, the European Union, the United States, and the Republic of Korea, among others, major private actors were invited to participate in the negotiating rounds, providing their views and expertise to official Chilean negotiators.

This chapter describes the interplay between public and private institutions in the recent evolution of trade policy-making and trade negotiations in Chile. The following section describes Chilean trade and foreign direct investment (FDI) during the 1990s. The subsequent section highlights the association between active trade promotion policies and the peculiar multi-track market access strategy that the country has pursued through the combination of unilateral liberalization, multilateral obligations and negotiations of bilateral preferential trade liberalization agreements. The penultimate section deals with cooperation and conflicts between interests and policy preferences of public officials and private agents. The final section summarizes the multifaceted Chilean negotiating agenda.

Trade and investment in Chile in the 1990s

There is ample literature covering Chile's transformation into an open economy since the radical trade liberalization imposed by the military regime from 1974 to 1979 that reduced the tariff structure to a single tariff level of 10 per cent.[1] The turmoil caused by the financial crisis of 1982/83 did not affect the preference of the government for a flat tariff though it was raised to 35 per cent until 1985. The second phase of trade reform in the latter part of the 1980s was more moderate. The military government introduced active instruments to promote export diversification: duty drawbacks for exporters, a subsidy for new exports and foreign direct investment policies favoring mineral and non-mineral exports that supplemented a further reduction of the flat tariff. Other structural economic reforms included a sustained wave of privatization in non-tradable sectors (Pietrobelli, 1993; Moguillansky, 1999). In addition, the experience with the financial crisis of the early 1980s alerted the authorities to the need for improved prudential norms in the domestic financial system. Sound fiscal, monetary and exchange-rate policies contributed to productive investment and export diversification.

The democratic government continued the policy of trade liberalization of the military regime. The low levels of domestic protection and the flat tariff were kept although they were combined with significant diplomatic efforts to secure market access through bilateral free trade agreements (FTAs). In 1991, the ruling political party of the Chilean congress proposed the reduction of the general tariff on imports from 15 per cent to 11 per cent. This was followed in 1998 by the approval of a plan to reduce the tariff by one percentage point every year, starting in 1999, until a rate of 6 per cent was reached in 2003. Hence, fair trade rather than purely free trade has inspired the Chilean *Concertación* administrations.

Product and market composition of Chilean exports

Exports of goods and services accounted for roughly 35 per cent of Chile's GDP at the end of 1990s. Imports accounted for a similar share of economic activities leading total trade to account for more than 70 per cent of Chile's GDP. Trade liberalization provided incentives to specialize according to comparative advantage in factors that were abundant in the country. As such, Chile incorporated labor- and natural resource-intensive commodities into its export basket during the long-term restructuring of exports. Despite these diversifying efforts, copper still accounts for nearly 40 per cent of Chilean exports of goods (total exports of mining and other unprocessed products account for more than 50 per cent of exports). The bulk of the exporting activity remains concentrated in a few enterprises (PROCHILE, 2002).

Between 1990 and 2000, the value of total Chilean exports more than doubled from US$8.5 billion to US$18.2 billion. The geographic destination of Chilean exports has also altered over time. In 1970, Chilean products were exported to 31 markets, mostly to European countries, that accounted for 61 per cent of all exports. In 2000, Chile was exporting to 174 countries and the European Union accounted for a little over 24 per cent of total exports. At the same time, Latin American countries increased their share from 11.5 per cent to 22 per cent of Chilean exports. Moreover, Chile expanded commercial ties with Asia Pacific countries. Asian developing countries almost doubled their participation in Chilean exports, from less than 10 per cent to almost 19 per cent during the period 1990–97. The financial crisis affected aggregated demand and exports destined for these countries shrunk to roughly 16 per cent of exports at the end of the century. United States and Japan are the first and second major importers, with shares of 18 per cent and 12.5 per cent of Chilean exports, respectively (ECLAC, 2003: Statistical Appendix).

In addition, there has been an increase in trade in services that is not commensurate to the role that services play in the domestic economy.[2]

As all Latin American countries, Chile remains a net importer of services. There is some incipient export activity in more sophisticated sectors that require skilled labor, such as for instance, information technology, telecommunications, consulting and engineering, health and social security services (Prieto, 1999).

FDI in Chile

FDI flows escalated during the 1990s, climbing from an annual average of US$720 million in 1985–89 to over US$5 billion annually in 1995–99.[3] Before 1995, FDI mainly targeted mining and other natural resources-based manufacturing industries such as paper and cellulose, which are mostly export-oriented industries. Post-1995 the bulk of FDI was directed to services, partly due to the privatization process, which Chile started the earlier than the rest of Latin America. The recent wave of FDI in Chilean services resulted from a process of mergers and acquisitions, most clearly illustrated by FDI in the electrical power industry and in telecommunications. The change in sectors is also associated to changes in the origin of investment. At first, the United States accounted for nearly 50 per cent of capital inflows, but over the 1990s even though the United States retained the first place, Canada and Spain became significant sources of FDI to Chile. Canada is concentrated in the mining sector whereas Spain has a strong presence in services (ECLAC, 2001b).

Nevertheless, Chile accounts for a reduced amount of FDI inflows to Latin America. From 1990 to 1999, these flows increased from US$9 billion to US$93.5 billion, whereas inflows to Chile increased from US$5 billion to US$9 billion. Chilean authorities expect that the country's dependable economic, political and legal institutions can attract foreign capital and offset the relative small size of the domestic market, since TNCs can use Chile as a reliable gateway to other South American markets. Other factors have intervened in the TNCs' decision process that have prevented the materialization of those expectations, except for Spanish investments in services (telecommunications, financial services, the electrical energy generation and distribution, and water and sanitation services).

There has been also some Chilean investment abroad. Foreign-owned Chilean firms participated in the privatization of the public utilities and financial services in neighboring countries such as Argentina, Brazil, and Peru in the early 1990s. Some locally-owned Chilean firms operating in retailing and agro-industries also began a process of internationalization through FDI in the same countries. In some cases, FDI was a complement to the firms' exporting activities (CCS, 1999). The Argentine and Peruvian economic crises negatively affected Chilean investment, that after reaching more than US$6 billion in 1996 was drastically reduced to a little more than US$2 billion in 1998, and to US$1.3 billion in 2001 (CCS, 2002).

Market access, export promotion and adjustment to multilateral rules

The validity of the export model of development is beyond dispute among Chilean economic agents although it is more difficult to find agreement on the ways and means to operate the model (Montero, 1997). There have been conflicting opinions on issues such as: (i) non-reciprocal unilateral liberalization versus discriminated trade liberalization, through bilateral FTAs; (ii) priority areas for negotiations; and (iii) strategies regarding the protection of the agricultural sector, including the adoption of more effective antidumping and safeguards legislation. The differences in opinion were exacerbated since the end of 1997, when Chilean economy was badly hit by the financial crisis that affected Asian markets and reduced the price of mining products to some of its lowest levels in many decades.[4] Furthermore, since middle 1990s, the economy has not been able to reach the extremely highs rates of growth to which the Chilean society had become used.

Open regionalism and the Chilean 'Lateral' trade strategy[5]

A strategy of international integration based upon the negotiation of bilateral *agreements* FTAs was defined in 1990 by the government of Patricio Aylwin, the first post-military democratic government in Chile. The Chilean administration concluded that the deepening of EU integration process and minimal progress in the Uruguay Round of multilateral negotiations were signaling a revival of regionalism. In Latin America, the Southern Common Market (Mercosur) was created and other sub-regional schemes were strengthened. Moreover, the US had legitimized preferential trade liberalization after signing a FTA with Israel in 1987 and another with Canada in 1988, followed by NAFTA in 1992.

The main argument for departing from previous non-reciprocal unilateral and non-discriminatory multilateral liberalization was that unilateral liberalization did not ensure a reciprocal move from trading partners. The adoption of FTAs, as an effective instrument for market access and for diversifying Chilean exports, could also sustain the liberalization process. In particular, FTAs with other Latin American countries of similar development would facilitate the export of Chile's goods and services more sophisticated. For a small economy such as Chile, FTAs offer the opportunity of combining the normal static benefits derived from trade liberalization with the dynamic benefits of economies of scale from extended markets (Sáez, 1999). The presence of economies of scale more than compensated static losses that could result from any eventual trade diversion. Furthermore, the negative effects would be minimal thanks to Chile's low uniform tariff. In addition, FTAs could contribute to accelerate the harmonization of trading partners' domestic rules, as well as to providing stable and transparent rules. Hence they could lead to decreasing transaction costs of conducting international business and contribute further to improve the investment climate.

At the bilateral level, since the end of 2000, Chilean diplomatic resources concentrated on negotiations with the US and the EU. Fully operational FTAs with Canada and Mexico laid the groundwork for a FTA with the US, concluded in December 2002, and a FTA with the EU was also signed in May of that year. In addition, the relations developed with Asian-Pacific Economic Cooperation Forum (APEC) countries contributed to negotiations launched for a FTA with South Korea and to preliminary studies for later negotiations with Japan.

Chilean FTAs are considered 'comprehensive' in nature and scope because they involve almost all trade-related areas of bilateral economic relations. In the case of trade in goods, they include aspects such as market access, rules of origin, customs procedures, and trade remedies including safeguards, antidumping and countervailing duties (AD). These agreements also cover services, FDI and standards (technical, sanitary and phytosanitary measures), trade-related issues (competition policy, intellectual property rights, government procurement), institutional issues (transparency, dispute settlement), labor and environmental issues (Direcon, 2000; ECLAC, 2002a).

According to official calculations, more than 90 per cent of all potential Chilean trade will be carried out under some form of preferential agreement by 2010. At present these trade agreements cover 20 countries (15 are already operational, five of which correspond to Economic Complementarity Agreements (ECA) completed under the umbrella of the Latin American Integration Association (LAIA) with the following countries and sets of countries: Colombia, Ecuador, Peru, Venezuela and Mercosur). Among the FTAs already signed, those with Canada, Mexico, and more recently that with the United States, which follow a NAFTA formula, and those with EU and Republic of Korea are broad in scope and depth of contractual obligations (Ortiz Mena, Chapter 3).[6] The agreement with Mercosur includes other areas of integration such as Chilean participation in the decision-making institutions of the sub-regional scheme, and joint projects of physical integration. It was the first to include all tariff lines in liberalization commitments, although sensitive agricultural products received the benefits of longer periods for adjusting to foreign competition.

The government claims that the Chilean strategy of integration to world markets through FTAs has improved its access to an aggregated market of roughly 858 million consumers. Nevertheless, the FTAs most visible effect on Chilean trade policy is the *de facto* adoption of a more differentiated tariff structure with tariff levels inferior to the flat tariff (6 per cent in 2003). Other effects such as the increase and diversification of exports toward FTA partners, and more stable trade flows that could counteract the effects of economic crisis, such as that of 1998–2000, cannot be fully attributed to the FTAs (Direcon, 2000). Evaluations of the impacts FTAs have had on trade are scarce, due to difficulties of isolating direct effects from those derived from specific conditions in participant countries that could influence the magnitude and the direction of trade flows.

The more recent FTA negotiated with industrial countries, which already have low average tariff levels, aimed much more at securing stable market access conditions and attracting investment on that basis. The FTA signed with the EU sought to stabilize market access conditions, particularly through the transformation of the Generalized System of Preferences (GSP) into permanent duty-free access for the same products, as well as the elimination of non-tariff barriers, tariff peaks and tariff escalation. Also, the FTA signed with the United States in December 2002, that had been a Chilean aspiration since NAFTA was signed, had similar objectives. Public officials and important segments of the private sector believe that the FTAs with the US and the EU will help to attract FDI from those countries. Other expected benefits are lower prices of intermediate and capital goods, heightened cooperation in the realm of the 'new economy,' better market access for Chilean goods and services,[7] and stricter trade remedy rules.

The Chilean government has been particularly cautious in negotiating the liberalization of trade in services with industrial countries. The purpose has been to strike a proper balance between the access to better and cheaper services, as inputs for Chilean production and exports of goods and services, and an equitable participation of Chilean services in high-income markets (Direcon, 2003).

Active export promotion policies

Together with improving and stabilizing market access conditions for its exports, Chile is also attempting to increase the product mix and the number of exporting firms. Hence, export promotion policies include instruments targeting both demand and supply conditions. The government has consolidated public instruments to promote exports through three main efforts: (i) expand the number of exporting firms; (ii) improve the competitiveness of existing exporting firms; and (iii) encourage new business areas, in particular finding ways to finance higher levels of internationalization among Chilean firms. The public sector has been careful to adjust domestic policy instruments to various international obligations, as it is shown below.

Chilean competitiveness policy was defined in a context of an expanding domestic economy and significant integration in the global economy in the early 1990s. The policy emphasized the neutrality of incentives across industries, encouraged association with the private sector in the execution of the programs, and defined co-financing programs within the framework of a gradual withdrawal of public participation.

The choice between sector-biased and sector-neutral (horizontal) instruments has polarized the discussions among economists in the country. Though the government has embraced the principle of *ex-ante* horizontal policies it has been suggested that Chilean trade-promotion policies have been selective in nature. The best examples are those policies that promoted infant industries that later became successful components of Chilean exports: in particular, forestry-derived products and the salmon industry (Pietrobelli, 1993; Agosin, 1997).[8] Efforts to improve the competitiveness of Chilean firms and products at the end of the 1990s centered on the second exporting phase, which was, at first, conceived as a move from natural resource-based exports to higher value-added products. Over time, the proposal came to include services as well as the incipient internationalization of Chilean firms through FDI, in sectors such as energy, retailing and finance.[9] Public officials have proposed policies targeted to new sectors such as biotechnology or information technology. Through the trade promotion agency (PROCHILE) the Chilean government has been actively assisting the participation of firms, particularly of small and medium size enterprises, in the new technology and knowledge-based economy (PROCHILE, 2000).[10]

Policy adjustments to the multilateral framework

Uruguay Round (UR) results represented a mix of challenges and opportunities for Chile, but they lack concrete meaning for the majority of the population. On the positive side, new institutional mechanisms were created, such as the Trade Policy Review that allows for a systematic analysis and follow-up of all countries' trade policies, the periodic notification of new trade-related measures introduced by individual countries and the dispute settlement body (Agosin, 1997; Direcon, 1999; Sáez, 1999). In addition, economic agents recognize the importance of multilateral rules related to trade defense mechanisms to protect a small economy from arbitrary rulings but believe that they have been ineffective in practice. Throughout the implementation period, Chilean exports were subjected to several dumping and subsidies investigations in the United States. These actions have mostly affected industries in which Chilean firms had been very competitive, such as the salmon, timber, and canned mushrooms (see ECLAC, 2001a,b).[11]

Besides, the UR resulted in very few market gains, in spite of the integration of agriculture into the multilateral trading system. Very high tariffs are permitted in agricultural markets and technical barriers were legitimized through the new agreements on standards (agreements on sanitary and phytosanitary measures and on technical barriers) (Fischer, 1997). In addition, carefully drafted disciplines in areas such as subsidies, FDI and intellectual property rights impinged on the government capacity to define and implement policies to upgrade the domestic export structure.

Major modifications in Chilean trade policy instruments were necessary because of obligations accepted under the Agreement on Subsidies and Countervailing Measures (ASCM), Trade-related Investment Measures (TRIMs), Trade-related Intellectual Property Rights (TRIPs) and Anti-dumping (AD) (WTO, 1997). At the WTO's outset, no great difficulties were foreseen in the adjustment of Chilean legislation and practices to the Uruguay Round Agreements, due to the horizontal nature of most of Chilean policies and the low level of the flat tariff.[12] Even so, the few instruments that had to be revised were deemed vital for export development, such as the Simplified Export Drawback System, the Deferred Payment System for imports of capital goods and the New Regime for the Automobile Industry.[13]

A few sectors gradually voiced their discrepancies with WTO commitments and requested greater protection. Disparities in productivity led domestic agricultural producers to question the degree of protection that the bound tariff of 31.5 per cent could provide, pushing the Chilean government to search for trade defense alternatives. In 1999, the Congress approved the Law of Safeguards.

The interplay between public and private interests: conflict and cooperation[14]

The institutional framework in the public sector

Within government institutions, a process of organizational restructuring and learning took place, parallel to changes in trade policies that were described above. The new trend of cost-sharing and gradual withdrawing of state involvement in the programs sought to render the interaction with the private sector more effective. Major institutions such as the trade promotion agency at the Ministry of Foreign Relations (PROCHILE) and the industrial promotion agency at the Ministry of Economy (Corporación de Fomento a la Producción – CORFO) exemplify the new trend. The coordination of the Ministry of Foreign Affairs with business associations, particularly in the negotiation and implementation of trade agreements, is another indication of the new public-private relations. Yet even this increased involvement of civil society in government activity has room for improvement. Critics cite a conspicuous absence of trade unions, scarce congressional participation (although it is increasing), and limited representation in terms of the range of firms and industries represented.[15]

The Ministry of Foreign Relations (MFR), which is responsible for all levels of trade negotiations, has set up inter-ministerial and mixed committees with private sector participation to ensure a fluid communication within the government as well as between the public and private sector. The Inter-Ministerial Committee on International Economic Negotiations, created in 1995, is coordinated by the MFR and has two major advisory organs: the Committee of Negotiators and the Committee of Private Sector Participation. The Committee of Negotiators, led by the head of the General Directorate of International Economic Relations (Direcon) of the MFR, reviews the various and simultaneous negotiating processes and makes clear recommendations to the President. Advisors drawn from the academia, private sector or public bureaucracies may assist the Committee. The Inter-Ministerial Committee is chaired by the MFR and comprises the Finance, Economy and Agriculture Ministers, and the Secretary General of the Presidency.

The Chilean design and implementation of trade policy faced opposition of the private sector, starting with the nature of the second exporting phase to the features of specific instruments. Disagreements abounded over the exchange rate policy, the priorities and the liberalization pace of the FTAs, the preservation of the flat tariff and the speed of tariff reduction, the adjustment of policy instruments to WTO disciplines, and the demands for protection of the domestic agricultural sector. Several government agencies took part in the formulation and resolution of these conflicts, allowing for fragmentation of policy objectives and priorities. On one hand, the Ministries of Economy and Agriculture were both interested in pushing forward the second exporting phase agenda, while on the other hand, the Finance Ministry and the Central Bank were in control of fiscal and monetary policies. The Ministry of Foreign Relations is the driving force behind bilateral agreements and the coordination of the negotiation process. The Ministry of Economy is responsible for adjusting domestic trade instruments to WTO rules and the Finance Ministry has developed proposals of trade defense mechanisms. The Ministry of Agriculture is also a very important agent in negotiations affecting the sector.

Within the ruling *Concertación* coalition, the process of trade negotiations has confronted different views on which partners to select for FTAs. The most critical situation occurred in the early 1990s around possible negotiations between Chile and the US. Officials from the Finance Ministry defended the opportunity offered by a FTA with the US whereas those from the MFR and Economy supported the alternative option of negotiating bilaterally with countries in the region. President Clinton's failure to obtain fast-track authority from the US Congress meant that the Chilean negotiating process concentrated on Latin American economies (Oppenheim, 1997). There are also divergent opinions concerning the benefits of full integration with Mercosur. The MFR supported this initiative believing that further opportunities could arise from negotiations between with the EU and Mercosur. Senior officers from the Ministries of Agriculture and Finance raised several objections, including the large gap between the Chilean flat tariff and Mercosur's common external tariff. The recommendation for preserving negotiating autonomy eventually won-out and Chile kept its status as associate member.

The institutional framework in the private sector

Likewise, the private sector is a more heterogeneous aggregate than was originally realized. Business perspectives on government involvement in trade policies vary across firms and industries. However, there is no disagreement over the need for a deep integration into the global economy. There are clear-cut discrepancies between manufacturing and agricultural interest groups in matters such as the choice between FTAs and unilateral tariff reduction. Business associations have also had some participation in the debate on the second exporting phase (Montero and Federici, 1997; Robledo, 1997).[16] Representatives of *small and medium enterprises* (SMEs) have tended to favor bilateral agreements against unilateral tariff reduction, and generally support the use of effective trade remedies. The interests of service sectors have been concentrated on FDI-related topics related to FDI such as double taxation agreements and the facilitation of international movement of personnel (Abugattás and Stephenson, 2003).

Business interests are organized at two levels. At the first level the Confederation of Production and Commerce (CPC), created in 1935, gathers segmented interests according to broad sectors. Affiliate associations encompass interests in agriculture (National Agricultural Society – SNA), in trade in goods and services (National Chamber of Commerce, Services and Tourism), in mining (National Mining Society – SONAMI), in manufacturing (the Society of Industrial Promotion – SOFOFA), in construction (Chilean Chamber of Construction) and in banking (National Association of Banks and Financial Institutions). Each of the associations that are part of the Confederation belongs to the first level of coordinated private interests. The second level of coordination takes place at business associations defined along industrial divides. At a operational level, the coordination is provided by a variety of specific committees created to disseminate information on government actions and establish channels to influence them.

The different positions and priorities that business associations hold with respect to the various modalities and topics of negotiations are derived from the especial nature of the productive activity of their affiliates. In particular, priorities differ between exporting and import-competing sectors, as has been described in the literature (Ventura-Dias, Chapter 1). For instance, private sector interests differ most strongly over the preferred treatment of the agricultural sector in trade negotiations.[17]

Chilean exporters are further divided according to the geographical destination of their exports, between business related to Latin American regional markets and those oriented to the EU, the US or Asia. On one hand, representatives of manufacturing interests, including agro-industries, have shown a preference for bilateral agreements with countries in the region, and integration with Mercosur, which they perceive as beneficial to manufactured exports. On the other hand, the traditional agricultural sector is more concerned with protecting the domestic market from undesirable imports originated in more competitive Mercosur countries. Similarly, the agriculture sector has misgivings about the FTA with the United States, although there is a relative consensus regarding the overall derived benefits among Chilean businessmen.

The CPC created an internal Area of International Negotiations with representation of all sectors in the early 1990s.[18] The SOFOFA acts as the technical secretariat and coordinates the affiliates with the public sector. Although SOFOFA has represented the economy as a whole in bilateral negotiations, the baton is passed back to the CPC whenever the coordination around specific issues or products becomes tangled. Two major channels are used. First, the Committee for International Negotiations monitors the evolution of FTAs and defines courses of action for each case. Secondly, the Council for the Area of International Relations prepares a monthly analysis of the evolution of negotiations and the general problems faced by the export sector, with participation of representatives from the public sector (SFF, 1998).

The existence of those formal mechanisms for coordination does not imply that all heterogeneous interests see their views represented in large associations. In particular, the SMEs prefer to use the Association of Manufacturing Exporters (ASEXMA) and the National Corporation of Exporters as their major agents. Although the different agricultural sectors all coalesce in the SNA, the views of the specialized associations of agricultural producers of fruit, wine, dairy products, and timber, must be taken into account, since they often formulate their interests in negotiations separate from the central body. Likewise, the services sector has only recently instituted a coordination body through the Committee of Exporters in Services (CES) in the Chamber of Commerce of Santiago (CCS). Previously, existing associations provided the coordination of their interests and their representation in negotiations. Formal representation in the CPC existed only in the case of retailing, construction and banking.[19]

The public–private interplay

Overtime and along the three *Concertación* administrations, the Chilean Government has striven to increase the transparence of the negotiating process and promote a serious engagement of the civil society in the process of negotiating the FTAs. Several meetings and seminars were organized by public officials with business organizations, trade unions, non-governmental organizations (NGOs) and parliamentarians, for a systematic debate on how these groups perceived that their interests could be affected by the outcome of the negotiations. Documents on each negotiation were made available electronically and promptly in the web page of DIRECON.

The earliest efforts to improve the links between business and the government in trade negotiations can be dated back to the Commission for negotiations in the LAIA in the mid-1980s. It was established by

SOFOFA to be a forum of information and discussion between the public and the private sectors. Later, as mentioned, the Committee of the Private Sector Participation and the Committee of Negotiators, which invites representatives from the private sector, provided a more permanent channel for the interplay of government and business associations.

The monitoring of the evolution of FTAs, modification of domestic trade instruments, and trade disputes (through Agreements Administration Commission), provide concrete instances that have contributed to a better interaction both within the public sector and between public and private sectors. Finally, the mobility of public officials in various trade-related governmental agencies may have also contributed to a better communication between the two sectors, as officials acquire negotiating experience in diplomatic missions as well as participate with their expertise in the private sector.

Business associations give a positive overall evaluation to their participation in FTA negotiations since the first government of the *Concertación*. The evaluation is less positive with regard to the effective conveyance of private sector views to the government on plurilateral and multilateral negotiations. Similarly, the government's assessment of the improvements introduced by business associations in their technical and organizational arrangements is quite positive, even when a plurality of representation channels prevents a clear identification of major commercial interests.

Trade unions are an important absence in the process of participatory decision-making in Chile. As such, the consensus-formation in trade negotiations in Chile is more backward than in Mercosur where specific channels provide for trade unions' participation. The authoritarian regime in the 1970s and 1980s negatively affected labor relations and disrupted labor organizations. In addition, the government has not been able to provide adequate training to trade unions in order to have staff capable of following joint meetings and of expressing organized labor interests in international negotiations.

Not surprisingly, labor unions have taken a more reactive than pro-active stand, attesting to their difficulties in assigning priorities in industrial restructuring or development policies.

Relations between labor unions, private and public sector representatives have been concentrated in domestic labor reforms. Discussions on association to NAFTA represented an exception to this low profile, when joint commissions were set up at DIRECON with trade union representatives.[20] Ultimately, the participation of organized labor in trade negotiations takes place mainly through the formal channels of civil society coordination such as those created by the process of integration itself.[21] It remains to be seen if such areas of international coordination will be able to permeate the domestic scene to provide better coordination between trade unions and other private and public actors.

Trade policy issues affecting broader interests in civil society, such as environmental or consumer associations are in a similar situation.[22] Consumer associations play a significant role in the definition of technical standards in the international arena that is not reflected at the national level. Some environmental protection organizations have had an active role, especially during the discussion of the possible accession of Chile to the NAFTA, and in the recently negotiated TLC with US. Individuals from the academic sector are represented in some consulting bodies for discussion of trade policy. In contrast to more advanced countries, in Chile there are no independent bodies to provide recommendations on trade policy (WTO, 1997).

Finally, the leading role assumed by some congressmen in public debates on trade policy adds a new dimension to the coordination of public actors. In particular, since the FTA with Peru was sent to the Chilean Congress in 1998, economic commissions demanded a greater role in the ratification of trade agreements. Some congressional representatives have questioned whether the new FTAs fall under the same ratification framework since recent negotiations have gone much further in scope and depth than previous FTAs that were confined to the LAIA narrowly defined trade liberalization.

The negotiating agenda

Producers, trade analysts and policy-makers are in relative agreement about the strategy of trade liberalization for Chile, and the need for a redefinition of its guidelines. However, the precise contents of this strategy, particularly export specialization and the selection of negotiating partners, are peppered with disagreements and misunderstandings. Recent economic trends have increased concerns on growth and employment opportunities. Despite the lack of accord, Chilean society must agree upon a well-defined strategy to follow into the future, especially with respect to the country's trade specialization. After a general assessment of Chilean industrial performance in the last few decades and of the limits to such a model of development perceived by the mid-1990s, the public and academic debate identified three courses of action. First, the neo-liberal model promoting the deregulation of the capital account, continued specialization in primary goods and services, and a possible transformation towards an international financial center. Secondly the

Asian model emphasizing industrial policy, leading to a stronger development of manufacturers, but encountering difficulties to comply with multilateral trade rules. Following this model, more support could be directed to the creation of technological capabilities, training and higher education as well as to export promotion, which would contribute to attract FDI. Thirdly, the 'Nordic' or Scandinavian model that advances through natural resource-based clusters with backward and forward linkages to other sectors amplifying the benefits derived from Chilean comparative advantages.[23] Each of these models and policy options are associated with distinct alternatives affecting priority areas in trade negotiations

Some of these ideas issued from the general debate conflict with the general guidelines for a negotiation agenda established by the government in the early 1990s, incorporating the debate about a trade-based growth strategy, which can be summarized as follows:

1. Reinforce the unilateral trade liberalization model with the results from multilateral agreements and bilateral and plurilateral FTAs under the framework of 'open regionalism', competitiveness and export promotion policies. To avoid the dilemma of selecting negotiating partners, the government decided to simultaneously move in all directions, negotiating with its major industrialized partners, while deepening economic and political linkages with other Latin American countries.
2. Combine trade liberalization with trade-related policies in areas such as services and FDI. There is special interest in competition policy, in order to level the playing field for Chilean firms in foreign markets, particularly in other countries of the region. Furthermore, the government has shown interest in the development of more stable multilateral disciplines on trade in goods and on effective dispute settlement (DS) mechanisms.
3. Enter into negotiations for global and across-the-board liberalization in different negotiating forums. Chilean representatives expressed their interest in negotiations without a priori selection of topics or sectors, in Seattle and Doha at the multilateral level. Similar proposals of non-sectoral selectivity were put forward in the APEC Forum and in the negotiations aiming at the creation of a FTAA, in efforts for the elimination of lists of exceptions in bilateral agreements, and in the Chilean refusal to sign the Information Technology Agreement (ITA) at the WTO. The treatment to agriculture has been an important exception to this neutral approach.
4. Establish a proactive agenda rather than a defensive one. The agenda included accelerated tariff reduction, extension of the scope of

negotiations, elimination of AD measures (initially, in the bilateral agreements), and strengthening of the DS mechanism.

With these basic guidelines in mind, the government has been able to compile a differentiated agenda for each individual negotiating forum, and has maintained a pragmatic approach to idiosyncratic differences with its partners in FTAs. Multilateral negotiations offer potentially important opportunities for market access in agriculture and services, and the Chilean government believes that further liberalization may ensure more stable and competitive conditions. Likewise, as a small economy, Chile strives for stricter multilateral disciplines in AD and safeguards and a more effective DS mechanism. At the regional level, the Chilean government perceives FTAA, and, secondarily, APEC negotiations as highly relevant from a medium- and long-term perspective. However, for many business associations the voluntary character and the vague preferential treatment of the APEC agreements do not warrant special efforts. In both regional agreements, emphasis has been placed on competition policies and on a framework for FDI.

Similarly, Chile is engaged in advancing liberalization beyond the traditional topics of market access to issues of trade in services and FDI at the bilateral level, which is clear in the most recently FTAs negotiated but also with Mercosur. Before the subregional crisis Chile hoped to accelerate tariff reduction, moderate non-tariff barriers, eliminate AD use, improve DS mechanisms and make headway towards macroeconomic coordination. Although trade figures between Chile and the Mercosur have worried private agents, according to official evaluations, regional agreements have relieved the effects of financial crises such as the long-lasting 1997 crisis, and helped to dilute eventual protectionist reactions from trading partners. The Argentine and Brazilian crises have proven to be extremely disruptive for the integration process.

Around this collection of multilateral, regional, and bilateral initiatives, some conflicting opinions have emerged within business associations, within the public sector and between business and the government. For example, differences exist on issues such as the implementation of trade defense instruments and a full incorporation of Chile into Mercosur. The proactive agenda still gathers considerable consensus. It is also generally agreed that public–private cooperation and convergence upon a unified national perception have been fundamental for success in the tasks to be confronted and in the implementation of a new course of action.

There is a wide consensus that Chile will continue pursuing a global export-oriented strategy of liberalization, in which the inclusion of services and further developments around natural resources seem to be generally accepted. Public macro- and microeconomic policies rather than a purposeful trade policy contribute to this course of action. Several questions, however, remain open. The first is how to convert the integration process into an effective engine of growth. Moreover, for many authors, growth cannot be separated from equity, and it is thus necessary to improve the quality of international integration in socially-inclusive terms. International specialization must sustain higher levels of real wages for larger segments of the Chilean population. To these demanding tasks, others would add the need for environmental sustainability in order to expand exports based upon primary products. It is also largely conceded that new advances in the specialization pattern are highly dependent on physical and technological infrastructure developments and higher quality productive factors, especially human resources and research and development.

It is not so clear how the Chilean society will achieve these goals, despite a broad discussion about who should lead the effort. Multilateral trade negotiations have not yet succeeded in involving economic and social actors but, on the other hand, there have been increasing government efforts to engage civil society in the FTAA process. The evolution of negotiations and the associated institutional mechanisms should give rise to new domestic arrangements that ensure civil society participation and greater transparency.

Notes

1. Edwards and Lederman (1998) stated that initially the military had not a precise idea about how deep and how fast the liberalization was going to be. Ffrench-Davis *et al* (1992); and Meller (1993, 1996a). See also Agosin (1997); Ffrench-Davis (1999).
2. The expansion of the Chilean economy has been fostered by the performance of the service sector. Between 1990 and 2000, the share of goods-producing sectors (agriculture, mining, fisheries, and manufacturing) declined from 38 per cent to 35 per cent of gross dermestic product (GDP) whereas that of services increased from 62 per cent to 65 per cent. Accordingly, more than 70 per cent of the labor force is currently employed in different sectors of services, including construction.
3. See Calderón and Griffith-Jones, 1995; ECLAC, 1998, ch. I sections B and C; CCS, 1999, 2000; Chudnovsky *et al.*, 1999; Agosin and Alvarez, 2000; Chile, CIE, 2000; and ECLAC 2000, 2001b, ch. II.
4. The stagnation in trade performance in the second half of the 1990s was partially a response to adverse macroeconomic conditions such as the appreciation of the domestic currency, but decreasing export growth was also a consequence of structural factors. Low investment in skilled labor, technology

and training, and difficulties in capital markets access are structural obstacles to the diversification and growth of Chilean exports (Agosin and Ffrench-Davis, 1998; Díaz and Ramos, 1998).

5. Sáez and Valdés (1999) use the concept of 'lateral trade policy' to refer to the policy of bilateral and plurilateral agreements implemented by Chile along the 1990s. See also Pizarro (1994); Agosin (1997); van Klaveren (1998); Chile, Direcon (2000).
6. Chile has FTAs with Costa Rica and El Salvador.
7. Although the average tariff in industrial countries is very low, some products that are important for Chilean exports, such as avocados and wine, face higher tariffs or non-tariff barriers.
8. The price bands have also granted a differentiated treatment to sensible agricultural products.
9. See Rosales (1993); Díaz (1995); and Meller (1996b), for a closer look at the second phase.
10. PROCHILE is the acronym for the Export Promotion Directorate of the Ministry of Foreign Relations.
11. The salmon case started with the petition in 1997 from producers in three states of the United States denouncing that the salmon imports from Chile were benefiting from subsidies (28 programs) and were damaging the local industry. After a greatly expensive procedure, the process ended without application of countervailing duties, but with anti-dumping duties at an average of 4.54 per cent (See also 'Contenciosos' in web page of Chile, Direcon: www.direcon.cl).
12. Several Chilean policies have been challenged in the WTO. The first complaint, filed by the EU in December 1997, questioned a special tax applied in Chile on sales of imported alcoholic beverages, which implies a discriminatory tax on whiskey with respect to the domestically produced pisco. After Chile modified the tax in question, basing the tax level on the alcoholic content as a parameter, the European Communities filed a second complaint and called for consultations, rejecting the tax modification and asking for a dispute panel. In April 2000, the EU presented a new complaint on the prohibition imposed by Chile on the use of its ports for ships engaged in swordfish fishing.
13. The modifications of these instruments were incorporated in the Act of Tariff Reform (Ministerio de Economía, 1998). See also Agosin (1997); Chile, Banco Central, (1997); and WTO (1997).
14. See a broader analysis in Silva (2000).
15. See Montero and Federici (1997); Robledo (1997); and Silva (2000).
16. See Montero and Federici (1997); and Robledo (1997).
17. In several significant agreements, the timetable for tariff reductions for sensitive agricultural products was as high as 18 years.
18. At the beginning of 1990, the CPC financed a broad assessment of the impact of an eventual Chile–United States Agreement (Coeymans and Larrain, 1992).
19. For a detailed description of Chilean sectoral organization of interests see Silva (2001, ch. 2).
20. Labor and ecological organizations were the main opponents to NAFTA (Oppenheim, 1997). The influence of labor unions in the United States and

Canada would have been determinant on a weak trade union movement in Chile, still unable to define its proper identity. The joint statement by the Chilean largest national trade union (CUT) and the AFL-CIO in favor of a bilateral agreement with the United States was envisaging the inclusion of labor clauses in the accession of Chile to the NAFTA (Alburquerque, 1994).

21. Such areas are the Committee for Civil Society Participation in the process toward the creation of a FTAA and the Economic and Social Consulting Forum at Mercosur, and the cooperation instances provided by the Agreement between Chile and Canada. See also 'Sociedad Civil' in web page of Direcon: www.direcon.cl.
22. See http://www.comerciojusto.terra.cl for an interesting example of an active interaction between a Chilean ONG that defends consumers' rights and the government.
23. See Díaz (1995); Agosin (1997); and Díaz and Ramos (1998).

3

Mexico: A Regional Player in Multilateral Trade Negotiations

Antonio Ortiz Mena[1]

Introduction

Mexico can be fairly deemed a special case in Latin America regarding to trade liberalization. To begin with, it launched a very ambitious and sustained program of trade reform in 1986, right after the country's decision to join the General Agreement on Tariffs and Trade (GATT). Physical proximity to the United States also distinguishes the Mexican case, particularly considering US participation in Mexican trade and the drive to constitute a North American Free Trade Area (NAFTA) since 1990. Furthermore, the Mexican reform was highly successful compared to other cases in the region, with the exception of Chile. Indeed, a decade after the reform began, exports and imports accounted for nearly 40 per cent of GDP and manufactured exports increased from 15 per cent to 85 per cent of total exports. Finally, unlike trade reform experiences in larger Latin American peers, Argentina and Brazil, Mexican private sector representatives and organizations actively and effectively participated in the design and implementation of the new policies.

This chapter seeks to determine the priorities of business and government for future multilateral trade negotiations, based on negotiation experiences in NAFTA and the Uruguay Round (UR). Moreover, it will outline possible points of convergence and contention among Latin American countries in future negotiations. The next section considers Mexico's move from unilateral reform to regional integration with special emphasis on NAFTA; there follows an outline of Mexico's current trade policies and then an assessment of the costs and benefits of Mexico's World Trade Organization (WTO) commitments. The penultimate section sets out government and business views on trade negotiations; and the final section considers the role of Mexico as a regional player.

From unilateral liberalization to regional integration

After the economic shocks of 1982, the Ministry of Trade and Industrial Development (SECOFI)[2] used trade policy instruments to pursue macroeconomic stabilization and economic growth. Unilateral reforms during the 1980s decreased the maximum tariff from 40 per cent to 20 per cent, eliminated official import prices and nearly abolished import permits. Liberalization facilitated the negotiation of regional trade agreements in the 1990s, notably with Mexico's largest trade partner, the US. NAFTA followed a *de facto* integration, as US participation in Mexican trade had surpassed 70 per cent for several decades. Politically it reflected a change in strategy from incipient efforts at trade diversification to acceptance of Mexico's reliance on the US. Mexico was able to make the most of a situation of trade concentration that was difficult to alter.

NAFTA

NAFTA modified Mexico's trade policy, influenced its stance in the UR, and affected trade and investment flows. The agreement was proposed in 1990, negotiated in 1991 and 1992, with further negotiations on labor and environment parallel agreements in 1993, and finally entered into force in 1 January 1994. The wave of reforms ushered in by NAFTA, either under explicit NAFTA commitments or NAFTA-related changes, left an indelible mark on trade policy. Mexico's trade concentration with the US meant that NAFTA-related reforms resulted in a substantial opening of the Mexican economy. More importantly, the agreement increased the political and economic costs of trade policy reversals and restrained trade policy with other countries to compatibility with (if not subservience to) NAFTA.

Exports produced in 'maquiladoras', or in-bond processing plants, constitute more than 80 per cent of exports. Duty drawbacks on non-NAFTA components were eliminated in 2001 as scheduled, but at the outset of 2002 the Mexican government extended a series of sector-specific promotion programs (PROSEC) to approved companies, which reduce Most-Favored Nation (MFN) tariffs to zero per cent or, in the case of maquila inputs, to 5 per cent. High priority was also accorded to textiles and steel sheets and tubes, as the textile industry employs nearly one million people and the automobile industry over half a million.

Sectoral sensitivities are revealed through exceptions and especially long tariff phase-out periods granted to certain products by the agreement. Mexico negotiated 10-year tariff phase-outs for automobiles, refrigerators, washing machines, poultry parts, pork products, potatoes, apples and vegetable oils. In fact, 60 per cent of Mexican agricultural imports are protected by 10 and 15-year tariff reduction schedules. Corn, beans and powdered milk are among the 1 per cent of products with a 15-year phase-out period; corn and beans provide employment for low-income peasants who would otherwise be displaced by cheaper imports. Mexico also maintained restrictions on foreign investment in the energy and rail sectors. The energy sector has long been politically sensitive and the Mexican Petroleum Company (PEMEX) still holds a monopoly over oil exploration and development, as well as sales of gasoline and fuel oil. Foreign investment is not allowed in oil exploration, production or refining. Investment was liberalized in secondary petrochemicals, and procurement by PEMEX and the Federal Electricity Commission for NAFTA suppliers was opened up.

Restrictive rules of origin in NAFTA, especially protecting the textile and auto sectors, have been a source of criticism (Hufbauer and Schott, 1993). For most textile products, the rule is 'yarn forward', meaning that a manufactured product must be cut and sewn from North American fibers to benefit from free trade. Similarly, there are a number of restrictions in the auto sector, including a high 62.5 per cent value-added requirement for autos, light trucks, engines and transmissions.

Liberalization of telecommunications affected the two-way long-distance telephone traffic between Mexico and the US, the most intense in the world. It provided access to value-added services, allowed the establishment of private networks and eliminated tariffs on trade of telecommunications equipment. The 1995 Telecommunications Law permits domestic and foreign private investment in long-distance services, in local value-added services and in local wireless services. The majority of local wire services are still provided by the former public telephone monopoly, the Mexican Telephone Company (TELMEX), which was privatized in 1990 (Bastos Tigre, 2003).

Market share restrictions for financial services were maintained under NAFTA. For instance, no single foreign-owned bank was allowed a share greater than 4 per cent of the market before the year 2000. After the December 1994 peso crisis, the rules on foreign participation in the financial services sector were liberalized on a unilateral basis and not restricted to NAFTA members.

Apart from substantive commitments, NAFTA established new procedures for trade relations, including dispute settlement mechanisms for anti-dumping (AD) and countervailing duty (CVD) cases (Chapter 19) and investor-state disputes (Chapter 11). NAFTA investment provisions, including dispute settlement, have been considered far superior to the URA on trade-related investment measures (TRIMs), and suggestions have been made that NAFTA serve as precedent for a future 'GATT for Investment' (Schott with Buurman, 1994). NAFTA also contains a general dispute settlement mechanism (Chapter 20) under which binational panels submit recommendations with possibilities of sanctioned retaliation (Weston and Delich, 2003).

Mexico undertook sweeping legal reforms both during and following the negotiations, owing to informal understandings reached during NAFTA negotiations and unilateral decisions. Of the total 204 federal laws in place in December 1996, 107 have been published and 57 reformed since 1992 (López Ayllon, 1997), many directly affecting trade policy instruments.

Other free trade agreements

Mexico pursued a myriad of free trade agreements (FTAs) in the wake of NAFTA, so that it now boasts preferential trade with over 30 countries worldwide. 'New generation' FTAs negotiated by Mexico with Latin American countries are closely patterned after NAFTA in terms of the range of issues covered and their procedural content. They are: Mexico–Bolivia (1995), Mexico–Costa Rica (1995), G–3 (Mexico, Colombia and Venezuela, 1995), Mexico–Nicaragua (1998), Mexico–Chile (1999), and Mexico–Northern Triangle (El Salvador, Honduras and Guatemala, 2001).[3]

The three extra-hemispheric trade agreements Mexico has signed are also quite comprehensive but stray from NAFTA precedents. The FTA with the European Union (EU), which entered into force on 1 July 2000, has by far the most potential effects on Mexico's trade and investment patterns. By 2003 virtually all industrial exports will enter the EU duty-free, and by 2007 EU exporters will reach full parity with their NAFTA competitors via duty-free entrance of all industrial goods into the Mexican market. Some matters were dealt with at the EU-level, while other issues, such as government procurement, were dealt with at the bilateral level with each of the 15 member countries. The agreement also has a democratic clause, contrary to NAFTA-like agreements that completely exclude any domestic political issues. The agreement with European Free Trade Agreement (EFTA), comprised of Iceland, Liechtenstein, Norway and Switzerland that went into effect in 2001, closely patterned on the FTA with the EU. A FTA with Israel that took effect in July 2000 is less comprehensive than the others, excluding investment, agriculture and services from coverage. Finally, preliminary talks for a FTA with Japan are under way. Japan has traditionally been reluctant to enter into any trade agreements apart from its multilateral commitments under the WTO and the loose commitments derived from the Asia Pacific Economic Cooperation (APEC), though an agreement between Japan and Singapore signed in January 2002 may pave the way for more bilateral deals with Japan.

Impact of the reforms

Unilateral and NAFTA-related reforms offered a face-lift to both trade composition and volume. Reforms in the 1980s precipitated a shift in trade composition, while the 1990s saw a jump in trade volume and a variation in trade patterns. In the early 1980s oil exports represented nearly three-quarters of total exports, but were replaced in importance by manufactured goods, which by the 1990s comprised more than 80 per cent of exports. With the boom in manufactured exports, and especially maquila goods, the 1990s saw a drastic surge in export volumes. Exports increased from less than US$30 billion in 1990 to US$166 billion at the turn of the century (see Table 3.1). By 2000, Mexico had become by far the largest exporter in Latin America and the second trade partner of the US, surpassed only by Canada. Trade with the US, already highly concentrated in 1982, became even more so by the close of the century. Increased concentration came largely at the expense of trade with Europe, as exports to the EU fell from 21 to less than 3 per cent between 1982 and 2000 and exports to the US expanded from 53 per cent in 1982 to 82 percent in 2000. These shifts in trade concentrations have meant that a large portion of Mexico's trade is covered by free trade agreements with its main trade partners, which should ease the subsequent implementation of URA commitments, reducing business resistance to additional reforms.

Table 3.1 Exports by major economic areas (fob in US$ million)

Year	*Extractive industries*	*Manufacturing industries*	*Agriculture and livestock*	*Total*
1980	10,410	3,571	1,527	15,512
1985	13,819	6,428	1,409	21,664
1990	9,538	14,861	2,162	26,839
1955	7,975	67,383	4,015	79,542
2000	16,903	145,334	4,217	166,454

Source: Secretaría de Hacienda y Cuentas Públicas, SHCP (n.d.).

Trade policy instruments[4]

Trade policies implemented in Mexico have been a by product of both unilaterally initiated and regionally coordinated reforms. The changes left trade largely liberalized both in terms of tariffs and non-tariff barriers (NTBs), and strengthened many related regulatory instruments.

Licensing requirements were virtually eliminated after Mexico joined the GATT in 1986. By December 1993 only 1.6 per cent of tariff lines were subject to licensing, but they amounted to 21.6 per cent of all imports, consisting mainly of agricultural products, petroleum products and motor vehicles. However, the use of import licenses resurfaced in the mid-1990s; by 1998 nearly 5 per cent of imports were affected by such licenses. Furthermore, some imports, like used cars, are prohibited altogether. NAFTA only allows imports of cars that are at least 30 years old, which in no way compete with auto production in Mexico (De Remes *et al.*, 1996). The rationale behind maintaining NTBs for these sectors included job displacement concerns in agriculture, sovereignty and symbolic concerns in the natural gas and petroleum industries, and the role of decrees in protecting the automobile industry (Lustig, 1992).

Applied tariffs for imports of non-agricultural products ranged from zero to 20 per cent by 1994, which is below the weighted average bound rate granted upon joining GATT (52.2 per cent) and the subsequent reduction under the URAs (40.3 per cent) (see Table 3.2). As a result of tariffication commitments under the URAs, Mexico's import duties on agricultural goods range from 36 per cent to 260 per cent, although agricultural goods represent a very small share of total imports. Moreover, license requirements were reduced from 1,200 tariff lines to 325, representing only 20 per cent of imports. The few remaining taxes on exports are restricted to petroleum derivatives, agricultural products and endangered species.

Participation in NAFTA and other FTAs restrained the use of increased protection in response to strains of the 1994/95 economic crisis. Nevertheless, some tariffs were raised, such as the 15 percentage point increase on apparel, shoes and manufactured leather goods from countries not part of an FTA with Mexico. MFN tariff increases of 3 and 10 percentage points in 1999 raised the simple average applied rate to 16.5 per cent in 2001 (WTO, 2002). The differential between MFN and FTA tariffs was thus widened; as the 1990s drew to a close Mexico's simple average MFN tariff was 13 per cent compared to the 2 per cent simple average tariff for imports from the US. The gap raises the possibility

Table 3.2 Liberalization of trade restrictions

	1982	*1984*	*1986*	*1988*	*1990*	*1992*	*1994*	*1996*	*1998*	*2000*
Import License Coverage[a]	100%	83%	27.8%	21.2%	13.7%	10.7%	12.9%	2.7%	4.4%	6.2%
Simple Average Tariffs[b]	27%	23.3%	22.6%	9.7%	13.1%	13.1%	12.4%	13.3%	13.2%	16.2%
Trade Weighted Average Tariff[c]		8.5%	13.1%	6.2%	10.5%	11.5%	5.7%	2.9%	2.6%	3.0%
Tariff Positions	16	10	11	5	5	6	8		8	
Maximum Tariff[d]	100%	100%	100%	20%	20%	25%	25%	35%	35%	35%

Source: OECD (1996), SECOFI, and EU (n.d.).
Notes: [a] Percentage of imports covered; [b] Arithmetic average of every tariff line's MFN tariff; [c] Trade data calculated on the basis of effective imports' tariff levels, weighted average of every tariff line on the basis of yearly import value; [d] Does not include tariff peaks on certain agricultural imports resulting from UR tariffication commitments, which reach 260 per cent.

of net trade distortions. The relatively low weighted tariff of 2.6 per cent in 1998 reflects Mexico's trade concentration with the US.

Despite these liberalization efforts, NTBs in Mexico affected a higher percentage of trade than in Argentina, Chile, Colombia and Venezuela. Mexico also has the highest incidence of AD and CVDs (1.4 per cent) among those countries, the second highest rate of non-automatic licenses (8.6 per cent included local content and/or export performance requirements) and was the only country other than Brazil with imports by state monopolies.

The 1993 Foreign Trade Law established safeguard provisions and revamped AD and CVD regulations that were issued around the time Mexico joined GATT.[5] Mexico is among the relatively few developing countries with a safeguard statute in domestic law, but it has rarely been used, as application standards are stricter and duties are imposed for less time than AD and CVDs. Aggressive AD and CVD use began about a year and a half before the peso crisis (see Table 3.3). Between 1991 and 1993, the number of cases submitted increased nine-fold. A record 1,125 per cent tariff was imposed on Chinese footwear in 1993. In 1994, 32 per cent of Mexican imports from China and 13 per cent from Indonesia were subject to AD and CVD duties. Organization of Economic Cooperation and Development (OECD) calculations show that,

Table 3.3 AD, CVD and safeguards resolutions

Year	*No. of resolutions*
1987	25
1988	38
1989	22
1990	28
1991	55
1992	89
1993	158
1994	109
1995	129
1996	91
1997	56
1998	66
1999	84
2000	86

Source: Unidad de Prácticas Comerciales Internacionales – (n.d.), 'Resultados de la UPCI,' available at http://www.upci.gob.mx

controlling for the size of trade flows, Mexico is one of the most active AD users in the world. Even so, the government publishes failed AD petitions in the *Diario Oficial* (*Daily Register*) with the apparent intent of dissuading frivolous petitions. Likewise, the amount of trade subject to AD and CVD duties is quite small, affecting only 0.5 per cent of trade in 1995 (OECD, 1996).

A total of 234 investigations regarding unfair trade practices and safeguards were initiated between 1987 and 2000 (see Table 3.3). There was a single safeguards case and 18 subsidies cases. The rest of the cases (91 per cent) refer to AD issues, the majority of which resulted in definitive findings affecting steel, chemicals, and the textile and apparel sectors. Exports from the US, China and Brazil were most affected. Different rules apply for each of these three countries: the US can make use of NAFTA Chapter 19 provisions, Brazil can make use of WTO provisions, and China, despite WTO membership since 2001, will only be able to seek redress in Mexican courts until the expiration of the waiver covering application of the WTO AD Code. The government argued that the high incidence of such actions was partly related to the strong peso, and while the incidence of AD actions did decrease somewhat after the December 1994 devaluation, it remains quite high.

The Foreign Trade Law seeks close coordination between SECOFI, which administers AD and CVD procedures, and the Federal Competition Commission (CFC), which is in charge of competition policy. SECOFI notifies the CFC when it believes a firm is engaging in monopolistic behavior, and the CFC is entitled to issue opinions on AD and CVD decisions. The Mexican system differs from that of other countries in that the same administrative unit (in this case SECOFI) issues the dumping determination and carries out the injury determination. Separating these two processes into different administrative units might improve the functioning of unfair trade laws by rendering the process more impervious to political influences (Tórtora and Tussie, 2003).

Further non-tariff protection comes from the use of standards, labeling and rules of origin. The 1992 Law on Standards and Measurements provides for both mandatory and voluntary standards, to be developed by the National Standards Commission and the National Standards Consultant Committee based on expert recommendations and public input. Complaints of protectionist use of mandatory standards have been raised by importers who argue that voluntary norms would have sufficed, that mandatory norms were 'excessively strict' (OECD, 1996: 42), and that the law generated a 'labyrinthine system' (WTO, 1998a: 227). Mandatory labeling and marking has also come under fire from importers.

They cite having to do the labeling before the products arrive in Mexico as a major inconvenience, since manufacturers rarely know the destination of their products. Related complaints arise over inspection requirements in customs areas rather than at the point of sale, which cause delays in clearing goods (OECD, 1996).

Though the aforementioned barriers have persisted, a wave of trade facilitating reforms was ushered in before the end of the century, including privatization and deregulation. There was a flood of privatization and closure of state-owned enterprises with the disappearance of 800 parastatal companies between 1982 and 1988 (OECD, 1996). The process continued into the 1990s with privatization of commercial banks and the telephone company. Some oligopolies endured, and prudential regulation and oversight of the financial system has proven woefully inadequate.[6] Regulation (especially competition policy) was emphasized less than privatization, though the government did issue the Federal Economic Competition Law in 1993. The law established the CFC and granted it powers to review mergers and acquisitions and make determinations about anticompetitive practices without Executive or Judicial interventions. Though the CFC is ostensibly an independent body, the President names its five commissioners to ten-year terms. Some CFC rulings have also been controversial, like the merger between Telmex and Televisa to provide cable services.[7]

Deregulation of the transport industry resulted in trade facilitation. A well-known shortcoming of the previous regime was that local monopolies forced trucks to return empty after making their delivery rather than transport goods from their point of the delivery to their home base. Deregulation of the telecommunications sector and the privatization of ports also had trade-enhancing effects and to some degree reduced the level of corruption prevalent in these sectors. The financial sector, the petrochemical industry, airline services and electricity generation were also deregulated during the 1990s. These reforms were carried out at the federal level though deregulation efforts have expanded to the state and municipal levels.

Beyond liberalization efforts, the government implemented various proactive trade facilitation instruments. Three programs for export promotion stand out: the Mixed Commission for the Promotion of Exports (COMPEX), the Program for Export-Intensive Industries (ALTEX) and the maquila and Temporary Imports Program (PITEX). COMPEX is a consulting mechanism between export industries and government officials that meets regionally every three months. Exporters bring complaints on bureaucratic and regulatory export obstacles and government officials try to solve them within a month. A national COMPEX gathering, in which cabinet members participate, tackles the most intractable issues. The ALTEX program awards export companies special administrative, fiscal and financial treatment. PITEX grants duty drawbacks to firms for temporary use of inputs for goods that are subsequently exported. Commitments under NAFTA and the URA on TRIMs required modifications, which took effect in 2001. The temporary import of inputs and components will still be tax- and duty-free if such inputs originate in a NAFTA country, regardless of export destination. Inputs and components that do not originate in NAFTA but are destined for export to Canada or the US are exempted from the lesser of the two applicable duties: duties that those inputs pay to enter Mexico and duties that the final product pays to enter the US or Canada. This measure seeks to avoid double taxation and free riding by non-members. These rules do not apply to machinery or equipment, which have paid import duties since 2001. In addition to these programs, the foreign trade bank (BANCOMEX) provides financing at competitive rates for exporting companies and helps them search for potential buyers and partners for joint ventures.

Sector-specific policies are aimed at strengthening the export sector by linking small and medium enterprises (SMEs) to larger and more dynamic exporting companies. It is hoped that through training and the facilitation of links between enterprises, SMEs can contribute to the inputs of larger firms. While these policies comply with WTO regulations, their effectiveness is not yet evident. A number of sector-specific promotion programs were implemented, beginning in 1998, to avoid adversely affecting the maquiladora industry with the changes to PITEX. The industries covered include electric, electronics, furniture, toys, shoes, mining, capital goods, photography, agriculture machinery, chemical, textile and garment, and auto. The duties paid by final goods, inputs and machinery are unilaterally lowered under these programs, such that the majority pays either zero or 5 per cent duties. These rules are in compliance with NAFTA commitments since non-originating goods no longer enter duty-free, but the reduction of tariffs means that in practice adverse effects to industries using non-originating components should be minimal.

A final effort at liberalization reformed the 1973 Foreign Investment Law, which put severe restrictions on foreign investment. With the 1982 economic crisis and the drying-up of voluntary lending by foreign commercial banks, the government opted to liberalize the legal framework governing foreign direct investment (FDI) gradually at first, allowing majority foreign ownership in certain sectors. Additionally, it re-classified petrochemicals to allow private sector participation in 1984 and 1986.[8] However it was not until May 1989 that the government altered FDI requirements, enacting a new set of regulations that allowed 100 per cent foreign ownership without previous approval by the regulatory body (the National Foreign Investment Commission) in a number of sectors and sped up the approval process in the rest. Policies were further liberalized under a new Foreign Investment Law in 1993, which, contrary to its predecessor, attempts to attract FDI. The 1993 law offers legal certainty and transparent rules, streamlined procedures for investment approvals, and opened new sectors to foreign investment.[9] There are no fiscal or other incentives (Chudnovsky and Lopez, 2003). The scope and coverage of the new law are similar to those of NAFTA Chapter 11, which contains provisions for opening to US and Canadian investment and an advanced investor-state dispute settlement mechanism.

WTO commitments[10]

Aggressive unilateral trade liberalization dovetailed with regional integration, to give Mexico a one-up on other developing countries in the UR. It was at the forefront of areas such as investment and intellectual property rights (IPRs) and gradually softened its position on eliminating export subsidies and tariffying imports in agriculture.

Mexico benefited from the URAs through market access gains without offering many concessions in return. The bound tariff rate for industrial goods of 35 per cent was actually higher than the tariffs Mexico was applying; it did agree to tariffy non-tariff barriers imposed on agricultural goods, but the resulting tariffs still award ample protection. By the close of negotiations, most trade legislation was already in compliance with the URAs, as a result of unilateral measures and FTA-related reforms.

Market access: tariffs

Industrial export products for which Mexico gained improved access as a result of URAs include beer, rum, tequila, pharmaceuticals, chemicals, furniture, glass, ceramics, some steel products, combustion engines and their parts, computers, and vehicle chassis. Tariffs for industrial goods were gradually reduced three percentage points annually for five years, reducing the bound rate from 50 to 35 per cent in compliance with URAs stipulating a 33 per cent reduction of outstanding tariffs. In practice, the URAs did not require Mexico to reduce any of its applied rates on non-agricultural goods, because bound tariffs are higher than many applied rates. This remaining gap between bound and applied rates, though lessened by the URAs, poses an inconvenience and a source of uncertainty according to trade partners (WTO, 1998). The increase in tariffs after the 1994 peso crisis shows that their complaints are not groundless. Recognition for unilateral tariff reductions within the WTO, as proposed by Mexico in the UR, would give greater incentives to lower bound rates than to the applied rates, thus reducing the uncertainty generated by the gaps and avoiding potential WTO-compliant tariff increases.

Agricultural exports that benefited from URAs include honey, fresh flowers, avocados, mangos, lemons, coffee, orange juice, oranges, papayas, onions and cantaloupes. Market access gains for some of the most important agricultural exports (fruit, vegetables and tropical products) were overshadowed by disappointment over the WTO's continued allowance of export subsidies. As a second-best solution, Mexico proposed developing countries be allowed to match other countries' subsidies, in order to defend products in third markets. Agricultural subsidies have been greatly reduced, as Mexico, together with other developing countries, agreed to a 13.3 per cent reduction in the Total Aggregate Measure of Support (AMS).[11] Subsidies for basic foodstuffs (corn, beans and milk) have likewise been reduced and subsidies for tortillas were eliminated in 1999. Though no export subsidies are awarded, Mexico included some in its UR commitments for corn, beans, wheat, sorghum and sugar, in order to leave open the option of subsidies should the need and ability arise. According to WTO calculations, Mexican tariffs imposed on agricultural imports will decline from an import-weighted base level of 77 per cent to an eventual bound level of 67 per cent after the ten-year transition period, in comparison with a minimum 10 per cent and 25 per cent overall reduction commitment. Although there are peaks in sensitive agricultural sectors such as corn, beans and powdered milk and overall import-weighted tariff levels are also quite high, it must be noted that these tariffs are bound, in contrast to the agreement on manufactured goods, where full coverage of bindings was not achieved.

Though Multi-Fiber Arrangement (MFA) quotas will be phased out, high tariffs will continue to hinder exports from developing to developed country markets (Schott with Buurman, 1994). Specifically, developed countries will reduce tariffs on textiles and apparel by a weighted average of 22 per cent, so that average protection levels after reductions will be 12 per cent. Although Mexico secured access to the US market for goods originating within NAFTA, it will still face high tariffs for goods not originating in the bloc.

Market access: non-tariff barriers

As mentioned before, Mexico uses safeguards infrequently, and has seldom been the object of safeguard actions by other countries. Mexico supported the stricter disciplines imposed by the UR Safeguards Agreement, such as the prohibition of voluntary export restraints (VERs) and the extension of special treatment to developing countries. Similarly, Mexico has not only been an active AD user, but its exports have also faced such duties. The main exports affected have been cement, iron and steel, cut flowers, synthetic and acrylic fibers, and sisal twine. Mexico favored stricter disciplines than those agreed to under the UR and has been among the proponents of substituting competition policy for unfair trade laws. Its AD legislation was basically in accord with URAs; some alterations to bring it fully into line have been made.

During the UR Mexico requested non-actionable status for certain environment-related subsidies, as well as for regional subsidies aimed at decentralizing production away from Mexico City and other large urban centers. The state company that provided fertilizer at subsidized prices was privatized in 1992, and the National Subsidized Staple Products Company (CONASUPO), which was in charge of domestic price supports and consumer and producer subsidies, was liquidated in 1999. The supports provided by the Direct Support for the Countryside Program (PROCAMPO) were exempted from UR subsidy reduction commitments and will not be subject to CVDs. It also proposed that countries be given credit for eliminating export subsidies ahead of the UR timetable. Mexico's preferences on non-agricultural subsidies were largely borne out in the URAs.

Mexico has advocated the transparent use of sanitary and phytosanitary standards, arguing that in most instances the imposition of NTBs for sanitary and phytosanitary reasons has no scientific merit. Its own practices are similar to those agreed to in the UR, largely resulting from NAFTA commitments. Mexico's exports have been subject to this type of NTB, including poultry meat, avocados, chili peppers, squash and strawberries. Before NAFTA negotiations, arguments for an FTA with the US often cited avocados: Mexico was the world's largest producer, the US was the world's largest market, yet Mexico could not export avocados to the US.

The URAs on rules of origin deal with discrimination among sources of supply for reasons other than Article XXIV of GATT 1994, as may be the case when goods from certain countries are subject to AD and CVD duties. Rules of origin are imposed to avoid triangulation and the sidestepping of such duties. Mexico does not apply specific rules of origin to imports from MFN sources; however, it does require certificates of origin when those goods are subject to AD and CVD action, especially in sectors such as textiles, apparel and shoes.

The use of import licenses has been virtually eliminated. In the few cases where they are still applied, Mexico argues that standards fulfill the provisions of the GATT Import Licensing Code. Nevertheless, some delegations to the WTO have questioned the transparency of award procedures for import licenses, especially when the fulfillment of compulsory standards is required (WTO, 1998).

Other URAs

The state-trading enterprise CONASUPO raised concerns among foreign exporters because of a limited quota on the import of powdered milk at low tariffs. The 'historical importer', CONASUPO Industrialized Milk (LICONSA), was granted the first option of filling that quota, essentially closing the market to all other importers. The majority of import permits for corn and beans are also allotted to LICONSA. In the 1997 Trade Policy Review of Mexico, several countries complained of CONASUPO's lack of transparency, and of the Mexican government's reluctance to give full and clear information on the practices of CONASUPO (WTO, 1998). However, CONASUPO has since been dismantled.

Government procurement policies have also come under fire, as Mexico seems unwilling to open this sector within a multilateral framework (WTO, 1998). Mexico did not sign the WTO Government Procurement Agreement, as it was not included in the single undertaking.

Local content requirements were phased out in the Mexican electronics industry in 1990, but they are still prevalent in the auto sector (36 per cent for small vehicles and 40 for large), in order to generate incentives for the use of local auto parts. These measures are inconsistent with the URA on TRIMs. It was agreed that all TRIMs are inconsistent with both national treatment and the prohibition of quantitative restrictions, and that developing countries must eliminate them. This is one of the largest challenges Mexico faces as a result of the URAs, especially as it overlaps with previous agreements under NAFTA. Countries have voiced their opposition to restrictive practices by Mexico in the auto sector (WTO, 1998). Nevertheless, SECOFI claims that Mexico is not obligated to amend or rescind its automotive decree (SECOFI, n.d.).

Unlike TRIMs, Mexico's TRIPs regime, in theory, is fairly state of the art. Mexico has made great leaps in the legal framework governing IPR. The 1976 Law on Inventions and Trademarks, which covered patents, trademarks, copyrights and trade secrets, was amended in 1987 to strengthen the protection accorded by law. US pressures led to a new IPR law in June 1991, which awarded patents for up to 20 years and trademarks for up to ten; it also gave greater teeth to judicial procedures against infringements.

Under the General Agreement on Trade in Services (GATS), Mexico made commitments in most areas covered by the negotiations except environmental services and recreational, cultural and sporting services. Its commitment on the movement of physical persons is limited to intra-corporate transfers and specialists. It maintains limitations on foreign ownership in a number of sectors; in financial services individual shareholding can not exceed 7.5 per cent and Mexican stockholders must maintain effective control. The cap on foreign ownership of commercial banks was raised by ten percentage points, to 30 per cent. In many services, such as accounting, auditing and bookkeeping, certain telecommunications and audiovisual services, construction, private education and health services, FDI may not exceed 49 per cent of the registered capital of enterprises. In other sectors, such as certain professional services and all scheduled distribution services, Mexico allowed up to 100 per cent foreign ownership.

As a signatory of several FTAs, Mexico is sensitive about changes to Article XXIV of GATT 1994. During the UR it argued, together with EFTA and the EU, against the Australian position of requiring that no major sector be excluded from a FTA. In the end, the changes to Article XXIV were only advisory.

Business and government views[12]

Business views

Manufactured goods account for more than 90 per cent of exports and imports, and five broad sectors (electric and electronics, autos, capital goods, textiles, and processed foods) represent nearly 80 per cent of all manufactured exports and nearly 70 per cent of manufactured imports. Some of the most dynamic export sectors, such as the textile and apparel sector and several industries of the processed foods sector, are also import-competing sectors, although they are not listed separately as such. To the contrary, in the Argentine case, export and import-competing sectors do not coincide (see Tussie *et al.*, Chapter 4).

The electric and electronics sectors are represented by the National Chamber of the Electronics, Telecommunications and Computer Industries (CANIETI). Many of the industries represented by CANIETI are linked to the maquiladora industry. Electric and electronics represent approximately 30 per cent of total manufactured exports and imports. The Mexican Automotive Industry Association (AMIA) represents all major assemblers in Mexico, including Ford, Daimler-Chrysler, General Motors, Renault, Volkswagen and Nissan. Despite its name, the National Chamber of Electric Manufactures (CANAME) represents a sizable share of the capital goods sector (around 10 per cent of total manufactured exports and 15 per cent of imports). A specialized office in the Confederation of Industrial Chambers (CONCAMIN) represents textiles and apparel, and the processed foods sector is represented by the National Industrial Transformation Chamber (CANACINTRA), a member of CONCAMIN. CANACINTRA represents approximately 5 per cent of total manufactured exports and imports.[13]

The electric and electronics sector regarded the URAs as positive, insofar as the Mexican government decided not to join the Ministerial Declaration on Trade in Information Technology Products (ITA). CANIETI preferred postponing accession, given disagreement within its ranks on the issue, but by mid-2000 members agreed on supporting accession. Most of the businesses represented are multinational corporations that in general favor free trade, and many of its concerns were already addressed through NAFTA. CANIETI's main concern was the commitment to phase out PITEX coverage for goods not originating in NAFTA countries if they were to be used as inputs for intra-NAFTA trade.

The auto sector looked positively upon the results of the UR because it was able to sidestep full compliance through a series of bilateral deals, and AMIA has been able to count on close cooperation with the Mexican government on these issues. The sector was opposed to the actual substance of the agreements, especially parts of the TRIMs agreement that relegated performance requirements of the national auto decree inconsistent with multilateral commitments. Local content requirements and import rules related to foreign exchange balances were to be removed by January 2000. South Korea and Japan have pressed Mexico on this issue, to no avail. Problems with the US are avoided as NAFTA rules prevail, which allow for the gradual liberalization of decree rules until the expiration of the decree slated for the end of 2003. Similarly, an understanding was reached with the EU during FTA negotiations whereby Mexico would allow the importation of auto parts from certain foreign industries, in contravention of the decree, in order to maintain the 2003 phase-out date. Mexico in principle gained a three-year moratorium on TRIMs and is cautiously optimistic of gaining a five-year reprieve through alliance with Brazil and India, so that full implementation will be postponed until January 2005.[14]

The capital goods sector considers the URAs irrelevant. CANAME argued that the largest share of trade is with the US, so most of the opening is already agreed upon. Their concern, if any, is linked with procurement. The Mexican government can unilaterally determine procurement rules for countries not included in a FTA with Mexico, and it has accepted bids from countries that have a closed procurement market. Furthermore, in turnkey projects, which have fallen out of favor elsewhere but are still sometimes used in Mexico, it is difficult to detect unfair trade practices.

The textile sector was satisfied with NAFTA results. CONCAMIN argued that the scope of the US market still allowed room for growth and a FTA with the EU would similarly open opportunities for export growth. The chamber did, however, indicate that significant increases may be limited as many businesses were already working at full capacity. A phasing-out of the MFA, which is assumed inevitable, would partially offset the gains from NAFTA. There was great concern over a flood of garments upon China's accession to the WTO.

Like capital goods, CANACINTRA regarded the URAs as irrelevant given trade concentration with the US. However, problems plague the bilateral relationship, including alleged dumping of beef and pork meat and lard exports, and barriers to access for Mexican sugar exports. NAFTA precipitated a breakup of national production chains and a concentration of producers and retailers, leaving small and medium producers and retailers out in the cold. Producers call for support or aid equal to the aid they claim many WTO members award to their local producers. CANACINTRA insists on securing a level playing field, focusing on the extension of supports like R&D investment, partnerships between universities and business, training for mid-level technicians, and a proactive SME policy.

While all sectors have relevant concerns, as listed in Table 3.4, only the electric and electronics and auto sectors have clear strategies. On one hand, CANIETI favors liberalization and membership in the

Table 3.4 Issues of concern for business association representatives

Sector	*Issue of concern*	*Response*
Electric and electronics	ITA	Possible support
Autos	TRIMs	Request five-year TRIMs moratorium
Capital goods	Procurement	Uncertain
Textiles and apparel	China in WTO	Uncertain
Processed foods	Level playing field	Uncertain

ITA. On the other hand, the auto sector seeks continued protection for TRIMs in the form of five additional years of reprieve. Other sectors voiced concerns, but offered no clear strategy to address them. CANIETI mentioned the need for a more proactive government support of WTO-compliant policies such as reducing taxation levels, investing in human resource training and streamlining customs procedures. Some concerns are directly linked to their relationship with the Mexican government, as is the case with the requested unilateral opening of procurement and increased support for agriculture.

The most vociferous criticism of Mexico's trade policies comes not from the traditional business organizations but from non-governmental organizations (NGOs) and 'unofficial' business organizations. The Mexican Trade Action Network (RMALC) represents a broad range of concerns including human rights, labor rights, democracy, environmental issues, SMEs, and small agricultural producers. Its stated goals are to replace Mexico's current economic policies with alternatives ensuring both sustainable development and equitable distribution of the costs and benefits of economic development. Their proposals include sweeping changes to central elements of trade agreements, such as favoring special and differential treatment instead of relying on national and MFN treatment, and modifying standard investor-state dispute settlement procedures on grounds that it is an affront to national sovereignty and favors the interests of multinational corporations instead of the public interest in issues like health and the environment. They also have more specific proposals, such as changes to IPR commitments under the WTO that allegedly allow 'bio-piracy' when multinational corporations patent biological processes and privatize the use of 'traditional' medicine, which may deprive indigenous groups of their traditional medicine. Their impact on Mexico's trade policy has been minimal, partly due to SECOFI's reluctance to make a conscientious and sustained effort to incorporate such groups' views in trade policy deliberations. Certainly their extremist positions curtail potential influence, as calling into question the backbone of the multilateral trading system, such as MFN and national treatment, making it difficult to find common ground with pro-free trade coalitions.

The National Association of the Transformation Industry (ANIT), a breakaway group of CANACINTRA and a member of RMALC, offers a more constructive approach. It represents the interests of some 3000 SMEs in the capital goods sector, which thrived under the import-substituting industrialization model but struggle in an open economy. ANIT recognizes that an economic policy shift was necessary, but argues that the initiation of various WTO-consistent measures could help SMEs. Its most specific suggestions are for the government to grant SMEs a share of the procurement market and a place at the foreign economic policymaking table. Moreover, the group calls for more liberal financing and flexibility of guarantee requirements for loans from BANCOMEXT, which could foster a revival of SMEs in Mexico. There are nearly four million SMEs, accounting for a large share of total employment, but few are members of a business chamber. In ANIT's view, the Foreign Trade Business Organizations Coordinating Council (COECE), which was supposed to represent all business interests, is in fact a relatively closed group that tends to favor big business interests.

Business–government relations

Government support during UR negotiations was regarded as ample by most peak associations, providing open channels of communication and highly capable negotiators. All sectors had direct access to SECOFI, which was the official source for URA information. Additionally, business organizations resorted to their respective chambers or the WTO web site for information. AMIA highlighted the excellent information the sector received from multinationals, which gather information from several governments and have detailed knowledge of market conditions in many countries. CANACINTRA noted that while information on the URAs was readily available, full and timely information on specific support WTO members received from their government was not. CANAME and CANACINTRA noted that less than full agreement with NAFTA or UR provisions was not necessarily a result of the lack of government collaboration, but a natural result of give-and-take negotiations among numerous sectors.

CANIETI classifies the support offered by the government during the round as mediocre. Because the sectors the chamber represented did not comprise a large participation in the economy during the round and they were not united behind an effective lobby, the government regarded them as neither as important as autos nor as sensitive as grains. In response to disassociation in the UR, CANIETI argued that the representation scheme had two basic flaws. First, CANIETI did not have direct access to the negotiators; it relied on CONCAMIN, which represented a large array of chambers and thus tended to better represent some chambers than others. Secondly, when a complex issue necessitated direct and timely consultations with CANIETI, the chamber was unable to consult its members for consensus. CANIETI seeks to have direct access to the negotiators for future negotiations.

Similar to the response to UR negotiations, all sectors classify participation during NAFTA negotiations as very intense and maintains that they worked in close collaboration with the negotiators. The Executive Director of AMIA, who has represented the sector since the outset of NAFTA negotiations, noted that NAFTA itself was used as a framework for the negotiation of other agreements, including the FTA with the EU. The expertise developed by both business and government proved extremely valuable in subsequent bilateral, plurilateral and multilateral negotiations.

Given the importance of NAFTA for many areas of the Mexican economy it is not altogether surprising that the government went out of its way to ensure close coordination with the representatives of key economic sectors. In turn, sectors of less importance were unable to gain direct access to the negotiators. For example, those sectors that could not present a sophisticated report on the state of their sector and their trade policy preferences were likely to be the first bargaining chips used. Thus, although formally COECE ensured widespread representation of business interests, some sectors were much better represented than others. Sectors controlled by the dominant Institutional Revolutionary Party (PRI) exercised the required 'discipline' by not venting public or private opposition and hence remained unheard. The main groups involved in the NAFTA negotiations were:

- The Free Trade Agreement Inter-ministerial Commission comprised of second-tier (deputy ministers) officials. It formally served as the coordinating unit for negotiation strategy design, though in practice key decisions were made by a smaller group consisting of the President, the Trade Minister, the Head of the NAFTA Negotiations Office (Deputy Trade Minister) and close advisors of the President.
- The Free Trade Agreement Advisory Council, comprised of representatives from the public sector, labor (the Mexican Workers Confederation (CTM) and other pro-government labor unions), agriculture (both PRI-affiliated groups and private sector groups representing agribusiness and livestock interests), business (trade associations as well as prominent businessmen, offering leading firms direct access to negotiators), and academia (heads of the nation's top public and private universities). In practice, the Advisory Council was rather passive, but it did allow businessmen to establish informal communication channels and rapport with top trade officials.
- The COECE is an ad-hoc group comprised of the presidents of the Business Coordinating Council (CCE) and major business organizations.

> COECE was divided into six sectors: agriculture, industry, banking, insurance, finance, and commercial and non-financial services. It coordinated a series of highly confidential studies, which were used to determine negotiating positions. Representatives from COECE formed small teams to work in tandem with the negotiators in each of the negotiation areas. These groups were involved in the day-to-day negotiations and remained in close contact with the negotiators throughout the process. During negotiations they participated via a 'next door room', whereby they would be close at hand in the negotiating venue so that negotiators could get immediate feedback from relevant private sector representatives.

Unlike the positive response to UR and NAFTA business-government relations, all representatives regarded the Free Trade Area of the Americas (FTAA) process with little optimism and scant concern. The capital goods, auto and food sectors focused on ongoing bilateral negotiations with Latin American countries, especially Brazil, rather than on the FTAA process. CANIETI sensed that neither the US nor Brazil showed genuine interest in establishing hemispheric free trade, and hence resorted to a 'wait and see' approach.

Government views

Mexico, together with a number of developing countries, claims that the benefits from trade liberalization have been less than expected due to incomplete implementation of URAs by developed countries. Mexico proposes developed countries ensure full and prompt implementation to smooth the initiation of the post-Doha work program. Mexico regards the issues traditionally addressed in the built-in agenda of multilateral negotiations as insufficient. It seeks, at bare minimum, full consolidation of the tariff structure for industrial goods. Nevertheless, a 'contamination' of the trade agenda with environmental and labor issues could actually revert the gains made in trade liberalization (SECOFI, 1999).

Agriculture: Mexico is concerned more with compliance of URAs than with a deepening of commitments, given there are several market access problems that adversely affect exports. Agriculture-related subsides are a non-issue, since Mexico already maintains levels lower than those allowed under the URAs. Regarding sanitary and phytosanitary measures, Mexico agrees that national provisions should be made on a 'scientific basis' and is willing to contemplate the discussion of this issue.

- *Export subsidies*: Mexico is essentially already in compliance, since NAFTA guidelines are based on the DUNKEL text, which in turn was also used with few alterations in the URAs. The only significant problem was with PITEX, given that it covered the duty-free import of industrial goods (machinery) with which temporarily imported inputs would be transformed and re-exported. Since the machinery itself would not be re-exported, it constituted an unauthorized export subsidy. PITEX was reformed in 2001 and should now be URA-compliant.
- *TRIMs*: Commitments obligate elimination of Mexico's automotive decree. Under NAFTA Mexico agreed to eliminate a number of provisions of the auto decree by 2004, but under the URA on TRIMs it would be forced to eliminate them by 2001, thus losing important concessions it gained in NAFTA. Mexico could argue for exceptions under Article 5 of TRIMs, but the matter may yet end up in dispute settlement procedures due to pressures from Korea, which wants to export cars directly without making local investments (WTO, 1998).
- *Services*: As the world's 13th exporter of services and the largest in Latin America, Mexico would gain from GATS negotiations through market diversification. Mexico is interested in as wide a sectoral coverage as possible, such as a horizontal approach whereby all sectors would be open for negotiation for a given type of service (Abugattas and Stephenson, 2003).
- *IPR*: Mexico seeks the establishment of a multilateral system of registry and notification of distinctive products for tequila and mescal, which are recognized as distinctive products under NAFTA Annex 313.
- *Dispute settlement*: Mexico, together with most developing countries, wants to keep dispute settlement procedures strictly inter-governmental, despite proposals by the US to incorporate NGO participation. Mexico is also concerned with the abuse of the appeals process, and argues that stricter guidelines are required.
- *FDI*: Mexico proposes that any eventual multilateral agreement on investment should avoid linkage with environmental and labor issues, should be compatible with current domestic FDI laws, and should not inhibit the country's regulatory capabilities.
- *Competition policy*: Mexico theoretically accepts the substitution of competition policies for AD laws. Nevertheless, there is a contradiction in Mexico's position; in its FTA with Chile Mexico did not accept the suspension of AD laws when a product enters tariff-free. Apparently, the Mexican producers did not want to award this benefit to Chile, and the government decided to use this issue as a negotiating card in future bilateral and multilateral negotiations.

- *Government procurement*: Though Mexico does not support the US's idea of an 'early harvest' on procurement issues, it does favor greater transparency of rules as pursued in the post-Doha work agenda. NAFTA rules have already subjected Mexico's procurement practices to substantial transparency, making such practices at the multilateral level a drop-in-the-bucket for Mexico.
- *Industrial goods*: Negotiations should seek commitments on the full industrial goods tariff structure, binding applied tariffs when those rates are lower than the bound levels. In addition, bound levels should reflect 'reasonable' tariff ceilings. Mexico is concerned that the buffer between bound ceilings and applied rates in sectors such as footwear, apparel, copper and cement may disappear in the next round.
- *Labor and environment*: Mexico accepts the need for deliberation of these issues in the WTO, but proposes that no formal commitments be made. Mexico has argued that the ILO is a more appropriate forum for addressing labor issues, and that the environmental committee established at the Singapore meeting could continue their work under the current terms. Pressure from Europe and the US managed to get environment included in the Doha work program.

Mexico as a regional player

Mexico is the eighth largest trading nation in the world, though its export markets and import sources are highly concentrated in the US. In the Doha work program Mexico will certainly seek to maintain the privileged access secured through NAFTA, as significant concessions by the US on a MFN basis would translate into an erosion of Mexico's privileged access.

Mexico represents a 'hub' in the 'hub and spoke' trade system,[15] given its agreements with other Latin American countries and its privileged access to the US and Europe. It is not clear if Mexico became a 'hub' haphazardly or by design; regardless, it now has strong incentives to sustain its position as long as tenable. Once this process gets going, vested interests in the hub will make it difficult to proceed with multilateral liberalization. Both business and government seem to support the idea of stagnated negotiations in the post-Doha work program. The WTO represents neither the root of problems nor the favored fora for the resolution of concerns. Some issues can be dealt with bilaterally, as in the case of procurement, or domestically, such as links between research and businesses, better representation, adequate financing, and WTO-compliance support. In any case, it will be important to seek solutions to legitimate concerns so that the potential benefits from trade liberalization can be realized by sectors and regions that have until now borne most of the costs.

Mexico will concern itself with ensuring improved access for its most important manufacturing and agricultural exports in the post-Doha agenda through full compliance with URAs rather than pursuing new commitments. Further disciplines on services, investment, IPR or AD are not of significant concern, given Mexican trade policy instruments' full compatibility with the URAs. It may favor deeper commercial defense disciplines, but will still make wide use of the practices. Similarly, it will be wary of forgoing AD and CVD actions in favor of competition policy at the multilateral level. China's accession to the WTO will only fortify Mexico's reluctance to forfeit its policy arsenal against unfair trade practices.

Mexico's post-Doha concerns will complicate establishing negotiating coalitions with other Latin American countries, except in a few areas, such as TRIMs and the auto sector (Narlikar and Woods, 2003). Gains in access to the EU agriculture market via the FTA eliminated a potential coalition issue. One of the few areas where the position of Latin American countries coincides is opposition to commitments on environmental and labor issues in the WTO (Paiva Abreu, 2003). Developing countries must come up with a positive agenda on which they can agree, and gain Mexico's support, as one of the world's most important trading countries, to fend off developed countries' advances on environmental issues in the post-Doha work program. More generally, the WTO must ensure that multilateral rules accommodate the interests of developed as well as developing countries to avoid a potentially dangerous slide into regionalism. Otherwise, Mexico could turn into a stumbling block for multilateralism (Motta Veiga, 2003).

Notes

1. I would like to thank Gustavo Vega Cánovas, Miguel Lengyel, Antoni Estevaordal, Pablo Rodas and colleagues at CIDE's International Studies Division for their comments. I also wish to acknowledge the contribution made by business and RMALC representatives for conveying to me their candid views on trade policy issues. I have attempted to faithfully represent their views, and any shortcomings are solely my responsibility. Alfredo González Reyes and Aurelio Nuño provided valuable research assistance.
2. SECOFI was renamed Secretaría de Economía (Ministry of Economy) in December 2000. The original name is used throughout this chapter, for ease of reference.

3. Some differences between the Latin American FTAs and NAFTA are worth noting: the exclusion of national treatment for Venezuelan textiles, and for Venezuelan and Colombian polystyrene; special treatment on rules of origin for chemicals, plastics, textiles, steel, copper and aluminum; and an extra-long transition period for rules of origin in the Mexico-Bolivia FTA. Other exceptions are the exclusion of trade in financial services in the Chile and Costa Rica agreements, and their formal inclusion in disciplines for the Northern Triangle agreement, with actual market access commitments to be negotiated at a later date.
4. This section draws heavily from OECD (1996).
5. See Tortora and Tussie (2003) for a discussion on commercial defense laws in Latin America
6. After the devaluation in December 1994 the economy suffered a severe downturn (GDP shrunk by more than 6 per cent in 1995), driving banks to the verge of or fully into insolvency. Bad loans were channeled to the government-sponsored Savings Protection Fund (FOBAPROA), creating a moral hazard incentive for borrowers and lenders. The total 'bad' loan portfolio was approximately US$65 billion. A re-structuring of FOBAPROA resulted in taxpayers assuming a large share of this debt.
7. Controversy arose when the CFC ruled on a merger between TELMEX (the former public telephone monopoly which is now a private company but still has the largest share of the market in virtually all its telecommunications activities) and a branch of Televisa (the largest of the two private television chains), in order to provide cable services. The argument against the operation was that a merger between these two very large firms would make it difficult for others to enter the cable communications market. The CFC disagreed, arguing that it represented an international trend and would allow the companies to be internationally competitive.
8. PEMEX is the only firm constitutionally permitted to produce 'basic' petrochemicals. Private domestic and foreign investment is allowed in the production of 'secondary' petrochemicals, following guidelines such as a 40 per cent cap on foreign equity shares. Instead of a politically costly amendment of the Foreign Investment Law, the government simply reduced the number of petrochemicals classified as 'basic' and increased the number classified as 'secondary.'
9. Among the sectors where certain restrictions remain are petroleum, petrochemicals, electricity, nuclear energy generation, radioactive minerals, satellite communications, and transport services. Restrictions range from participation ceilings to outright prohibition.
10. This section draws heavily from OECD (1996).
11. AMS is the sum of all domestic support measures provided to agricultural producers that are production and trade distorting.
12. This section is a summary of information gathered through interviews with business representatives. The following interviews were conducted in 2000: Edgar Ubbelohde of CANAME, the CONCAMIN representative in charge of NAFTA textile negotiations, two representatives of RMALC, and ANIT President Adán Rivero. Interviews were carried out with peak associations and they are not necessarily representative of all business sector views. Information was also

gathered at the seminar on the Millennium Round held at SECOFI on 5 October 1999.

13. For an overview of these business organizations, see Luna (1995), Alba (1996b and n.d.), and Arriola (1997).
14. Mexico concluded a two-year interim agreement with Brazil in 2000, under which both countries opened their markets for certain models of vehicles under an 8 per cent tariff-quota arrangement. This could be a turning point in Brazil–Mexico trade relations, which have been quite tense.
15. Wonnacott (1991) characterizes the political economy of overlapping free trade areas as hub and spoke arrangements. Under FTAs, gains from free trade with one country are increased by additional gains from free trade with a new partner. Wonnacott argues that, conversely, under hub and spoke arrangements, the partner would probably incur losses as the hub signs new bilateral agreements. The hub will have a locational advantage, allowing its firms to source from and export to all countries with which there are bilateral arrangements. The spokes, on the other hand, would only be able to source from and to export to the hub itself. Hence additional spokes strengthen the hub at the expense of the spokes.

Part II

The Management of Trade Liberalization in the Mercosur

4

Argentina: In a Logic of Nested Games

Diana Tussie, Gabriel Casaburi and Cintia Quiliconi[1]

Introduction

In December 2001, after a four-year long recession and a yearlong drain on reserves, Argentina came to grief. President de la Rúa was forced to step down by fierce opposition and widespread rioting. One institutional crisis led to another; a default on a US$130 billion-plus debt was declared; the fixed exchange which had endured for a decade was wiped out; social unrest and political fragmentation flared; the fall in gross national product was calculated at 11 per cent over the year. Such a momentous collapse in a country heralded as a model of structural reforms in the 1990s begs many questions, whose answers will reverberate throughout the developing world and spill over to issues of systemic management. Trade liberalization was certainly at the core of the reforms, and at the core of social discontent. The difficulties of compliance with international trade commitments which had been taken in times of past plenty and innocence became a central concern of both public opinion and public policy-making. Because all discussions over the rate of exchange had been all but shunned from serious public discussions, disputes became deflected to discrepancies in effective rates of protection. Particularly after the recession began to bite sharply after 1998, trade policy came to be seen as a tool to mitigate macro-economic distress.

Argentina had high hopes for the result of the Uruguay Round Agreements (URAs) as a potential beneficiary of more open global food markets and higher export prices (Tussie, 1993). The potential benefits, however, were misperceived and the costs were greater than anticipated, an imbalance that became increasingly more evident as the deadlines for implementation were reached. This chapter explores the main benefits, dilemmas and tensions generated by the management of trade policy commitments undertaken in the URAs. Selected sectors are analysed, focusing on business views and their role in shaping trade policies. The analysis draws on a set of interviews and questionnaires submitted to business associations representing import-competing and export-oriented sectors. The following section offers a review of Argentina's practices; after which an analysis of the implications of World Trade Organization (WTO) commitments for private sector interests, looking both at costs and benefits, is provided. The subsequent section highlights Mercosur's influence on trade policy. Argentina is a small country with negligible influence in international trade. Bloc bargaining with other Mercosur partners increases its share of world trade from 0.2 per cent to 1.3 per cent, while intra-regional trade could potentially be an asset to increase its competitiveness. Members are now bound together by an unusually dense, though not always smooth, network of shared interests, affiliations and communications. The penultimate, section explores the life cycle of the public-private interaction. The final section closes with an analysis of the nested games involved in the domestic, regional, multilateral arenas.

The creation of Mercosur, conceived to increase bargaining power in the WTO, opened up a host of other games. Mercosur thrived in the policy spaces left by multilateral disciplines, such as the TRIMs agreement, which paved the way for the regional treatment of the auto sector. At the same time multilateral disciplines have mutually served to tie the hands of regional partners in two-way interlocking games. The WTO has thus also served as a parameter and a pillar that sustained regional integration. Interlocking and revolving games (see Putnam, 1988) were set in motion between regional and multilateral disciplines. On one hand, regional tariff disciplines made multilateral ceiling bindings operational; on the other, multilateral commitments catalyzed the regional agenda.

Trade policy revisited

Widespread reforms were implemented briskly from 1990 to 1993. Over 20 state-owned firms, including the national oil company and major public utilities, were entirely or partially privatized. Similarly, the most heavily trafficked highways became privately-held concessions with the right to charge tolls. Almost two-thirds of total investment came from foreign savings. Privatized companies performed reasonably well in terms of growth and quality of services. But services were offered at excessive prices due to regulatory deficiencies and the concession of monopoly positions (Nogués, 2003). The Convertibility Act enforced from 1991 to 2001 restricted the supply of pesos to reserves at a one-to-one parity on a one-to-one basis. This fixed exchange rate served to anchor inflation, despite the lack of progress on fiscal balances. Capital inflows financed fiscal deficits and eventually gave way to currency appreciation.

Average tariffs fell to 13.5 per cent in 2000 from prevailing rates of over 30 per cent in the 1980s. In the Uruguay Round binding commitments were expanded to cover the entire tariff schedule; the ceiling was reduced from 140 per cent to 35 per cent, which nonetheless implied an average of over 20 per cent between bound and applied rates (WTO, 1998). Import prohibitions and import licenses, key instruments of the protectionist arsenal, were eliminated; but the openness coefficient (exports plus imports as a share of GDP) touched only 17.6 per cent in 2000. Exports never went beyond 10 per cent of GDP. Import liberalization coupled with a fast appreciation currency led to a much faster rise in imports than exports. The resulting trade deficits were all too comfortably financed by the massive inflow of foreign savings (Fanelli, 2000), until the process gradually dried up, first with the Asian and Russian crises in 1997–98; later the Brazilian crisis in early 1999, leading to the final crash in late 2001.

The volume of trade quadrupled over the 1990s, but composition changed only marginally. The growth of mining, fuel and electricity, and auto exports allowed some export diversification, while imports remained concentrated in capital goods and intermediary inputs. Mercosur became an important anchor of the trade policy framework; every tool became the object of mutual scrutiny and intense negotiations. Regional interdependence also has increased the sensitivity of trade flows to swings in bilateral exchange rates. Table 4.1 highlights the centrality of Mercosur in trade flows.

Table 4.1 Trade by regions, 2000

	Exports (%)	*Imports (%)*
Mercosur	31.8	28.4
Rest of Latin America	15.0	5.8
USA	11.8	18.7
EU	17.8	22.9
Rest of the World	23.6	24.2
Total	100.0	100.0

Source: CEI (2002).

Table 4.2 Export promotion instruments: WTO status

Instrument	*Status**
Convergence factor	U
Fiscal incentive (Reimbursement to regional exports: Patagonian ports)	U
Fiscal incentive (Reimbursement to mining in western provinces)	U
Special Tobacco Fund	P
Export credit	NA
Export processing zones	NA**
Fiscal incentive (reimbursement/remission of tariffs)	NA
Fiscal Incentives (duty drawback)	NA
Fiscal Incentives (Tax free temporary admission of imports)	NA
Scientific and technological development	NA
Tax incentives (Exemption from indirect taxes)	NA
Market information (Fundacion Export-Ar)	NA

Notes: *U: under discussion, P: prohibited; and NA: non-actionable.
**EPZs are WTO compatible as long as the incentives granted are themselves compatible.
Source: Based on Tussie and Lengyel (1998).

The pressure of fiscal disequilibria severely restrained the room for active trade and industrial policies but, as the country's competitive position weakened, micro-economic instruments were applied, often to compensate for the exchange rate misalignment. Table 4.2 summarizes the main export promotion schemes and their status under WTO agreements. These are described in the following paragraphs.

Under the aegis of the Ministry of Foreign Affairs, the foundation Export-Ar gives horizontal support to exports: guidance and support for strengthening export activities, information on foreign markets, international procurement, etc. Export-Ar's activity amounts to less than a drop in the ocean; its budget is minuscule, barely amounting to about five per cent of trade-promotion organizations in similar countries (IERAL, 2001). Some assistance for fulfilling foreign export regulations is also provided to small- and medium-sized firms. The mining and forestry sectors were granted fiscal incentives as part of regional promotion and export development schemes. Duty drawback and tax reimbursement mainly benefit industrialized goods. Export taxes are meant to encourage domestic processing of rawhides and skins. A law for export processing zones (EPZs) was passed in 1994 with crudely political criteria. Each province was given the right to set up an EPZ without clearly defined criteria for incentives. This led to a free for all: one of the provinces granted a WTO-prohibited subsidy (exemptions from social security contributions) and others raced to follow suit. However, the room for conflict soon evaporated, as the WTO-prohibited subsidy was lifted at the end of 2003. Similarly, reimbursements were granted to exports shipped from Patagonian ports south of the Colorado River in an effort to promote regional development. Only goods produced in this region qualify for the reimbursements, which range from seven to 12 per cent of fob value, increasing gradually for the southernmost ports of exportation. This export subsidy has been duly notified to the WTO and must be phased out by 2007.[2]

The Special Tobacco Fund has been in force since 1972 to help tobacco growers in the relatively backward northern provinces. Briefly rescinded from 1991–94, it was then rejuvenated by the pressure of a coalition of farmers' cooperatives, labor unions, provincial governors, and Congressional representatives. It is financed by a 7 per cent excise tax on cigarette sales, which amounted to over US$180 million in 2001. The Fund was notified under the Agreement on Agriculture as a *de minimis* provision, which would go untouched by reduction commitments. The amount was mistakenly thought to compose the Aggregate Measure of Support (AMS), as a function of the gross value of total agricultural production. This interpretation had to be corrected to compare the domestic support for tobacco with the gross value of tobacco production, rather than total agricultural production. The support level offered to tobacco then surpassed the ten per cent *de minimis* level allowed for developing countries. Consequently, the subsidy is now subject to a 13.3 per cent reduction over ten years.

In mid-2001, in the last throes of the struggle to stave off debt default, boost competitiveness and revive growth, a fiscal mechanism was created to increase export reimbursements. Exports, with the exception of fuels, were granted an additional reimbursement whereby dollar receipts were converted into pesos equal to the average of the peso–dollar and the peso–euro exchange rates. The same procedure was applied in reverse for all imports, including goods from Mercosur. This so-called 'convergence factor' was destined to be a temporary convergence mechanism on the way to Euro-dollar parity, so that, once the Euro reached parity with the US dollar, the Argentine currency board would include Euros in the pegging of the peso to the average of the peso-dollar and the peso-euro exchange rates. This fiscal support to exports was short-lived; it was eliminated after the peso was left to float in January 2002, paving the way for more cordial intra-Mercosur relations.

WTO commitments: a mercantilist overview of costs and benefits

The general lowering of protection unveiled a number of simmering tensions, as the impact was felt distinctively among upstream and downstream producers, importers, consumers and exporters. In addition, the broad coverage of the Uruguay Round added new tensions, which gradually intensified over time and the imbalance between the concessions granted (in lower protection levels) and received (in greater access to world food markets) was made evident. The most valued benefit expected had been the Agreement on Agriculture, and among the most important costs is the Agreement on Trade-Related Intellectual Property Rights (TRIPs), which especially affected the pharmaceutical sector. These two sectors maneuvered at opposite ends of the spectrum: agriculture expecting to benefit from potential export opportunities and the pharmaceutical industry suffering restrictive legislation adjustments to comply with the TRIPs agreement. In between fell a number of slightly narrower issues that affected business incentives and required readjustment to comply with new commitments.

Commitments

The TRIPs agreement has become a source of bitter dilemmas over required legislation incorporating the new protection standards. Implementation costs have fallen upon the domestically-owned pharmaceutical industry. The industry as a whole represents significant interests, with annual domestic sales reaching US$5 billion. Surprisingly for a developing country, locally-owned firms account for nearly half of the market, some of which also export to regional markets. Many of these firms, especially the smaller ones, benefited from lax enforcement of a 19th century patent law, gladly taking advantage of loopholes in the legislation. A heated confrontation sparked between local firms and multinational corporations over a new patent law meant to comply with TRIPs commitments. The precise interpretation and compatibility of clauses was at debate, such as those relating to parallel imports (Article 6 and 28) and compulsory licenses (Article 31). The passing of a law in 1996 became a *cause célèbre,* a protracted and murky Congressional debate. A tense struggle surfaced between the camp that supported multinational firms' interests and the camp that favored national laboratories. The initially approved legislation took advantage of the ten-year grace period offered to developing countries for the incorporation of TRIPs requirements. The US, however, opposed a grace period and

Table 4.3 Specific concessions obtained in the UR

EU	• An increase of (so-called Hilton) beef quota to 11,000 ton (in compensation for higher subsidies on oilseed products) • *A 50% MFN tariff reduction on pears and apples
Japan	• *A 50% MFN tariff reduction on vegetable oils
US	• Allocation of a 20,000-ton beef quota • A quota increase to 1850 ton for hard and semi-soft cheese • A commitment to maintain the bilateral allocation of the sugar quota, despite multilateralization • Allocation of quotas for peanuts and peanut butter • *A 33% MFN tariff reduction on fruit juices, grape must, lemon essence oil, corned beef and cooked beef

Source: author's own data.

demanded GATT-plus legislation with a shorter transition period and stricter intellectual property conditions than those agreed upon under the WTO regime. The US lobby successfully persuaded President Menem to veto the original version of the law and introduce clauses including their demands. When the final legislation was approved, an unsatisfied United States Trade Representative (USTR) retaliated by withholding half of the benefits granted to Argentine exports under the Generalized System of Preferences (GSP). Argentina had no chance to register a complaint with the WTO because the non-binding nature of GSP allows the offering country to unilaterally modify preferences according to changing interests. The struggle continues to flare-up from time to time as both sides try to take advantage of loopholes in the agreement. The US has opened consultations with Argentina complaining of scarce protection of microorganisms, compulsory licenses, and strict enforcement of property rights. Both parties are expecting to rely on the case law of WTO panels to settle their differences.

Market access gains

The Agreement on Agriculture was a massive disappointment. Gains that could have accrued to Argentina from overall global liberalization were much reduced by the token reduction of export subsidies and dirty tariffication that resulted (Josling *et al.*, 1996). The specific concessions Argentina obtained under are listed in Table 3. The items marked with an asterisk were obtained on an MFN basis by virtue of the principal supplier rule. The rest of the items are bilateral quotas sanctified under the Agreement on Agriculture. Overall market access gains were hardly significant. On the whole these concessions amounted to a mere 8 per cent of total agriculture exports (Finger *et al.*, 1996).

The US decision to allocate a 20,000 ton beef quota after a 70-year hiatus was a product of the Sanitary and Phytosanitary Agreement's loosening of tight US regulations. Sale of Argentine fresh beef had been banned in US markets since 1927 because of foot-and-mouth disease. Before the URA, the US had had a 'zero risk' sanitary evaluation policy, which Argentina questioned as lacking substantial foundation and, moreover, as discriminatory. US sanitary policy has shifted to 'minimal risk' of this disease and it is hoped that other countries will follow suit, thereby paving the way for an increase in Argentine beef exports to world markets. Now Argentina must show that it can permanently control the disease, which had an outbreak as recently as March 2001. Still access problems pepper bilateral relations, affecting Argentine exports of peanuts, beef, milk, fruit and fruit juices. Sanitary and phytosanitary problems continue, for example, in the case of fresh fruit with the US and in labeling requirements for genetically modified soy and corn with the EU.

The proliferation of regional agreements has displaced many Argentine agricultural exports, as was the case with oilseeds in Mexico and Chile. Before the creation of NAFTA, Argentina was the main supplier to the Mexican market with an MFN rate of ten per cent, but Mexico's reduction of tariffs with the US and Canada has jeopardized Argentina's participation in the market. As noted by Ortiz Mena, Mexico has assumed the role of a hub in a 'hub and spoke' trading system, so that regional agreements signed by Mexico will hurt the spokes, in this case Argentina (Ortiz Mena, Chapter 3). A similar situation occurred in Chile, where bilateral agreements with Canada, Paraguay and Bolivia have discriminated against Argentine soy flour and oilseed exports.

Meanwhile, margins of preference also limit access of lemon juice to the US market. The MFN tariff for concentrated juices oscillates between 35 and 50 per cent, but competitors (Israel and Mexico) in the US market benefit from free trade agreements. Similarly, confectionery exports to the EU face a very high MFN tariff. These bilateral problems resulting from the worldwide mushrooming of discriminatory practices clearly trigger sectoral interest in both regional agreements and a new global round to overcome discrimination.

Administration of multilateral commitments

Twined with the progressive overvaluation of the currency, Argentina's trade reform process was riddled with tensions and conflicts. As sectors stepped-up their demands for protection, tariff policy was used pragmatically. Since the applied average tariff was well below the 35 per cent ceiling bound by the WTO, there was significant room to tinker without breaking commitments. The application of the convergence factor to imports is a case in point. Similarly, a so-called 'statistical levy' on imports was introduced when international capital markets began to deteriorate after the Mexican crisis of 1994. The levy operated as a 2.5 per cent across-the-board tariff surcharge, and was notified to the WTO at the close of the Uruguay Round. It drew strong objections from the US, and a panel investigation was requested to determine its proportionality to services provided. The panel was resolved against Argentina and the levy was formally lowered back to 0.5 per cent. When the 1997 East Asian crisis began to affect the current account deficit, Mercosur agreed upon a 3 percentage point increase to the CET, which offset the reduction requested by the panel but was legally feasible because of the gap between applied and bound tariff levels.

UR disciplines on antidumping, countervailing duties and safeguards led to the creation of the *Comisión Nacional de Comercio Exterior,* a technical quasi-independent body under of the aegis of the Executive. The Commission is charged with handling business petitions for trade relief against unfair foreign practices affecting the domestic market. The procedure replicates the two-track US model, in which the Commission investigates injury to industry while establishing the presence of the unfair practice is in the hands of the Secretary of Trade. The division of duties was established as a way to defuse lobbying pressures on political appointees. The rules did not save Argentina from rising to the top of the league in the use of anti-dumping, as declining tariffs levels and currency appreciation badly shook import competing interests. In the period from 1995 to 2001, as organized business became quite dexterous, the Commission was inundated with petitions to investigate injury.

The trade liberalization process and its relation to macroeconomic conditions and financial volatility explain the evolution of the number of investigations. When the first wave of unilateral trade reforms rocked the region at the end of the 1980s, there was a surge in the use of anti-dumping and safeguard policies. Governments and the private sector saw them as appropriate 'compensation' for the unilateral liberalization. The pace of trade defense leveled off in the mid-1990s, coinciding with higher rates of growth. Finally, trade remedy policies peaked again following the 1999 financial crisis (Tortora and Tussie, 2003).

Although the number of trade relief applications was on the rise prior to the unpegging of the peso in early 2002, the volume of imports covered by antidumping was negligible (well below 1 per cent). Over two-thirds of all investigations opened were against China and Brazil (followed by Taiwan, Korea, Italy and Spain). While China provided four per cent of total imports, 1.2 per cent of its imports were investigated; 2 per cent of Brazilian imports were investigated of a one fourth import share. Not surprisingly, antidumping was a bone of contention that soured intra-regional relations, and few steps were carried out to implement common trade relief procedures.

Textiles and footwear obtained specific duties above the bound 35 per cent tariff ceiling, challenged by the USTR and the EU in the WTO (with Hungary and India reserving the right to participate as third parties). The dispute settlement panel decided against Argentina in October 1997. The footwear sector applied for a safeguard to offset the decreased protection, which was similarly challenged by the EU and India. A new panel in the WTO finally ruled that the safeguard measure was incompatible with Articles 2 and 4 of the Agreement on Safeguards and Countervailing Measures. To comply with the ruling, authorities dropped the safeguard covering the whole footwear sector in February 2000 and crafted a solution to comply with the panel's requirements by distinguishing between two segments of the market, accepting the presence of injury for athletic footwear segment (coming from Asia), but not for non-athletic footwear (coming from Brazil). Argentine and Brazilian producers subsequently agreed to a voluntary export restraint.

The textile sector applied for a three-year quota on cotton textile products from Brazil, China and Pakistan under the safeguard provision of the Agreement on Textiles and Clothing (ATC).[3] Brazil objected strongly and registered a complaint with the Textile Monitoring Body (TMB) of the WTO, the first dispute between regional partners taken to the WTO. The TMB recommended the safeguard be lifted because the calculation of injury did not provide up-to-date data. However, since the TMB recommendation is not a binding decision, Argentina maintained the safeguard and Brazil resorted to arbitration by Mercosur's Ad-Hoc Tribunal (see Weston and Delich, 2003). The Tribunal concluded that safeguards of any kind were incompatible with Mercosur's foundational treaty.

The auto sector benefited from TRIMs that should have been eliminated by the end of 1999. But in contrast to the conflict over TRIPs, which faced-off national and international pharmaceutical firms, the local auto firms were able to rely on the bargaining power of their parent companies. Agreement among auto firms in both Brazil and Argentina on third-party protection was not hard to come by. However, tensions did arise over protection to be granted to auto parts and over location incentives, especially after Brazil launched a 15-year program to attract firms to northern states (see Chudnovsky and López, 2003).

In sum, this panorama suggests that both costs and benefits of WTO multilateral agreements have been exaggerated. The WTO has served as a retaining wall for trade policy, but the room to maneuver remains relatively ample on all sides. On one hand, the benefits accrued from the Agreement on Agriculture fell far short of expectations and a myriad of loopholes allowed OECD countries to leave their distorting agricultural practices intact. On the other hand, agreements affecting the import-competing sectors had loopholes that required new legal capabilities to exploit them creatively. Nonetheless, the constraints on trade policy tools became very visible to Argentina as it attempted to use them to mitigate the misalignment of the exchange rate.

Costs and benefits aside, the joint impact of the WTO and Mercosur commitments on the process of trade policymaking has been considerable. Not only have trade-related rules been necessarily curtailed to be URA-compatible, but new institutional structures were also created to deal with these instruments. Undoubtedly, the room to maneuver has been reduced. Without turning to counterfactual history, it can be safely assumed that without the outer ring limits to its trade policy provided by URAs and Mercosur, Argentina would have implemented a more dramatic protectionist turnaround in the face of the 2001/02 crisis.

The regional constitution: Mercosur

Mercosur was initially notified in the WTO under the Enabling Clause, rather than under Article XXIV, which contains the main provisions for customs unions and free trade areas. This legal coverage was questioned by major WTO members and an agreement was subsequently reached so that it would be scrutinized by the Committee on Regional Trade Agreements under Article XXIV.[4] Regional free trade agreements have been the most prominent new 'clubs' sustaining liberalization (Hurrell, 1995; Kahler, 1997; Woods, 2000). True to the global trend, the Mercosur Treaty constitutes an integral strain of the trade reform strategy. The bulk of intra-Mercosur trade is now exchanged duty-free with the exception of the so-called 'special sectors': sugar and autos. Here intra-regional trade remains overtly managed. Argentina applies the maximum-allowed 35 per cent tariff on sugar to intra-Mercosur imports and the auto sector operates under the umbrella of the Trade Related Investment Measures (TRIMs) Agreement.

Taking stock of the agreement at the end of the 1990s, the elimination of trade repression led to a rapid growth of intra-bloc trade, which more than doubled as a share of members' total exports. Argentina sustained a surplus with regional partners throughout the decade. As Brazil became Argentina's main trade partner, exports to Brazil more than quadrupled from US$1.4 billion in 1990 to US$8.0 billion in 1998. The first burst of economic integration rested on absolute as well as comparative advantages. Argentina's generous endowment of energy and temperate agricultural products is a complement to Brazil's structural deficits in these two sectors, generating Argentine surpluses quite regardless of the relative exchange rates. It is in the more sophisticated intra-industry trade, particularly developed over the second half of the 1990s, that exchange rate misalignment caused serious trade frictions. Negotiations stagnated in the face of difficult policy decisions.

While intra-regional liberalization has made progress, in contrast, the teeth of the common external tariff (CET) have been softer. First, Argentina had to raise its lower tariff level to reach the 1995 agreement on the CET; and second, the CET has been observed more in spirit than to the letter. The CET set a tariff range of 0 to 20 per cent. Countries were unable to agree on the protection to be afforded to information technology, telecommunications and capital goods: Argentina, Paraguay and Uruguay were inclined to allow duty-free treatment while Brazil preferred higher rates of protection. A compromise was reached that allowed the maintenance of national tariff rates subject to convergence by 2006. In addition, each country was allowed a number of country-determined exceptions; by 2001 the Argentine list had fallen to 100 products. The tariff escalation of the CET is quite significant across all sectors, with oil refineries being the sole exception.

Even if the convergence schedule for national tariffs is ever met, Mercosur will still be far from becoming a full customs union: common trade policy instruments are missing (described below) and the CET is lackadaisically applied. All goods remain subject to rules of origin, thus eliminating one of the expected benefits of a customs union over a free trade area. The applied CET is below the WTO binding level; the gap has allowed room for disagreements and lax enforcement. By way of a recent example, seconds prior to the final demise of the peso, all but choked by overvaluation in late 2001, Argentina applied for a waiver from the CET that allowed a raise in national applied tariffs on consumer goods to the WTO-bound 35 per cent ceiling binding – an example of how the WTO binding served as a useful brake on even wider oscillations; and how the WTO can thus be seen as embedding the regional association.

The motivations underlying this regional engagement are first to increase inter-regional trade and gain scale advantages by specialization, and second to increase collective bargaining power. This power in numbers was pursued by Argentina in free trade agreements with Chile (Silva, Chapter 2) and Bolivia in 1996 to be completed in a timeframe of ten years. Similar negotiations with the Andean Community of Nations (ACN) and Mexico broke down and led to the temporary extension of existing bilateral agreements, further eroding the CET. More recently, Mercosur also began to negotiate a Bi-regional Free Trade Agreement with the EU. At the procedural level, coordination among Mercosur partners frequently allows joint presentations in the negotiations aiming at the creation of a FTAA. However, the FTAA has not yet reached the critical point of exchanging concessions.

The divergence of macroeconomic paths between the two main partners rose was reflected in tense trade relations. Clashes were initially managed pragmatically with political muscle, as evidenced by Brazil's readiness to direct government purchases of oil and wheat to reduce the bilateral trade imbalance. The collapse of the Brazilian currency in early 1999 marked a turning point, with the serious shake up of relative competitiveness. Trade conflicts erupted overtly and the formalized procedures of the dispute settlement mechanism were first tested in late 1999 (Weston and Delich, 2003).

The numerous trade relief measures and 'orderly marketing arrangements' that sprung-up sought to manage competitive pressures at a micro-level in poultry, pork, dairy, footwear, textiles, paper and steel. Common solutions seemed hard to come by; a tit-for-tat followed, with Brazil's application of sanitary and phytosanitary measures on honey, cereals, fruits and vegetables. Cases submitted to the dispute settlement mechanism subsequently multiplied. As is well documented for other countries when the trade balance is blown out of the water by imbalances between income and expenditure or the rate of exchange becomes appreciated, protection becomes all but irresistible (Bloningen and Prusa, 2001).

The auto sector: regionalization of TRIMs

The commitments of the Trade Related Investment Measures (TRIMs) agreement provide an example of how multilateralism can catalyze the regional agenda in unexpected ways and lead to a new set of interlocking and revolving games between regional and multilateral arenas. TRIMs played a paradoxical role opening a window of opportunity to streamline the car sector in regional perspective. Since the first stages of import substitution in the late 1950s, the auto sector in Argentina had suffered from lack of scale with an annual output of barely 100,000 units, a situation compounded by production atomized in too many plants with too many models. It had never managed to compete with Brazil or to become export oriented. When the TRIMs commitments became due they provided an opportunity for Brazil and Argentina to hammer out a common policy. At the time the Argentine car sector was in the midst of an overhaul begun in 1991. The car regime in place consisted (in a nutshell) of the following measures:

- a nominal tariff of 35 per cent (the highest granted to any industry)
- local producers were allowed to import finished cars but required compensating imports with exports;
- non-established producers were allowed an import quota equivalent to 10–15 per cent of total domestic production;
- local content requirements were lowered to 60 per cent;
- preferential import tariff on car parts and components of 2 per cent for terminal plants.

The costs of adjustment were thus borne by the parts and components industry. Established terminal plants could import parts and components at a 2 per cent tariff, whereas the tariff was 18 per cent for auto companies not established in the country. This aspect of the regime conferred great bargaining power to the assembly plants that were already established, both with regard to foreign competitors and to the parts and components domestic industry. The outputs of the parts sector grew at a considerably lower rate than that of the terminal plants, which had been all generously endowed with an effective rate of protection amounting to nearly 100 per cent. Argentina became a net exporter of finished cars to Brazil and a net importer of parts and components from Brazil. Only in 1996 was the special tariff regime for the terminal plants extended to the parts and components industry, but without the need to compensate imports with exports.

The TRIMs agreement committed signatories to phase out local content, trade-balancing, foreign exchange-balancing and domestic sales requirements. It required strict notification procedures of all such measures within 90 days of entry into force of the agreement (i.e. 30 March 1995). Measures were then to be eliminated within five years (in the case of developing countries). Application for an extension of the deadline (which became due in 2000) could only be accepted if notification procedures had been complied with. Argentina promptly notified the measures to the WTO under TRIMs agreement. Brazil did not, despite applying similar performance requirements and thus forfeited its right to apply for an extension when the 2000 deadline expired. In contrast, Argentina (together with Indonesia and several other developing countries in a similar situation) was able to obtain an extension.

The extension became a window of opportunity. Argentina used it as a lever to entice Brazil into planning a broad base inclusive regional regime. Brazil's chances of holding on to its national TRIMs hung on the process of a regional convergence. Each national regime would converge into a regional policy which could use Argentina's notification as an umbrella. As the deadline to dismantle the un-notified, and hence soon untenable, Brazilian TRIMs approached, the negotiation of a regional regime became a war of attrition, aggravated by the fall of the *real* in early 1999 and the move by local governments in the Brazilian Northeast to jumpstart the race, offering incentives to attract FDI. As framed, they would be excluded from the scrutiny of both WTO and Mercosur disciplines. The future of the car sector in Argentina lay on an uncertain foundation. During the year Argentina's bilateral surplus in finished cars was wiped-out. When, in late 1999, the new government was sworn in, in late 1999, it rushed to avoid runaway plants seeking investment subsidies and a more favorable exchange rate in Brazil. Argentina had the upper hand as far as the WTO umbrella was concerned, but could not match Brazilian competitiveness, favored both by incentive packages and the bilateral exchange rate.

With the leverage provided by compliance with the WTO notification procedures, the Argentine government made a proposal, pushing for a common policy that would allow the domestic car parts sector to increase its share in the regional content requirement that would be jointly submitted to the WTO and given legal coverage. An agreement was reached in mid-2000, stipulating bilateral compensation of exports and imports and apportioning one half of the sum total of regional content for Argentina (30 over 60 per cent). Both the trade balance and the allocation of a pre-established share of car parts were seen as leveling the playing field for the domestic parts and components industry undermined by falling competitiveness.

Roadblocks to an implementation of the agreement surfaced almost immediately. Disagreement ensued on procedures to calculate the share of 30 per cent share. Subsequently, the seriousness of the Argentine collapse impeded implementation and the agreement fell apart. The disintegration of Argentine domestic demand increased surplus capacity in the industry; imports could not be absorbed and the commitment to a balanced trade became untenable. Keenness to export the surplus to Brazil (and beyond) without balancing requirements increased. Soon after each country was able to reach agreements with Mexico and Chile before the joint auto regime for the bloc was finished. The incentives for a regional policy in this field have therefore withered away.

The life cycle of the public–private interaction

Business is highly divided over trade policy with positions depending upon the degree of concentration of production, location in the production chain, whether sectors are producers of tradeables or non-tradeables, and whether sectors are exporting or importing. Trade flow fluxes and competitiveness problems mould sector preferences and thus alter the micro-management of trade policy.

A major cleavage occurs between the export interests of the Argentine Rural Society and the predominately import-competing sectors of the Argentine Industrial Union. Further splits occur along the chain of production, illustrated by the auto sector where representatives of the major firms were pitted against small parts producers. Major firms never complain about their access to information or dialogues with the trade officials. Moreover, they expect their respective headquarters to protect their interests in any meaningful negotiation regarding compliance with TRIMs deadlines. In 1998 representatives of both the Argentine and Brazilian trade associations presented a joint proposal for the new regime to their respective governments and traveled to Geneva to discuss their proposal with WTO authorities. Application of a lower differential tariff for autos from firms with assembly plants in Mercosur stood out among the issues proposed. The Argentine auto parts business association rejected the idea because of the loss of market share it would entail, while auto firms would continue to enjoy very high effective protection rates. Medium and small companies in the auto parts market had limited access to the government's negotiation strategy; they claimed to have information only on Mercosur negotiations, not on multilateral negotiations. These small parts firms complain of being sandwiched by the protection granted at the beginning and the end of the production chain for steel and auto firms respectively. The re-negotiation of the TRIMs agreement with Mercosur brought the struggle to the light of day.

Steel production is highly concentrated, and can easily access trade and industrial policy-making channels. The sector has dexterous caucusing abilities and is able to make its preferences felt in a wide array of issues. An advertising campaign was mounted in major newspapers with their counterparts in Mercosur to demand equal treatment along the production chain so that both steel inputs and parts were granted the same high protection as that granted to auto assemblers under the Mercosur auto regime.

The footwear sector is divided between local producers and importers. Importers complain of government indifference to their interests, whereas producers maintain a fluid relationship with the public sector and both cooperated closely for the application of safeguards. However, the most modern producers, which use imported inputs and final products to complement their own production are uncomfortable with both extremes. A similar polarization exists in the pharmaceutical sector, in that two business associations coexist: one brings together national laboratories and another represents international companies. During the long battle to update and adapt to the TRIPs, both lobbied at various government levels in distinct ways. Interestingly, both associations believe the other yields more power in the molding of government decisions. By the same token, both are equally dissatisfied with the official representation of their interests.

Finally, the very competitive agricultural sector, a net exporter, is the sole sector with a positive and monolithic vision of the WTO process. The sector's ability to maintain a cooperative relationship with all government agencies may be explained by several factors, including the competitiveness of the sector, the professionalism of the sector's associations, and their history of active participation in the Cairns Group.[5]

The public private interaction may be understood as a process involving four-stages. Different logics of action are involved at different stages and the form in which interaction evolves hinges upon the particular stage of the process. Interests change along the continuous process of reform and negotiation, together with the shape and intensity of the public-private consultation. Trade liberalization and regional integration in Argentina were first pushed from above, but as liberalization progressed it changed the policy preferences of business. The initial step of a grand decision to reform is usually a government decision, nudged at the margin by a particular sector that needs access to markets. In WTO negotiations, the push is provided by agricultural producers; in Mercosur the push came from the auto sector and food exporters. During a second stage of rule-making and cumbersome technicalities, consultations are intermittent. On one hand, very few business associations are equipped to deal with technical issues. On the other hand, incentives to get involved have not yet materialized, as the costs of the negotiation take time to be registered by the relevant sectors. Subsequently, when market offers are on the table and product-by-product haggling takes off, business becomes more alert and consultations are intensified. Lastly, when enforcement of the agreement begins and disputes over interpretation arise or trade relief is sought, private representatives take the initiative to submit applications to the relevant government agency to seek redress.

Completion of the life cycle is not inevitable. Discontinuities in the process of trade policy in a highly foreign-capital dependent economy have not been affected by the partisan composition of the government but rather by the ups and downs of macro-economic cycles. In fact, party politics remained irrelevant because of the overriding macro concerns; prior to the currency collapse in early 2002 all governments tried to remain insulated from societal pressures in order to carry-on a disintegrating macro program. However, decision-makers are not immune to the entreaties or even the purses of major corporations. At the micro-level, particular interest groups are powerful and tend to develop symbiotic relationships with those government agencies that make decisions directly affecting them. The idea of permeable or porous bureaucratic rings where decisions on particular issues are crafted fairly depicts the policy-making process at that level. Public officials can overcome pressure, but only when exercising political leadership to mobilize broadly held sentiments within the general population, or to use the constraints imposed by international markets to resist domestic lobbying.

Generally, business views WTO negotiations as largely inaccessible and impermeable to their influence, noting the limited access to information on the negotiations provided by the government. Quite to the contrary, business organizations have been actively engaged in Mercosur negotiations, as they struggled to retain and even gain profitability with the regional liberalization program. Opinions on FTAA negotiations fall somewhere in the middle, since business has been officially invited to participate, but participation is still at a high aggregate level through the Business Forum of the Americas and the private sector presentations to the Governmental Representatives Committee created in the FTAA. Business engagement differs along the life cycle of negotiations and according to the costs and benefits experienced or expected. As the number of negotiations, multiply the pressure for systematic consultation gains momentum, especially when market offers are made or enforcement and disputes arise.

The logic of multiple games

The ten-year long fixed exchange rate shifted the burden of economic policy making to an intensive use of trade instruments, but both the WTO and Mercosur agreements imposed limits on grandiose reversals. Although the wide oscillations of the past were hindered, they were not altogether impeded. Public policies are now required to move within the general margins of international practice and policy instruments may no longer be arbitrarily managed. The number of instruments negotiated with Mercosur partners and consultations opened within the new WTO dispute resolution system demonstrate the increasing importance of playing by the rules and how these rules bind succeeding governments to the broad generalities of a liberal economic program.

Argentina's main export interest in the multilateral negotiations continues to focus on greater access to international agricultural markets. Nevertheless, the WTO process now affects sectors that had previously enjoyed high levels of protection in the domestic market, which are consequently more alert and stirred to participate in the process. Liberalization has intensified the search for competitiveness and access to inputs at world market prices, as decreasing protection has reduced the extent to which local industry can keep the domestic market captive. Imports have established a limit to the increase of internal prices, preventing the transfer of increased costs to consumers. As a result of this pressure, businesses are paying more attention to cost reduction as a way to gain and even retain markets. Efforts to reduce costs in the local market have increased the rivalry between upstream and downstream producers, with the consequent emergence of conflicts among and within sectors. Suppliers of raw materials, parts and manufactured goods mutually cast the blame on each other for inefficiencies in the production process. Faced with this heterogeneity of situations and interests, policy makers find it very difficult to define a single, homogeneous national interest, and have turned trade regulations inside-out in search of loopholes.

Interaction between the public and private sector has changed fundamentally. Business participation in the negotiations has intensified, especially in regional and sub-regional fora, where the brunt of opening was most felt. The experience can now be transposed to other negotiations, especially the WTO, once felt to be distant and arcane. Unceasing trade negotiations show a four-stage process of interaction. After a first stage of government-led reform, negotiations navigate into deeper waters and business becomes progressively more involved. When negotiations only involve rule-making and cumbersome technicalities, channels of consultations are not systematic. Expertise resides in professional bureaucrats, who move the process along. Subsequently, the channels of consultation are gradually intensified when market offers must be made. When enforcement of the agreement begins to bite, a new public-private relationship emerges in which business must provide justification for the use of trade relief measures or prod the government to seek redress for violations made by partners. Access to these measures is frequently related to the organizational capacities of the industry.

The domestic market, together with the expanding regional market, continues to be the mainstay for production. The agriculture sector constitutes an exception thanks to its highly competitive orientation towards extra-regional markets. Therefore, the WTO agenda is driven by the hopes of liberalizing world food markets. Post-Doha negotiations could have potential benefits for agriculture with concessions in other import-defensive sectors such as services and industry, but such an outcome will depend upon Argentina's ability to defend its goals.

The market power of Mercosur could become an important element of each member's negotiating power, although collective negotiations have not been a roaring success (Phillips, 2003). The mere presence of Mercosur has significantly altered the negotiating scenario. The internal coordination within Mercosur is and will be particularly intense, and simultaneously the external environment may catalyze Mercosur's incomplete agenda. Member countries will not only have to define criteria for negotiating but also establish the depths of commitments that are to be made in the numerous existing negotiation forums. This is no small challenge, considering the well-known difficulties that have plagued policy coordination within the region.

But by and large, WTO disciplines are entrenched in regional structures through a process of mutual encirclement. In addition, multilateral negotiations offer a 'hidden' incentive of opportunities to tie neighbors' hands for eventual gains in regional agreements. The WTO thus provides a public good to counterbalance regional and hemispheric partners. The GATT game of enlightened mercantilism (Krugman, 1992), whereby countries have an individual incentive to be protectionist but can collectively benefit from rules-based free trade, is replicated in the regional arena. In sum, there are multiple games played simultaneously, so that national policies are in some sense the precipitate of multilateral commitments, regional negotiations and domestic forces. Neither of the three games can be ignored by policymakers so long as interdependence has gained weight and the country has become involved in increasingly participatory trade policy-making. Policy formulation takes place at the intersection of these three vectors and the challenge ahead is to move forward the still-unfinished business of maximizing synergies among them. The political complexities are staggering, quite apart from the technical economic complexities.

Notes

1. Thanks are due to Miguel Lengyel for insightful comments to the final draft and to Marisa Diaz-Henderson for inputs into earlier drafts, 'Argentina and the WTO: As Good as it Gets,' unprocessed.
2. The compatibility of this program with the UR Agreement on Subsidies is under discussion. Argentina has been up for consultations with the EU, Japan, Korea, Poland and the US in the WTO.
3. Some months after this safeguard, the Argentine government also decided to impose another safeguard on polyester textile imports from Korea.
4. The revision has not been completed.
5. Only some associations in the sector, mainly representing very small farmers and domestic-oriented food production like dairy, call for more protectionist measures. Their main claim is that with distorted world agrifood markets, all food imports are basically unfair: 'why should we allow any French cheese or wine in, when is virtually impossible for us to sell a single product in their market?'.

5

Brazil: The Fine-Tuning of Trade Liberalization

Pedro da Motta Veiga and Vivianne Ventura-Dias

Introduction

Beginning in the late 1980s and throughout the last decade the Brazilian economy was subject to structural and regulatory reforms. Developmental policies that the nation followed for many decades were adapted without dismantling the web of interests installed in the Brazilian State. The adoption of policies aiming at the liberalization, privatization, and deregulation of domestic markets was at first caught in the middle of an institutional crisis, and was later subordinated to macroeconomic stability objectives. Pragmatism rather than a blind conviction of free trade benefits has guided the design and the implementation of Brazilian trade policies. Understandably, macroeconomic variables were the most influential factors in the formulation of entrepreneurial strategies. Over a period of less than 10 years, Brazilian society had to adjust to three radically different situations. In this brief interval, the economy moved from decades of highly distorted domestic prices – that included periods of hyperinflation – to inflation control combined, however, with an overvalued domestic currency (*Real*), the escalation in public debt and high interest rates. The third phase started in January 1999, when the reverberation of the international financial crises of 1997–98 led to the decision to float the *Real* freely, resulting in its devaluation.

Brazilian decision-makers went through a difficult process of learning the new international agenda while also facing a changed domestic system of incentives in a volatile global economy. The implementation of market-oriented reforms in Brazil generated distributive tensions among social groups and to severe disparities in the distribution of derived costs and benefits since all players were not upgraded as the playing field was progressively leveled. In fact, the capacity of firms to compete in the new environment as well as their bargaining power varied according to size, capital ownership and the nature of their economic activity. Social inequities increased as labor was disproportionately penalized both in terms of job creation and wage level.

Domestic, regional and sub-regional initiatives captured the imagination and efforts of economic agents and it was not until late in the decade that multilateral topics were included in the national debate. In general, the meager results from the Uruguay Round agreements in market access were felt to be disproportionate to the costs of the new obligations that had been accepted by Brazilian negotiators. In addition, the creation of a free trade area in the Southern Cone, and later the process towards the establishment of a Free Trade Area of the Americas (FTAA), demanded more attention from the nation. Throughout the past nine years of operations of the World Trade Organization (WTO), however, Brazilian private and public actors underwent a deep process of self-education as their involvement in trade-related negotiations proceeded at the bilateral, regional, sub-regional, inter-regional, plurilateral and multilateral levels.

This chapter looks at the political economy of the Brazilian commercial negotiating agenda after the Uruguay Round. The following section examines the transformations in Brazilian trade and investment policies during the 1990s. The contradictory impacts of trade liberalization on Brazilian production and trade in a context of overvalued currency and high interest rates are then discussed. The subsequent section summarizes the views of prominent public and private actors on the Brazilian trade agenda and the weights that they assign to negotiating fora to defend their interests. The results are based on direct interviews with private and public sector representatives. The penultimate section presents the Brazilian trade agenda in WTO as well as the strategy of combining topics and negotiating fora. Finally, the last section briefly presents some final considerations and suggestions for further studies in this area.

Trade and investment policies

The evolution of Brazilian industrial and trade policies in the 1990s bears little in common with a gradual implementation of the liberal paradigm. Rather than a progressive movement towards a less interventionist state and greater operation of market forces, the sequence of policies that were enacted revealed the existence of conflicts in views and of interests between technocrats and pressure groups, but also among technocrats as well. Some discontinuity was to be expected due to the institutional crisis of the beginning of the decade, when the first president democratically elected since 1960 (Fernando Collor, 1990–92) was ousted after remaining in office less than three years. There were differences also in the nature of industrial and trade policies in the two periods of the Fernando Henrique Cardoso presidency (1995–2002) that followed the former Collor administration after the interim government of Itamar Franco (1993–94).

The radical cutback in tariff and non-tariff protection started in 1990 and was completed by the end of 1993. But it was only after price and income effects of the successful price stabilization program (*Plano Real*) concurred with exchange rate appreciation that the impact of the unilateral trade liberalization was felt. Imports became considerably cheaper than domestic goods while exports fell behind. The accumulation of trade and current account deficits demanded more attention from the economic team with increased vulnerability of the Brazilian economy to external shocks.

Substantial macroeconomic imbalances still persist due to the extent of the public debt that forces high domestic interest rates. The access to external or public long-term credit became a critical component of individual firms' investment capacity, closely influencing their capacity to introduce technological and organizational changes and to reach higher levels of international competitiveness.[1] Traditionally, in the Brazilian context, the access to sources of long-term credit has varied among firms, according to the industries in which they operate, their size and capital ownership. The financial restriction under which local firms have had to perform was reinforced by strong fluctuations in the level of domestic economic activity in a context of depressed profit margins and high fiscal burdens.

Trade liberalization

The program of tariff reduction, which had started cautiously at the end of the 1980s, gained speed and consistency in the first months of the Collor administration. Radical tariff reductions and the elimination of non-tariff barriers included *inter alia* narrowing the local content requirements that entitled domestic enterprises to public loans and substantial modification of the national information technology policy. The unilateral trade liberalization removed a wide range of non-tariff barriers and reduced average tariff from a level of above 32 per cent at the beginning of 1990, to roughly 13 per cent by the end of 1993. Tariff dispersion and escalation were also reduced. In parallel, the new Brazilian government promoted the conversion of a bilateral trade agreement with Argentina into a free trade agreement. Whereas the previous Alfonsin–Sarney agreement had been crafted around sectoral agreements, the Collor–Menen agreement had a built-in provision aiming at a gradual, automatic and general elimination of import duties in bilateral trade over a short period of time. The negotiations included Uruguay and Paraguay, giving birth to the Mercosur (the Southern Common Market) as a free trade area in 1991, with the intermediate objective of becoming a customs union by the end of 1994.[2]

Consonant with liberal economic policies, domestic industrial incentives targeted to industrial and regional development were replaced by horizontal instruments of automatic application, with few provisions for coordination and interaction between public and private sectors. In fact, the design and implementation of the whole program did not include the participation of the private sector. However, new channels of communication between the state apparatus and private entrepreneurs were rapidly established.

The liberal project was aborted when the government became the object of heavy accusations of corruption that eventually led to the impeachment of the President. During the interim government that finished the mandate of the inculpated President, *ad-hoc* industry-specific incentives and other industrial policy instruments complemented the liberal agenda. Traditional fiscal and credit instruments of industrial policy at the sectoral level were reintroduced.

Inaugurated in January 1995, the government of Fernando Henrique Cardoso, who had been the Minister of Finance in the interim government, signaled that the triple process of unilateral, plurilateral (Mercosur) and multilateral liberalization had come to its end. The government had no intention of reversing the trade liberalization process but was not contemplating any further opening. There was a growing consensus in the country that domestic industries and enterprises had to be upgraded in order to face up to the new competitive but highly volatile international environment, especially following the Mexican payments crisis. Increased consumer purchasing power resulting from the stabilization program combined with an overvalued domestic currency led to increased inflows of relatively cheap imported goods. In several sectors, competition with imported goods squeezed the profit margins of leading firms, which until then had retained considerable power for price setting. New procedures for the application of trade-remedies (anti-dumping, safeguards) began to be noticeably used together with instruments for investment and export promotion.[3] Additionally, the design and implementation of industrial and investment policies gained force in sub-national spheres (Motta Veiga and Iglesias, 1997).[4]

The management of trade and investment policies remained closely subordinated to the priority of macroeconomic stability that, since the end of 1995, included the urgent need to monitor the growing trade deficit. Nevertheless, a neo-activism in industrial and foreign trade policies gradually emerged; it went beyond mere emergency measures that could be justified on macro or microeconomic grounds.[5] The trade liberalization process reached its height in the first quarter of 1995 in terms of the average level of tariffs and their degree of dispersion. Since then there have been several episodes of tariff increases, differentiated by sectors, which have increased the degree of dispersion of the tariff structure (Baumann *et al.*, 1998).

Brazilian industrial and trade policies did not fall under the uncontested hegemony of the 'liberal paradigm' except for a brief period. Trade and investment policies were concentrated on manufacturing segments facing difficulties in competing with cheap imports from Asia, like the toys industry, and, increasingly, on sectors with large trade deficits. In these cases, trade policies were associated with the promotion of new import-substituting investments or with specific actions for restructuring sectors affected by external competition.[6] In addition, in spite of apparent drastic changes in the overall development strategy, the same sectors that were major targets for industrial and export promotion policies during previous decades became major beneficiaries of discriminatory trade liberalization. Industries such as motorcars, electric and electronic goods, and capital goods were assisted by significant levels of trade protection within a highly heterogeneous structure of protection (see Table 5.1).[7] Likewise, the Brazilian Development Bank and the National Bank of Economic and Social Development (BNDES) offered relief credit to the textile and footwear industries.

Controlling imports, while attempting to increase and diversify exports, characterized the evolution of Brazilian trade policy since 1996. The federal administration has made great use of WTO-compatible trade remedies. Since the second half of 1997, the Brazilian administration has also employed different types of *ad-hoc* administrative measures to restrict imports. Some imports are subject to non-automatic licensing although formally there are no import surveillance mechanisms. A *similarity test* is still applied to discourage imports where a comparable good is produced domestically.

Table 5.1 Nominal and effective tariff protection in selected sectors, December 1995

Sectors	*Nominal protection* %	*Effective protection* %
Electric material	21.5	31.3
Machinery and tractors	18.2	20.8
Electronics equipment	22.1	24.9
Cars, trucks, etc.	55.5	270.9
Weighted average	11.5	12.9

Source: Kume, Honorio (1996).

The public system for export promotion was gradually reorganized on improved grounds. Special financial funds and interest rate equalization facilities were created, new mechanisms to assist exporters with credit insurance were established and instruments of fiscal exemption were defined. The PROEX is an export credit program that compensates exporters for high domestic interest rates. Public financial institutions such as the state-owned Banco do Brasil and the BNDES became increasingly involved in export financing. In 1998, the Brazilian Government created the Agency for Export Promotion (APEX) as well as financial mechanisms to attract small and medium sized enterprises (SMEs) to export activities.

In the period immediately following the devaluation of the Real in January 1999, Brazilian trade policy became less active based on the assumption that the devaluation of the Real would restore the international competitiveness of domestic firms. At the same time, volatility in the international environment at the end of the decade inhibited the use of fiscal and credit instruments for export promotion. The impact of the devaluation on the expansion of Brazilian exports, however, took longer than was initially forecast, and several sectoral programs of industrial and trade promotion still persist (Bonelli, 2001). Moreover, later in 1999, the WTO Dispute Settlement Body ruled against the PROEX. The decision was the result of a Canadian claim on behalf of Bombardier, an enterprise that was challenged by Embraer's (the Brazilian aircraft enterprise) success in the market for regional aircraft. Canada claimed that the PROEX constituted export subsidy, a type of subsidy that is prohibited by the WTO Agreement on Subsidies and Countervailing Duties.[8] The credit program was subsequently modified.[9]

Foreign direct investment (FDI) liberalization, deregulation and privatization

Throughout the import substitution period, Brazilian foreign direct investment (FDI) regulatory regime was only slightly discriminatory as compared to local trade policies. In opposition to high tariff and stringent non-tariff barriers, the investment regime embodied just a few 'horizontal' reservations and conventional sector-specific restrictions. The restrictions affected a precise number of industrial branches (mining, hardware information technology, among others), but were particularly relevant and persistent in the majority of service sectors. Some regulations excluding service sectors from FDI still remain in place. In WTO terms, Brazil had a 'negative list' in FDI, extending national treatment to foreign investment in all sectors except for a few that were reserved for local capital firms.

Besides being relatively liberal, the Brazilian investment regime is characterized by an unusual legal continuity; from the early 1950s the same constitutional provisions and one single piece of legislation (Law no.4131) remained in force. The 1998 Constitution reaffirmed, and even reinforced prior restrictions. At the same time, it provided the President of the Republic with discretionary powers to authorize the entry of foreign firms in areas formerly reserved to local capital and the access of such firms to public credit sources as well as to fiscal benefits.

The debt crisis of the 1980s, and the inflationary process that followed, drove the country out of the map of investment flows until stable macroeconomic conditions were restored. By 1995, macroeconomic stabilization, unilateral trade liberalization, the consolidation of Mercosur, the expansion of domestic market and the regulatory *aggiornamento* carried out by the government (privatization of state enterprises, softer rules for public concessions and public monopolies'), *inter alia*, promoted huge inflows of FDI. The inflows of FDI reached US$4.9 billion in 1995 (almost four times as much as in 1993), US$15.3 billion dollars in 1997 and US$28.5 billion in 1999. In 1998, Brazil accounted for 14 per cent of FDI flows received by all developing countries, ranking second among recipients in this category.

Nevertheless, at least four recent trends must be taken into consideration in the analysis of the FDI flows. In the second half of the 1990s, due to the privatization program almost 80 per cent of capital inflows went to services or non-tradables, namely telecommunications, energy and financial services.[10] Secondly, within the manufacturing sector, motor vehicles, electrical and electronic products and food and beverage industries have increased their share in FDI flows. Thirdly, the United

States remained the main investing country, although some European countries, and in particular Spain and Portugal increased their share. Finally, a reduced part of investment inflows consisted of greenfield investments, this is to say new productive plants. Growth in foreign ownership was accomplished mainly through mergers and acquisitions of domestic firms (Lacerda, 2000).

Brazilian production and trade

The assessment of the impact of trade liberalization on Brazilian industrial structure and productivity has been controversial. Criticism was focused on the way in which the unilateral trade liberalization was implemented without taking into account the short-term adjustment problems of Brazilian enterprises. Other authors claimed that Brazil had gone through a process of des-industrialization, epitomized by the contraction of the domestic capital goods industry. Conversely, other studies, even though recognizing the difficulties imposed by structural reforms, have concluded that trade liberalization induced gains in productivity as well as in industrial efficiency throughout the 1990s. These gains were associated with higher import coefficients in the production of most goods, as well as lower profit margins and costs for manufacturing enterprises (Hay, 1997; Moreira and Correa, 1997). The process of trade and capital liberalization was accompanied by a considerable increase in the participation of multinational firms in food and beverages, household appliances and auto parts, among others.

There is no evidence that the pessimistic conjectures on the transformations of Brazilian industrial structure have materialized, although it is true that the industrial dynamics of the 1990s was unable to launch a virtuous circle of new investments (Fonseca *et al.*, 1998). Aggregated data do not show significant changes in the composition of Brazilian manufactured production that could be imputed solely to trade liberalization.[11] It should be considered, however, that in the 1990s, new opportunities and risks were introduced in the business environment, following the generalized retraction of investment combined with stagnated production and low industrial productivity of the preceding decade. The perverse combination of high interest rates and currency appreciation, upon which the stabilization program was anchored, introduced great disparities in the distribution of costs and benefits of trade and investment liberalization. The benefits from the new opportunities as well as the vulnerability to risks were not evenly distributed in the business community. On the contrary, firms faced discrimination according to their size, capital ownership and the nature of their economic activity, features that tend to be highly correlated. Industrial branches in which multinational firms prevail have constituted the dynamic core of Brazilian manufacturing industry, in terms of new investments, competitiveness, introduction of organizational changes and quality control systems.

As was mentioned above, initially the drastic reduction in average tariff levels and the elimination of a great part of non-tariff measures had little effect on the level of imports. The tariff escalation in the Brazilian trade liberalization kept a reasonable degree of tariff protection for final goods, since tariffs were reduced mostly for raw materials and industrial inputs. For a while, producers of final goods could benefit from cost reductions without facing competition in their markets. It was only after the full implementation of the *Plano Real* that the simultaneous consequences of the Real appreciation and the expansion of the domestic demand were felt in increased import flows. Thereafter, trade liberalization acted as a factor of inter and intra-branch discrimination among firms in domestic markets, according to their levels of productive efficiency and their ability to adapt to a new competitive environment. Bonelli (2000) showed that between 1991 and 1998 the average productivity of labor increased at 2.5 per cent yearly although with great discrepancies among industries. The 'structural heterogeneity' of the Brazilian economy – inter-sectoral divergence in levels of productivity – that was already high at the beginning of the 1990s, increased even further.

The competitiveness of Brazilian exports, measured by its market share in world exports, reached a peak in middle 1980s, around 1.4 per cent. Thereafter, due to internal and external factors, the participation of Brazilian exports in world markets was reduced to 1 per cent in 1998 (Mortimore and Peres, 2001). The declining trend was particularly steep in manufactured exports, a process that has not yet been completely reversed. The chaotic macroeconomic situation of the second part of the 1980s and beginning of the 1990s was a severe constraint for the upgrading of enterprises. From 1995 to 1999, the appreciation of the *Real* also played a fundamental role in curtailing the price competitiveness of Brazilian exports. Between 1994 and 2001, Brazilian exports increased 1.3 times whereas imports increased 1.7 times. After the accumulation of trade deficits over the period 1994–2001, the situation was reversed and moderate trade surplus were obtained (mostly due to depressed and repressed demand). Nevertheless, deficits in the service account remained highly negative, leading to significant current account deficits (see Figure 5.1).

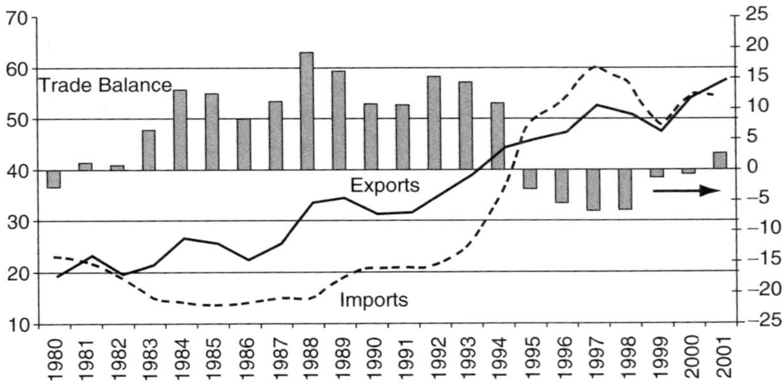

Figure 5.1 Brazilian trade balance, 1980–2001 ($billion)
Source: ECLAC, International Trade and Integration Division, on the basis of official figures.

Trade liberalization did not contribute to alter the product mix of Brazilian exports that had been inherited from the 1980s, as it did not eliminate the pervasive sector bias in the mechanisms for export-promotion and protection of domestic production. At the end of the 1990s, less than 41 per cent of Brazilian exports had grown at rates equal or above world exports and less than 21 per cent had high technological content (IEDI, 2000 quoted by Miranda, 2001). Nevertheless, the determinants in the reduction of Brazilian market shares in OECD manufacturing imports were both price and non-price components of the international competitiveness of those exports rather than the product composition of those exports (Fonseca and Veloso, 1998; Martins and Moreira, 1998).[12]

Brazilian industrial and trade structure was also affected by two important factors: the privatization program and the process of sub-regional economic integration, with the creation of Mercosur in 1991. In fact, Brazil illustrates the hypothesis that regulatory reforms and preferential trade agreements tend to benefit large domestic economic groups (Garrido and Peres, 1997). Through special links that they maintain with State bureaucracies these groups have access to privileged information on major privatization programs and are also able to exercise great influence in preferential trade liberalization negotiations. National groups include large multinational firms already established in the country. The involvement of these groups in Mercosur 's negotiations was quite effective in guaranteeing a significant level of protection in regional markets to industries such as capital goods, automobiles, information technology and telecommunications.

The management of trade liberalization: the views of public and private actors

Brazilian public and private sectors have experienced a multilevel and manifold process. It is a multilevel process because it encompassed a complex dialogue within and between public and private spheres of decision-making. The process included different segments of the state bureaucracy, a great heterogeneity of industry-specific trade interests, and the incorporation of new actors, organized labor and a broadly defined civil society. It is manifold because it entailed the generation of consensus in a society with little tradition of democracy and lacking adequate participatory institutions on ways and means of opening up the domestic economy and integrating it into a volatile and mercantilist world economy. The process is far from being over but considerable ground was covered in the past years.

Not until the end of the Uruguay Round had Brazilian commercial diplomacy been exposed to the need of identifying and harmonizing conflicting interests of local import-competing and exporting sectors before exchanging concessions with trading partners – actually, it was not used to exchange concessions due to the principle of concessions based on the largest supplier of the GATT. Negotiations started to move away from the control of experienced diplomats that had to coordinate the definition and implementation of the national trade agenda with other segments of the government. In previous negotiations representatives of the private sector participated in governmental meetings providing their view but, at the end, accepted the tutelage of the Brazilian bureaucracy.

This section summarizes major findings from interviews with representatives of private and public sectors whose interests impact the design and implementation of Brazilian trade agenda.[13] The purpose was to understand how public and private actors stand in terms of several aspects of trade negotiations. First, how would those agents assess the impacts of WTO rules on their particular industrial branch as well as on the domestic policy-making machinery. Secondly, what topics compose their general trade agenda and how do they evaluate the relative importance of various trade negotiations (especially processes so radically different as the Mercosur, the FTAA and WTO). In addition, how do these actors perceive the relative effectiveness of formal and informal communication channels between public and private actors in those negotiations.

The survey showed that the nature of international integration of the industrial branch in which the enterprise operates is critical in shaping business interests, setting up a negotiating agenda and in selecting the negotiating forum.[14] In fact, the industry-specific pattern of integration to the international economy is central to the formation of perceptions and positions of the business sector. Two sets of trade agenda emerged according to the import-competing or export-oriented characteristics of the industries. The first one is typical of global traders sectors, such as agribusiness, iron and steel. The trade agenda is essentially multilateral with market access as the central axis of concern. The second one is characteristic of sectors with low export coefficient and that compete in the domestic market with imports from the rest of the world, such as automobiles, textiles and apparel, electric and electronic goods. Negotiations with South American countries have a higher priority *vis-à-vis* multilateral negotiations combined with a clear interest in trade defense measures.[15]

Needless to say, the picture is still incomplete. Several groups were left out of the survey although they became increasingly influential in Brazilian policy-making. First, large domestic exporters, highly diversified in terms of their investments and business operations, were not included. They are concentrated on the production and exports of industrial commodities but have also diversified their investments to non-tradable sectors (energy, infrastructure services, financial services and retailing) through their participation in the Brazilian privatization program (BNDES, 1997). Second, the Brazilian media and the National Congress were not covered this study.

The impact of the Uruguay Round Agreements (URAs)

Representatives from both public and private sectors share a similar assessment of the impact of the URAs. The technical secretariat of the National Manufacturing Association (CNI) believes that a major impact was that domestic trade and investment policies can now be sanctioned by the WTO. Likewise, Brazilian bureaucrats tend to see multilateral commitments as a liability. These multilateral obligations restrict the type of instruments that can be used in trade and investment policies, limit the scope of these policies and reduce the discretion of the Federal Government to implement trade initiatives. Further restrictions are associated with ratification requirements and drafting complementary legislation that gives a major role to the National Congress in trade policy.

In the first years of WTO operation, the obligations derived from the URAs seemed quite abstract to Brazilian entrepreneurs who were still trying to cope with the impact of domestic trade liberalization. As mentioned, in 1993, when the Uruguay Round was reaching its conclusion, Brazil had completed the radical program of tariff reduction and elimination of most non-tariff barriers. By the end of 1994, Mercosur was a free trade area and a Common External Tariff was effective for 80 per cent of intra-regional trade. The amplification of tariff reduction effects after the *Plano Real* coincided with the beginning of WTO operations in 1995. In effect, the average tariff was reduced to roughly 13 per cent whereas the level of tariff binding for Brazilian industrial tariff schedules in the Uruguay Round was almost three times higher (35 per cent). There was, therefore, a wide convergence between unilateral, subregional and multilateral liberalization, which diluted the impacts that could be credited specifically to the URAs.

The Brazilian government also agrees that any assessment of the impacts of the URAs in Brazilian policy-making have first to consider the other parallel processes of trade liberalization. Federal administration representatives recognize, moreover, that multilateral obligations had a marginal effect in restraining the use of traditional instruments of protection. The country has enjoyed considerable freedom in handling its tariff protection as well as the use of short-term *ad-hoc* administrative measures without violating multilateral commitments.

Nevertheless, the URAs affected the process of trade policy formulation, particularly the legislation for trade remedies and trade promotion as well as in the creation of effective enforcement institutions. The country had to revise its legislation on trade defense mechanisms to meet the terms of the Agreement, to set up a Department of Trade Defense at the Ministry on Development, Industry and Trade, and to open the discussion of rules on antidumping, subsidies and countervailing duties in Mercosur.[16] From the perspective of export promotion and investment policies, the URAs initially supported the government objectives of restricting the previous business sectoral 'activism.' Even the recent sectoral bias of Brazilian trade policies has been tempered by the restrictions of WTO obligations. In general, the Brazilian government has been very careful to avoid any flagrant violation of the multilateral agreements in the use of incentive instruments.[17] The impact of the Agreement on Trade-Related Aspects of Intellectual Property Rights (TRIPs) was also relevant, although the

Brazilian legislation on Intellectual Property Rights was enacted before the end of the transitional period.

In terms of market access, the aggregated effects of the Uruguay Round were very moderate even for sectors that were re-introduced in the multilateral system of rules such as agriculture, textiles and apparel. Professional managers in agroindustrial enterprises evaluate positively the impact of the Agreement on Agriculture, even though they remain skeptical of the effective fulfillment of the obligations assumed by developed nations. The positive results refer not only to the inclusion of agriculture under the GATT disciplines, but also to expectations of reduced agricultural subsidies, and the advances embodied in the Agreement on Sanitary and Phytosanitary Measures. Exporters of agricultural products are especially pleased with the principle that sanitary barriers has to be justified in scientific terms.[18]

Similarly, for the textile and clothing sectors, integration into the GATT/WTO disciplines is considered positive. However, textile decision-makers recognize that the productivity of Brazilian enterprises is still below the level of their international competitors. At first, managers of these Brazilian firms looked at the Agreement on Textiles and Clothing (ATC) from the point of view of import-competing interests rather than from market access improvements. They were concerned about the strict rules included in the application of safeguards by importing countries, under the ATC as compared to those under the Multifiber Agreement. They are wary about the possible growth of imports from Asia, as well as illegal imports or 'triangular' operations via Mercosur.

In iron and steel, the improvement on safeguard disciplines and anti-dumping measures is perceived as a mild guarantee against the arbitrary use of discretionary actions by large importers. The limited protection has been effective since 1998, when Brazilian steel exporters were again subjected to arbitrary restrictions in the United States market. Anti-dumping duties were imposed and Brazilian producers had to accept a voluntary export restriction agreement (an instrument that had been formally banned in the Uruguay Round) (see ECLAC, 2001). In fact, Brazilian industrialists were led to believe that after the privatization of iron and steel enterprises and the removal of several subsidies, there would be no justification for anti-dumping and subsidies actions. Conversely, the expansion of steel imports in Brazil, parallel to the general movement of trade liberalization and the expansion of world exports, resulted in a greater use of anti-dumping measures requested by Brazilian steel producers.[19]

On the other hand, the motorcar industry complains of the failure by the Brazilian government to present a notification to the WTO within the deadline defined in the Trade-related Aspects of Investment Measures (TRIMs) Agreement. Without the notification, Brazil was forced to protracted bilateral negotiations with each of its main trade partners that forced the government to give additional concessions.[20] In the last few years, the main priority for the sector has been the negotiation of a common automobile regime within the Mercosur. The automobile regime shall keep the import tariff at 35 per cent (which is also the maximum level bound by Brazil at the WTO for industrial goods).[21] Recently, the motor car industry became the main supporter for the renewal of a bilateral trade agreement with Mexico. Furthermore, the sector has also been active in pressuring for favorable market access conditions from Chile and other countries in South America. It is interesting to note that this pro-exporting posture has been restricted only to bilateral agreements, while the industry defends the preservation of the same high levels of protection that it enjoys in the domestic market.

Finally, for the electronic sector, WTO and the Uruguay Round are not relevant issues. The industry representatives are more concerned with the impact of unilateral trade liberalization, intra-Mercosur liberalization and with imports originated in other Latin American countries, particularly from Mexico.

The Brazilian trade agenda in various negotiating forums

Brazilian competitive exporting sectors, mostly agricultural and industrial commodity producers, are global traders – that is, they export to all different regions of the world, including Mercosur, although member countries have a limited weight in their sales abroad. They identify the WTO as the most relevant negotiating forum to defend their market access interests. For instance, the poultry meat sector has taken a quite assertive position in market access conditions. The industry has successfully lobbied for the formation of a panel at the WTO against the European Union regarding its management of poultry meat imports.[22] The international agenda of the sector includes the effective implementation of the Agriculture Agreement in terms of industrial countries' commitments to market access and reduction of subsidies. Argentina is the second national market for Brazilian poultry exports, leading the industry to be moderately interested in Mercosur and in FTAA negotiations. On the other hand, although iron and steel producers fall in the category of global traders, the sector has redefined its external priorities due to protectionist measures in its major importing countries. In market access, more weight has been given to the Mercosur and to the revision of bilateral trade agreements with other countries in the Latin American Integration Association (LAIA).

Conversely, other sectors for which the domestic market is more important assign greater weight to Mercosur. Consistent with their import-competing situation, the establishment of a hemispheric free trade area is perceived as a threat rather than a positive challenge. Textile and clothing producers are the exceptions since they are interested in preferential access to the United States market. Textile representatives support the creation of a negotiating subgroup on textiles and the elimination of the principle of single undertaking, a key negotiating element in the strategy of Mercosur countries in the FTAA (see Table 5.2).

As it will be developed below, the Brazilian negotiating position starts from a general recognition that the country is a global trader in terms of product and market composition of its exports. Therefore, the negotiators believe that the WTO should be the privileged forum for trade negotiations. In the first years of the WTO, Brazil's agenda as a *demandeur* was more defensive than assertive. The government was reluctant to

Table 5.2 Priority Issues in the trade agenda of selected Brazilian industries

Sectors	*Priority issues*	*Secondary issues*
Steel and iron	Trade remedies Access to markets: Mercosur and anti-dumping	Trade and environment
Automobile	Automobile regime (TRIMs) in Mercosur Agreement with Mexico	FTAA (tariff liberalization/ larger access to domestic market)
Electro-electronics	Trade defense and access to Mercosur market	FTAA (idem)
Textile	Trade defense (customs valuation, among others) and FTAA (sector agreement implementation)	Labour and environmental rules at WTO and FTAA: favorable position
Clothing	Trade defense (customs valuation) and Mercosur (illegal imports)	FTAA (access to United States market)
Poultry meat	Reduction of subsidies to exports and multilateral trade liberalization	Sanitary and phytosanitary measures
Orange juice	Reduction of tariffs and barriers to exports	Labour rules

pursue a more 'positive' trade agenda because of the vulnerable conditions of most enterprises and industries. The intra-sectoral heterogeneity of Brazilian industries converted any negotiation into a 'two-edged knife,' as the gains resulting from better market access for a few competitive sectors would be negatively balanced by the costs inflicted on greater number of less competitive sectors and firms.

The interviews suggested that government priorities in trade negotiations are influenced by considerations about the impacts of possible concessions on employment or the technological upgrading of domestic production and trade, as well as the performance of sectors with a significant weight in industrial structure. Hence, industries such as clothing and textiles, automobiles, electric and electronics, chemical and iron and steel, all of which – with the exception of the latter – are essentially import-competing and play an important role in the formulation of the Brazilian negotiating strategy. Conversely, resource-intensive exporting sectors seem to suffer a kind of 'tacit discrimination.'

The private sector participation in negotiations

Greater participation by private actors in trade negotiations still faces difficulties. Federal bureaucrats, especially at lower echelons of government, complained of insufficient familiarity of the business sector with the multilateral trading system rules and procedures. There are also difference of views within the Government, as between the Ministry of Foreign Relations and the Ministry of Development, Industry and Commerce, that affect the overall coordination within the government and among the various bureaucracies and the business sector.

Nevertheless, there has been an intensification of relations between public and private sectors, particularly in the process of structuring the FTAA. Some governmental negotiators perceive this involvement positively because it confers legitimacy to the government position and reinforces its bargaining power in different negotiating fora. On the other hand, however, negotiators are wary about the internal negotiating process since it could hinder the definition of a positive agenda for negotiations later on.

In general, businessmen perceive a significant improvement since 1995, when the government adopted a more flexible stance toward suggestions from the private sector.[23] At the same time, the business sector is getting more familiar with negotiating matters. In the interviews, the lack of technical expertise in the private sector as a valid interlocutor to the government was recognized, but the paucity of government initiatives to reduce the gap was also pointed out. The first years of Mercosur are quoted as the paradigm of non-participation of the private sector and the government opposition to any attempt in that direction. The business sector concluded that the costs of not being involved in the first years of the Mercosur negotiating process were very high. Learning from past mistakes, since 1994 the business sector, through its associations, became intensively involved in the negotiations that followed. Moreover, that process provided the stimulus for a strong and growing participation in the pre-negotiation phase of the process for the establishment of the FTAA. Organized around the National Manufacturing Association (CNI), the Brazilian Business Coalition was created combining business associations from all industries (manufacturing, resource-based and service industries). The Coalition has been able to coordinate, consolidate and present consistent Brazilian business position in relation to the FTAA. Although, at the beginning, the coalition adopted the defensive position of the Brazilian bureaucracy, it has been gradually evolving toward a more independent and strategic position in which both defensive and as pro-active views are combined.

The establishment of the Brazilian Coalition was a landmark for two reasons: first, because business associations accepted that access to important markets (investment, services and government procurement) could result from exchanging concessions among partners. Secondly, because the Coalition was an autonomous expression of the business community with respect to the Brazilian government. Therefore it helped to determine a trade agenda based on a different rationale. In this sense, the result of the self-education of entrepreneurs and public bureaucrats may be a multiplicity of 'national positions' and other coalitions may arise on a more decentralized basis than in the past, when negotiations were confined to a bartering for tariff concessions.[24] This contrasts with the previous situation, when business participation was restricted to sectoral negotiations in the LAIA and bilateral negotiations within the Multifiber Agreement, in the case of for textiles and apparel industries and the Agreement on Voluntary Restrictions of Exports imposed by the United States on Brazilian iron and steel firms. The agroindustrial sectors closely followed the evolution of the Uruguay Round, but scarcely had any participation in the formulation of the negotiating position of Brazil.[25]

In the FTAA process, there has been some convergence of views between the private and the public sectors. The private sector endorsed the Brazilian government position, especially in what refers to negotiating principles and time schedules in market access negotiations. Nevertheless, the business sector complains that access to information is still restricted, and that the government arbitrarily decides the level, nature, and degree of consultations. In general, the presence of the private sector at the negotiating table is not allowed. Furthermore, the participation of government agencies in the negotiations has been criticized: the most common refers to the discontinuity in the composition of the staff of negotiators and lack of coordination among the ministries and agencies involved.

Labor Unions[26]

Foreign trade and international integration became important topics in the international relations agenda of the Brazilian trade union, the CUT (*Central Unica de Trabalhadores*). The political consolidation of the CUT coincided with the beginning of the Mercosur and the intensification of the liberalization of the Brazilian market. However, Mercosur was not perceived as part of the trade liberalization process but as a regional political process. The integration was associated with the idea of a greater bargaining power for individual countries in their dealings with powerful industrial countries. On the one hand, the Brazilian organized labor movement admired the higher labor standards reached in Argentina. But on the other hand, there was some concern about employment and wage effects in Brazil of sub-regional business strategies of oligopolistic sectors (automobile, food). Some defensive positions among trade unions emerged together with localized bilateral conflicts between Brazil and Argentina.

The CUT became involved in Mercosur negotiations after a technical subgroup on labor questions was set up in 1992 to study labor relations, employment and social security in the four member countries. Later its participation was expanded to include the discussion of public policies not directly related to labor. Currently, the CUT is permanently in close communication with trade unions in other Mercosur countries. With the Brazilian government it negotiates the country's position on labor-related questions. In association with the CNI, the CUT proposed the creation of the Economic and Social Consultative Forum in the FTAA, like the Forum that had been established in the Mercosur through the Ouro Preto Protocol in December 1994.

Conversely, the trade union is more critical of the FTAA due to the impact on domestic production and employment of opening Brazilian markets to the United States. It supports the strengthening of Mercosur to counterbalance the power of the United States in FTAA negotiations. It was also quite active in the creation of an Americas Labor Forum of the FTAA in 1997 to have a voice in the FTAA process similar to that of the corporations. In contrast to trade unions in the United States and Canada – which are more concerned with the inclusion of labor conditions to the agenda of the FTAA – the Brazilian trade unions advocate a broader defense of labor interests in all topics of the negotiating agenda. In spite of this divergence, the CUT maintains a permanent dialogue with its North American counterparts.

Multilateral negotiations and the WTO are still remote issues for the CUT, in part because the Brazilian government has selected labor rules (or social clauses) as the single multilateral topic that could be of interest to the labor movement. Since the issue is not likely to be included in the WTO agenda there remains little room for consulting and negotiating with trade unions. Recently, the CUT suggested the creation of a joint Committee WTO/ILO to discuss labor standards and to prevent their use as disguised protectionist measures.

The Brazilian trade agenda in the new round of multilateral trade negotiations

Access to markets and ensuring fair competition in external and in domestic markets is crucial for the expansion of Brazilian exports. A great diversification of products and markets distinguish Brazilian integration to world markets from that of other Latin American countries'. Brazilian commercial diplomacy has assigned a high priority to multilateral negotiations for market access while other viable alternatives such as the Mercosur were established. Throughout the Uruguay Round Brazilian negotiators strove for a balanced and transparent system of multilateral norms enforced through an effective dispute settlement mechanism. The defense of multilateral rules has been carried out, however, with a high degree of pragmatism, in the belief that a system of rules would not restrain industrial countries from protecting their markets and special interests through arbitrary measures. Consequently, efforts towards multilateral rules and multilateral liberalization had to be combined with others aimed at strengthening schemes of subregional and regional cooperation. Multilateral and regional actions are perceived as complementary to each other and supportive to the global economic integration of the Brazilian economy (Barbosa and Panelli César, 1994).

It should be recalled that the WTO became operational in January 1995. By then, NAFTA had been implemented since January 1994;

Mercosur had completed the intra-trade liberalization process; the process of the FTAA was beginning the preparatory work and the negotiations between Mercosur, Chile and Mexico with the European Union were also taking shape. It was with great internal and external difficulties that Brazil, initially a lonely voice, could extend to the other members of Mercosur its cautious approach to the FTAA.[27] Later on, Mercosur established the practice, inaugurated by the European Community, of having a rotating speaker on behalf of the sub-regional group. As the process towards a FTAA evolved, a basic concern of Brazilian diplomats, and increasingly of Brazilian society, has been to guarantee the survival and the strengthening of Mercosur (with the creation of a Southern America Free Trade Area, as a related objective).

The failure to launch a new Round at Seattle in December 1999 contributed to greater interest on the part of public and private decision-makers in the two major regional initiatives: Mercosur and the FTAA. Mercosur, however, went through a difficult period after the devaluation of the Brazilian currency in January 1999, which was later compounded by liquidity problems in Argentina and the eventual devaluation of the *peso*. Under these circumstances, the preservation of Mercosur identity within the FTAA became the central concern of Brazilian diplomacy, which implied the adoption of actions to deepen commitments in fields where the sub-regional scheme had remained at the stage of a free trade area. Services, investment, government procurement, competition policy and unified trade defense instruments made up the 're-launching' agenda of Mercosur in April 2000. The financial vulnerability of the two major economies forced their governments to assign greater importance to solving pressing problems that led to the postponement of widening and deepening their integration commitments.

Since the first WTO ministerial meeting in Singapore at the end of 1996, Brazilian negotiators began to fear the worst scenario of having to accept either trade-related rules defined bilaterally or to endorse sector-specific negotiations such as had occurred in service sectors and in information technology products. Therefore, they began to advocate a wide-ranging round of trade negotiations in which countries could bargain for a balanced agenda to address both developing and developed countries' interests under the ruling principle of a *single undertaking*. In addition, the reforms that were introduced in domestic regulations, particularly in services, investment and in strengthening the protection of intellectual property rights strengthened the Brazilian negotiating position.

The Brazilian trade agenda is concentrated in two broad areas that are being advanced at the bilateral, plurilateral and multilateral levels: a drastic reduction in the agricultural protectionism of industrial countries and a revision of trade remedies rules, particularly of anti-dumping. Moreover, in order to keep the balance between concessions at the various negotiating fora, it is crucial for Brazilian diplomacy to synchronize WTO negotiations with those that the country is undertaking with the two major trading partners – the United States in the FTAA and the European Union, for a free trade agreement Mercosur–European Union. Otherwise, it could extend concessions to the United States for trade preferences that might later be eroded by multilateral commitments (Abreu, 2002).[28]

In the Brazilian evaluation, the results of the Uruguay Round were unbalanced and the benefits accrued disproportionately to rich countries. The rules on subsidies differentiated agricultural from manufactured products, since export subsidies were prohibited for manufactures but not for agricultural products. Brazilian exporters of agricultural products (poultry meat) had to face competition from subsidized goods in third markets. Negotiators asserted: 'Brazil wants its exports to have the same degrees of market access and the same disciplines that industrial countries expect to find in our market for their exports.'[29]

Two other areas of concern refer to: (1) rules on export credit for manufactured goods; and (2) the compatibility between the protection of intellectual property rights and legitimate measures either to defend public health, or to protect genetic resources and traditional knowledge. Brazil was very active in negotiating a Ministerial Declaration on TRIPs and Public Health in the Fourth Ministerial Conference in Doha, Qatar. At Doha, Brazilian diplomats also put forward several other topics that been raised by the private sector in the preparatory work for the WTO Ministerial meeting. Most of those topics fell under the broad title of 'implementation of the Uruguay Round Agreements.'

Concluding remarks

The central objectives of this chapter were to look at the political economy of the Brazilian trade negotiating agenda and to provide insights into the Brazil's strategy of a multi-level bargaining game. There is an extensive agreement in the country that the results of the Uruguay Round were highly unbalanced. The impact of the URAs on the design of trade and industrial policies in Brazil were not commensurate with the direct and indirect gains, in terms of greater and better market access in industrial countries. The agreements did contribute to the consolidation of Brazilian trade liberalization policies, conferring some degree of commitment and irreversibility to the reforms. Nevertheless, representatives from competitive exporting enterprises expressed their frustration with a set of rules that do not protect them from unilateral measures in industrialized countries. Basically, they feel that they continue to have restricted access to developed country markets, while facing unfair competition from their subsidized products in third markets.

In the words of the Brazilian Ministry of Foreign Affairs, any trading negotiation is made of two complementary processes: a domestic negotiation, in which negotiating positions are defined through a wide consultation with the business sector and with civil society as a whole; and an external negotiation, with representatives from other governments (two-level bargaining game).[30] In the past, industry-specific interests have molded Brazilian trade and industrial policies, successfully presenting their own agenda as a legitimate national agenda. A federal bureaucracy with an authoritarian bias and protectionist tradition supported the hegemonic trade agenda of essentially import-competing sectors. Therefore, a trade agenda negotiated directly between the government and carefully selected sectors tended to be more defensive and less market-access-oriented.

An outcome of the participation of business and labor sectors in the domestic negotiations around the FTAA and Mercosur is a new perception of national interest that goes beyond a mere juxtaposition of industry-specific interests and that challenges the monopoly in the definition of national interest by those groups that had privileged access to the public sector. Non-traditional players such as organized labor, agricultural workers and consumers, among others, forced their way into the debate and were recognized as important partners in the domestic negotiation. Although necessarily full of contradictions, since not all social and economic sectors will gain in the external negotiation, the process of consensus-formation requires higher levels of transparency and a broader assessment of costs and benefits of internal and external concessions.[31] Moreover, it requires an independent search for information and training, which are readily available in the era of e-formation. Consequently, civil society can escape the tutelage of the public sector and contribute to the debate with greater autonomy.

One possible follow-up of the present study could be a better understanding in different national experiences of the process of consensus building (see Motta Veiga and Iglesias, 2002). Another suggestion concerns further studies on industrial policy instruments that are WTO-compatible. Such instruments tend to be intensive in coordination requirements and their success is dependent, in general, on particular conditions of implementation. These conditions are not easily created in developing countries such as Brazil. Nevertheless, while the use of discriminatory policy instruments and rent-seeking practices should be discouraged, the need for the technological and organizational upgrading of the productive apparatus and the reduction of intra-branch productivity heterogeneity is legitimate. The discussion should therefore move in the direction of identifying new ways for state action that should be compatible with multilateral rules but, above all, should be compatible with democratic rules and the process of nation-building.

Notes

1. The opportunity cost of capital became the major strategic variable to investment decisions of Brazilian enterprises (Miranda, 2001).
2. The Asunción Treaty that created the Mercosur established a timetable for tariff reduction of 7 per cent every six months after an initial reduction of 47 per cent that led to a duty-free internal trade by the end of 1994 (see Baumann, 2001).
3. Over 1996–99, 72 anti-dumping investigations were initiated and definitive duties were imposed in 36 cases. By end-1999, Brazil had some 46 anti-dumping measures in force (OECD, 2001).
4. From 1995 on, investment policies at the State level were added to federal instruments normally targeted to the same industries.
5. From the very beginning, the Cardoso administration adopted several measures aiming at discriminating against imports, and also providing incentives to production and investment for domestic firms. Thus, tariffs for artificial and synthetic fibers were raised to 16 per cent. Tariffs for fabrics and clothing went up from 15 per cent to 70 per cent, to be later reduced to 21 per cent. In addition, quotas in clothing were established for imports coming from China and other countries. Furthermore, between May 1996 and June 1998, a Program for the Textile Sector was instituted at the BNDES (Brazilian National Bank of Economic and Social Development).
6. A safeguard measure for toys, particularly from China, was extended to the end of 2003. Brazil also applies transitional safeguard permitted by the WTO Agreement on Textiles and Clothing.
7. The review on Brazilian trade policy undertaken in 1996 by WTO identified the existence of tariff variations across products that reflected mostly the substantial tariff escalation by stage of processing. Calculations for the 1996 applied tariff show that the simple average for all raw materials was 6.5 per cent, compared with 9.2 per cent for semi-processed goods and 15.7 per cent for finished goods (WTO, 1996a).
8. The dispute started in June 1996 when Canada requested consultations with Brazil on the use of the PROEX to support the purchase of aircrafts from

Embraer. In March 1997, Brazil requested consultation with Canada, regarding the subsidies that the Canadian government at the federal and sub-national levels provided to the exports of Bombardier aircrafts. In July 1998, the two countries requested a WTO Panel to rule on their claims. Both claims were accepted by subsequent Panels and Appellation Groups (see the documentation on WTO Web page: www.wto.org). See Goldstein and McGuire (2002) for an overview of the dispute.

9. On 21 December 1999, the government issued new regulations for PROEX, by Decrees MDIC no. 374 (equalization) and 375 (direct finance to exports), with the objective of improving the management of the resources.
10. It should be emphasized that the privatization program was carried out in Brazil without an effective regulatory framework (except in telecommunications). Major players were institutional investors such as the pension funds of state-owned companies associated with large national and foreign private groups.
11. See Bonelli and Gonçalves (1998; 1999) and Kupfer *et al.*, (1998).
12. Research on the evolution of Brazilian exports to the United States in the 1990s assembled empirical evidence on the secondary importance product composition plays in explaining the weak Brazilian export performance during the decade (Motta Veiga *et al.*, 1999).
13. The survey included interviews with representatives of the major national manufacturing association (Confederação Nacional de Industrias – CNI), as well as of business associations at branch level. CNI has taken an important coordinating role for Brazilian business both in FTAA and in Mercosur negotiations and has also been quite active in disseminating information on the various negotiations among entrepreneurs and in training business men and women in international negotiations. For the complete description of the survey see Motta Veiga (2000).
14. Three exporting manufacturing industries and four import-competing industries were selected: steel, orange juice and poultry-meat in the former, and automobiles, textiles, apparel, and electric and electronic appliances.
15. Some sectors such as footwear and iron and steel combine both strategies.
16. Governmental officials believe that the utilization of these instruments *per se* does not indicate a protectionist stance, since there has been a restricted recourse to safeguards and the application of non-extreme margins to anti-dumping duties, among others practices.
17. The rulings of the Dispute Settlement Body at the WTO on the use of the PROEX to finance the exports of regional aircraft contributed to a wide diffusion of WTO by the media and to become part of the national debate.
18. The orange juice industry constitutes a particular case. It is composed by a handful of large domestic and foreign enterprises that had an active participation in the Uruguay Round, when it lobbied for tariff concessions, under the Agreement on Agriculture. As a result of these negotiations, a 20 per cent reduction in import duties levied by the European Union was obtained, with a phasing-out period of six years. The industry is still hampered by a high import tariff in the United States. For this sector, multilateral negotiations should be centered on tariff reduction.

19. In May, 2000, the government imposed anti-dumping duties to imports of stainless steel from a number of countries (Mexico, France, South Africa, among others), following the appeal of a domestic firm, controlled by French capital.
20. In march 1998, Brazil settled with the United States the last bilateral dispute on this subject. The road to similar agreements with the other partners was expedited by the accession, in 1996 and 1997 of European and Asian firms to the sectoral regime of incentives.
21. This is a reversal of a previous decision to reduce tariffs for the import of finished vehicles in Mercosur to 23 per cent by the 2000. The Mercosur regime should replace the national regimes of incentives adopted by Braziland Argentina and will be in effect until 2004, when it shall be discussed again.
22. See the Web page of WTO (www.wto.org) (WT/DS69/R and WT/DS69/AB/R).
23. In 1996, the SENALCA (National Section of the Coordination of FTAA-related Issues) was created in the Ministry of Foreign Affairs, as part of the process of coordinating the FTAA negotiations. It is composed of several Ministries and Federal agencies and the business sector. Trade unions have been invited at the discretion of the government (Motta Veiga and Iglesias, 2002).
24. For instance, some of the persons interviewed stressed the importance of a greater involvement of the Brazilian government in establishing multilateral parameters in the related topics of trade and environment and labor standards. Particularly for competitive exporting sectors such as orange juice, the establishment of multilateral rules would reduce the leeway for unilateral protectionist moves by larger trading partners. After a wide program of information dissemination about the non-utilization of child labor among their associates, the business association (ABECITRUS) signed a public commitment with the ILO and UNICEG to recommend to their members, and to all supply chain participants the exclusion of any kind of child labor.
25. The poultry meat sector has had a long experience in participation on trade negotiations, having being present at the GATT since 1983.
26. A single interview was carried out with a representative of the permanent Committee for International Affairs of the largest labor union federation in the country. The *Central Unica de Trabalhadores* (CUT) is the main Brazilian confederated labor union, representing some 2,600 local unions and 10 million workers. It is solidly rooted in the rural sector, among the public employees and in the modern industrial and service sectors. Two-third of the CUT affiliates belong to the private sector of the economy. The CUT makes use of a rather large staff of technical consultants for policy formulation, especially in areas new to the trade-union agenda.
27. See Feinberg (1997).
28. 'There are issues, however, that cannot be adequately addressed in regional negotiations. It is the case of agricultural subsidies in which concessions that we can extract from the European Union will benefit the United States and vice-versa. It will be easier to move forwards, therefore, in one forum in which all major interested parties will be present. Hence, the gains that could be obtained in WTO in anti-dumping, subsidies, technical barriers or

sanitary and phytosanitary measures are complementary to the elimination of tariff and non-tariff barriers in the Hemisphere and in the European Union. With clear, transparent and objective rules in WTO, and preferential access to the United States and the European Union, we will have effective conditions of access for our exports' (Speech of Celso Lafer, Ministry of Foreign Relations, in the XXI National Meeting of Foreign Trade, Rio de Janeiro, 30 November 2001, Web page of the Brazilian Ministry of Foreign Affairs, www.mre.go.br/sei).

29. Speech of Luiz Felipe Lampreia, Minister of Foreign Affairs, during the III WTO Ministerial Meeting in Seattle, 30 November 1999.
30. Presentation by Celso Lafer, Minister of Foreign Affairs, Ministerial Conference in OECD, 'Trade and Development', Paris OECD, 16 May 2002.
31. In a recent paper, Aráujo Jr (1998) referred to the existence of institutional arrangements, which are capable of simultaneously preserving the consistency of national policies and the legitimacy of industry-specific interests, thereby providing transparency on trade protection and promotion policies that could be adopted by the government.

6
Uruguay: Trade Policy in a Small Economy

Marcel Vaillant and Vivianne Ventura-Dias

Introduction

With little more than three million inhabitants, Uruguay is the second smallest country of Latin America, after Panama, despite its large territory. It was a prosperous agricultural economy throughout the first part of the 20th century but the dream of a premature welfare state was brought to reality by unilateral changes in the conditions of access to agricultural markets in industrial countries. In the second half of the 20th century, the Uruguayan society had to cope with the gradual reduction in rents derived from its abundant natural resources while the size and age composition of the population did not facilitate the diversification of production and trade.

Integration to international markets is crucial to Uruguay. The opening-up of the Uruguayan economy started in 1973 under the military rule, after the model of import substitution showed its limitations for a small economy. Democratic governments lent support to liberalization policies after 1985 but balance of payment problems and the debt crisis of the early 1980s reduced the scope of the first liberalization effort. It was widely debated in the late 1980s and into the 1990s whether to continue the process of unilateral and multilateral trade liberalization given the country's highly concentrated export basket. Alternatively, liberalization could be pursued regionally under the assumption that the intra-industry nature of reciprocal trade would contribute to reduce the adjustment costs of trade liberalization. The newly created customs union, Mercosur (Southern Common Market), offered the opportunity to test the alternative way. Uruguayan economy was already closely associated with the economies of the other three members of Mercosur (Argentine, Brazil and Paraguay).

A relatively homogeneous and educated society, which has consistently scored high Human Development indicators, Uruguay has not been able to find a path of sustainable development. Moreover, the economy has been extremely vulnerable to the economic and financial crises of its neighbors, Argentina and Brazil, that negatively impacted regional integration as a viable growth strategy.

This chapter describes the recent evolution of trade policy, including major trade institutions in Uruguay, as well as the interaction between private and public actors in the definition of a national trade agenda in the WTO round of negotiations. The next section examines trade and trade policy in Uruguay. The subsequently section summarizes trade institutions and business organizations. The penultimate section discusses the Uruguayan multilateral agenda in the World Trade Organization (WTO), centering on market access for agricultural and agroindustrial products and on the preservation of contingency trade measures. The final section concludes with observations on major challenges posed by regional, hemispheric and multilateral negotiations for a small developing economy.

Trade and investment policies

Trade liberalization in Uruguay differed from the rest of Latin America. First, it started early in the 1970s through the elimination of quantitative restrictions, the simplification of the import regime, and a new set of export promotion instruments (Anichini *et al.*, 1978; Vaillant, 1992). Secondly, it was preceded by significant liberalization of capital account and deregulation of the banking system.[1] Also, unlike Argentine and Brazilian experiences, Uruguay never suffered a protracted period of hyperinflation.

In 1974, the economy lacked the flexibility to quickly adapt to changes brought by the first oil shock, when the country had to cope simultaneously with losing important beef markets in Europe, and the erosion in the price of major commodities such as beef, wool, and leather. The economic crisis that followed put an end to the import substitution strategy and facilitated an early trade reform (Cardoso and Galal, 2002). Uruguayan trade policy, at the beginning of the 1970s, was a vast and not always consistent set of rules and regulations.

In addition, in the recent trade liberalization, there were few regulatory changes in terms of privatization, except for the elimination of state monopolies in alcoholic beverage production, electricity generation, and home mortgages. Likewise, there was little transformation of the public sector, except for changes in the social security system (Laens, 1998).[2] Transfer of some activities to the private sector under contract, concession or sale resulted from a 1991 law on state reform, including ground services and operation of the cargo terminal at Montevideo's International Airport; domestic air services; and the construction and operation of a new airport in Punta del Este. The state-owned insurance monopoly was dismantled, and two of the three banks that had been taken over by the government because of bankruptcy in the 1980s were re-privatized in the 1990s (WTO, 1998b).[3]

As a result of the economic opening, international trade became gradually more important for Uruguay (Casacuberta and Vaillant, 2002). Trade reforms altered significantly the price ratio between exports and import substitution industries in favor of the former. Hence, both imports and exports expanded steadily. The ratio of trade in goods and non-factor services to GDP, in constant prices, increased from 65 per cent to 80 per cent in the 1990s.[4] Agriculture and agroindustry constitute almost half of Uruguayan exports, although services (mostly tourism) are also included. Total employment grew slowly in a context of intense reallocation across sectors, and increase in labor productivity. However, the destruction of jobs in import-substitution industries was not matched by job creation in export industries of goods and services.

Uruguay's economic performance is increasingly linked to that of Brazil and Argentina. Consequently, any slowdown in these neighbor economies has spillover effects in Uruguay. For this reason, Uruguayan governments continued to diversify its trading structure by eliminating structural impediments to growth in sectors with export potential to new markets and by developing new products and services. It is an uphill battle, due to rigid supply structures concentrated on a few commodities (food products, textiles and apparel, and leather products) and the distance from major consumer markets.

Trade and investment

In the 1990s, after several decades of stagnation, Uruguayan exports expanded at the world average growth rate. Uruguayan exports rose continuously from 1992 to 1998 to a value of more than US$2.8 billion, twice that of 1988. In the same period, imports increased even faster, in large part due to the appreciation of the domestic currency, leading to the accumulation of significant trade deficits. Since 1998, the contraction of Brazilian and Argentine imports drastically affected Uruguayan exports. At the end of the century, Uruguayan exports totaled a little over US$2.3 billion, an increase of just 30 per cent since 1990.

Export composition has not changed significantly in the 1990s, although a diversification had occurred in the preceding decades. Until the 1970s exports consisted only of meat and wool products. In the following decades, manufactured processing of natural resources increased, but major products are still beef, wool, rice, hides and leather, dairy products, and fish. Raw agricultural products accounted for roughly 18 per cent of all exports in 1990 and just a little over 16 per cent in 2000. The participation of agroindustrial products increased from 31 to more than 37 per cent whereas exports of autos to Mercosur countries increased from 1.4 to almost 7 per cent of total Uruguayan exports (ECLAC, 2002).

The development of Mercosur, first as a free trade area and later as an incomplete customs union, supported the Uruguayan process of unilateral liberalization.[5] Integration with Mercosur countries has resulted in trade concentration, as trade with Argentina and Brazil increased at higher rates than trade with third countries. Exports to Mercosur increased from 34 per cent to 51 per cent of total Uruguayan exports in the 1990s. Brazil became Uruguay's main export market, purchasing 38 per cent of its exports. Overtime, Argentina reduced its relative significance as a market for Uruguayan goods, but increased its weight in the strategic services sector (especially financial services and tourism) (WTO, 1998).[6] Commercial services accounted for more than 35 per cent of total exports of goods and services in 2000, compared to an average of 17 per cent for Latin America in general (ECLAC, 2002b).

Patterns of trade specialization with Argentina and Brazil are remarkably different. Trade with Brazil is quite similar to Uruguayan global trade, with products such as grains and live animals predominating. Trade with Argentina has become more diversified, encompassing industries such as automobiles, plastics, machinery and electric tools that were more associated with the previous period of import substitution (Laens, 1998).

Foreign direct investment (FDI) is a relatively recent phenomenon in Uruguay, especially in the manufacturing industry. Expectations that Mercosur and the expanded sub-regional market would enhance the locational advantages and improve the attraction for FDI in Uruguay were partially fulfilled. The proportion of FDI in industrial value added was stable at around 14 per cent in 1968–78, but increased to more than 33 per cent in 1996. Nevertheless, this sector was not a major FDI recipient in the 1990s. Services totaled more than 60 per cent of accumulated FDI inflows over the past decade, with tourism accounting for roughly 40 per cent of that amount. Two-thirds of this investment originated in industrial countries and the other third came from developing countries, mostly Mercosur countries (Bittencourt and Domingo, 2001).

Trade and investment policies

Starting in 1973, one of the pillars of economic policy in Uruguay was a trade reform with an outward-looking orientation. Despite some temporary alterations in the reduction of tariff levels, Uruguayan economic policy has been relatively stable. It is possible to distinguish five stages in the process of trade reform: the export promotion (1974–78), the unilateral opening (1979–84); the continuity in trade reform (1985–89), the deepening of the trade liberalization process (1990–94); and the convergence to the Common External Tariff in the Mercosur process (1995–2000).

Soon after democratization in the mid-1980s, Uruguay resumed the process of unilateral liberalization that had been pursued under the military regime. Nevertheless, the civilian government retained the non-tariff measures, abolished during the authoritarian rule, in order to protect domestic enterprises from import competition. Parallel to the reintegration of administrative barriers into trade policy, the Uruguayan government tried to reduce the persistent anti-export bias by encouraging export expansion and promoting new export products and services.

Tariff reduction has accelerated since April 1990. The average tariff was reduced to 13 per cent in 1995 with a minimal spread.[7] As a result of the Uruguay Round Agreements (URAs), Uruguay bound all tariff lines in Chapter 1 to 97 of the Harmonized System, mainly at ceiling rates of 55 per cent for agricultural goods and 35 per cent for manufactured goods. These bound rates far exceed the unweighted average applied rate of 12.2 per cent in 1998 (WTO, 1998b).

The Mercosur Common External Tariff (CET) came into effect for Uruguay on 1 January 1996, a year after the deadline for Argentina and Brazil. Since then, applied tariff structure in Uruguay has been largely determined by the program of convergence towards the CET. Uruguay exempted about 963 tariff items from duty-free treatment within Mercosur, applying a new timetable of gradual but automatic reduction from 1996 to 2000.

Tariff peaks and tariff escalation are still employed in a pattern of protection similar to that which prevailed under import substitution, although the variation is not as pronounced. On average, the tariff structure offers low nominal protection for inputs, providing higher effective protection for final goods than can be inferred from nominal rates. Increased protection will still be present for some items after full adoption of the CET. The effects of tariff escalation are reinforced by fiscal incentives including tax and duty exemptions, duty-free temporary admission and duty drawback for goods used in export production, and free trade zones.

Uruguay has a long history of using customs valuation and later reference prices to protect targeted local production. Actually, these systems were used as contingency trade measures in response to 'unfair trade practices' by foreign enterprises. Reference prices were eliminated in 1994; but minimum import prices are set under the so-called minimum export price (MEP) system. In 1998, the MEP system covered some 117 tariff lines including sugar, textiles and clothing.[8] It was expected that the coverage of goods affected by MEPs would be reduced following enforcement of anti-dumping (AD) legislation and expanded AD use (WTO, 1998b).

In April 1996, the government issued a decree (192/96) governing all matters related to AD and countervailing duties (CVDs). AD procedures are relatively simple but in the first three years only two investigations have been initiated and none reached the stage of judicial decision.[9] In 1999, a decree regulating safeguards was also sanctioned (299/99), which gives discretionary power to the Executive. The impact on 'national interest' was added to the traditional reasons for restraining imports (high penetration of imports, damage to domestic industries).

The adjustment costs to the new competitive conditions were therefore, not evenly spread in the society. There were compensatory mechanisms and gradualism in the implementation of trade liberalization measures, but these were not oriented to the most vulnerable sectors. In addition, the instruments used to protect certain industries from import competition did not contribute to make the enterprises more competitive. They simply postponed the moment when those industries would have to make the required adjustments.

Besides the Mercosur Competition Protocol, Uruguay implemented a national regulatory framework for the defense of competition based on Laws 17243 (June 2000) and 17296 (February 2001) together with the Competition Defense Decree of March 2001.[10]

FDI was regulated by the Foreign Investment Law of 1974 (Law 14178), under which investment contracts secured tax and duty exemptions, access to financial markets, and repatriation of capital and profits. In 1998 a new investment law, the Law of Protection and Promotion of National and Foreign Investment (Law 16.906), was approved. Basically, Law 16.906 granted full national treatment to foreign investors while redefining traditional mechanisms for industrial promotion already included in Law 14178. Official authorization was required to invest in areas such as electricity, hydrocarbons, basic petrochemicals, atomic energy, exploitation of strategic minerals, banking and finance, railroads, telecommunications, radio, television, press and certain activities entrusted by law to state-owned enterprises. With the new law, equity participation in mining, hydrocarbons, and banking and finance was granted (WTO, 1998b). The law consolidated the investment regime that was previously granted by two competing texts (the Foreign Investment Law and the Industrial Promotion Law, both of 1974) into one text. The law defines a very open foreign capital regime in which prior authorization or registration is not required. Total convertibility for transfer abroad of capital and utilities is conceded with no further authorization (Bittencourt and Domingo, 2001).[11] The Law 16906 links investment and trade policies since on the one hand, the purpose of investment promotion is the expansion and diversification of Uruguayan exports, and on the other, trade policy instruments are used as fiscal incentives for export promotion.

State involvement in Uruguay is still substantial, especially in the services sector.[12] Electricity, railroads, ports, water, sewage and telephones are just a few examples of state-owned or state-managed enterprises. In the 1990s some changes were introduced in the structure of the markets in which state enterprises operate. For instance, the reforms carried out in the electrical energy sector aimed at introducing competition in the generation of electrical energy through the creation of a wholesale electricity market, while the public firm retains its monopoly in transmission and distribution. The state telephone company, ANTEL, has retained its monopoly in fixed telephones (local and long distance national calls) but it has to compete in the provision of several services including long distance international calls, cellular services, and data transmission (Forteza *et al.*, 2002). The National Ports Administration operates and administers all ports although many port services were privatized. The state also controls most water and sewage services except in some small resorts on the Atlantic coast.

Government, business organizations and the civil society

Public institutions and trade policy-making

In Uruguay, the Executive branch has handled trade policy since 1958 through a wide assortment of presidential decrees based on a single legal text. Only a fraction of domestic legislation was made with parliamentary participation.[13] Thus trade policy design and implementation has not been influenced, directly or indirectly, by democratic mechanisms of parliamentary representation. The government in office has constitutional powers to define, select and apply trade instruments using its own judgment. Uruguay trade laws and regulations were drastically altered upon adoption of the WTO Agreements, which were incorporated into domestic law via Law 16.671 of 1994.[14]

The basic framework for Presidential decrees on tariff levels is the Law of Exchange Rate and Monetary Reform (Law 12.670) of 1959. Originally intended to eliminate a system of multiple exchange rates, the 1959 law allowed several Uruguayan governments to impose administrative barriers including partial or complete prohibition of specific imports.[15] It was used later in the 1970s as the backbone to an outward model of growth based on export promotion combined with unilateral and regional trade liberalization. Institutional changes in the country did not affect the use of the basic legal instrument for trade management, although tariff and non-tariff measures were combined in proportions that varied in different administrations. After re-democratization in 1985, non-tariff measures gained prominence in the protection structure.

The Executive formulates and implements trade-related policies mainly through the Ministry of Economy and Finance. The Ministry of Economy and Finance, through its General Directorate of Foreign Trade, is responsible for the coordination of the national position on bilateral, regional and multilateral trade negotiations. The Ministry of Foreign Affairs (MFA) represents Uruguay in international forums and ensures the follow-up of the country's international commitments. Both Ministries are also responsible for export and investment promotion policies. The General Directorate of Foreign Trade provides links between public and private sectors as well as among different public agencies. The original objective of the General Directorate was to assist exporting firms with market information. Other public and private agencies also provide access to trade data banks with useful information for small and medium enterprises.[16] Chambers of Commerce began to develop similar activities, further weakening the relevance of trade services provided by the bureaucratic agency.

Uruguay has a long tradition of participation in multilateral negotiations and the MFA is particularly well equipped with skilled and qualified diplomats. The MFA is a major link between the WTO and the Uruguayan government. The diplomats posted in the various departments follow the implementation of URAs and ensure that the country complies with the different notifications that are required by the WTO process.

Mercosur negotiations contributed to the creation of a new institutional framework. The formal institutions of the sub-regional integration helped to gradually establish a more permanent coordinating scheme in the Uruguayan bureaucracy, exemplified by the national inter-ministerial representation at the Common Market Group. The inter-ministerial group is comprised of the Ministry of Economy and Finance, the Ministry of Foreign Affairs, the Central Bank, and the Planning and Budget Office, with the Ministry of Economy taking the lead role in structuring the group and the general orientation of the negotiations. To a large extent, the long stay of skillful officials in their positions reinforced the positive institutional impact of Mercosur. The greater involvement in negotiations of agencies, such as the Ministry of Foreign Affairs, who had initially served only a secondary role, had a similar effect. The institutional framework erected during the Mercosur process was further fortified by the continuity of the especially trained team. Moreover, the MFA, which initially did not have an important role in the negotiations, became increasingly more involved.

Business and labor organizations

There are no independent bodies in which the private sector is represented that formally advise the Government on the formulation of trade policy. However, the private sector is consulted in an informal basis through its business associations including the Chamber of Industry, the Rural Federation, the Chamber of Commerce, the Exporters Union and the Superior Business Council. Nevertheless, individual private interests are not clearly represented by business associations.[17] Consultation with business associations provides a general view on the content and operation of some specific rules. In addition, lobbying takes place during the actual implementation of the rules in a more direct and decentralized way that is not well documented.

The Chamber of Industry (Cámara de Industrias del Uruguay) has existed for more than a century and represents the interests of large manufacturing firms (private and public) grouped around 60 Chambers. Its members have traditionally adopted a defensive approach toward the domestic market, and have opposed economic liberalization, favoring higher rates of protection for the domestic manufacturing industry. Lately, the Chamber assumed a more flexible position on trade liberalization and export promotion. Though foreign multinational corporations are less active in Uruguay than in many other Latin American countries, in some manufacturing industries such as agroindustries, a pattern of close cooperation between domestic and foreign business interests emerged on the basis of joint ventures and licensing arrangements. The banking system was taken over by European and North American conglomerates in the 1970s and 1980s.

Agriculture and cattle producers, which includes the Rural Association and the Rural Federation (*Federación Rural*) lobby for the interests of Uruguay's large landholders, as does the Agriculture and Cattle Feeration to a lesser extent. These associations are better organized to lobby the government for favorable tax and exchange rate policies than on trade matters *per se*. Trade policy issues have been restricted to the historic demand for exporting agricultural products *in natura* as a means to limit the monopsonic power of agro-industrialists and food retailing firms. Other commodity exporters have their own association.

The Uruguayan Exporters Union (Unión de Exportadores del Uruguay) was founded in the early 1970s. Although its directors come from leading enterprises operating in different industries, its main support is in export-oriented firms (both traditional and non traditional goods) since its actions have been focused on promoting exporters' interests. There has been a conflictive relationship between the Union and the other chambers, which has limited its actions scope. Nevertheless, the Union has generated its own co-ordination spaces both at the domestic and regional level, particularly with the creation of the Mercosur Council of Foreign Trade (Consejo de Comercio Exterior del Mercosur – MERCOEX) to coordinate the activities with other exporter unions within Mercosur.

The Superior Business Council (Consejo Superior Empresarial) includes all of the above-mentioned associations and chambers (except the Exporters Union), as well as some important sector-specific chambers, such as the Uruguayan Banking Association. In particular, the Council represents the business community in the Social and Economic Consulting Forum of Mercosur, as well as in the Free Trade Area of the Americas (FTAA) Business Forum (see Motta Veiga and Ventura-Dias, Chapter 5).

Labor is organized in a single trade union (PIT–CNT), formed by various branch-level unions from both the public and private sectors.[18] It has a Commission of Integration Affairs focused on trade policy issues. The role of the trade union has been determinant for the creation and development of the Social and Economic Consulting Forum of Mercosur. In general, the labor movement does not favor the trade liberalization process at the multilateral level or at the FTAA. Nevertheless, it has endorsed the sub regional integration with neighboring countries.

Regional, hemispheric and multilateral negotiations

The multilateral agenda from Uruguay's point of view

In December 1994 the Marrakech Act was ratified by the Uruguayan Parliament through Law 16.671, which incorporated the multilateral agreement into domestic legislation (Vaillant, 1995). The WTO law contains a provision that states that the condition of Uruguay as a developing country should not be disregarded and, conversely, that special and differential treatment (S&D) should be accorded in the implementation of specific articles of the URAs. Although the Uruguay Round of trade negotiations was launched in Uruguay in 1986 (Punta del Este), the URAs were not considered a relevant trade issue in the country. The Uruguayan government believed that the rules and disciplines were an important achievement. However, WTO market access results, particularly for agriculture, should be viewed only as the starting point.

Multilateral trade issues have not been prominent in the country's policy debates. First, the URAs did not initially impose severe binding obligations, as the unilateral opening process went further than that at the multilateral level. The country also used the provisions in the URAs that allowed for transition periods in adjusting domestic instruments for trade protection and promotion.[19] Secondly, the scarce returns from the agreements turned the attention away from the WTO. The lack of substantial market access gains derived from the Agreement on Agriculture was used by agricultural exporters to justify their subsequent lack of interest in the WTO. As a member of the Cairns Group, Uruguay committed precious diplomatic resources to get agriculture back in the international trading system.

Moreover, the WTO's initiation came at a critical time for the region. More urgent matters required immediate attention in the WTO's first year of operation, as it coincided with the Mexican financial crisis that had critical economic effects in Argentina and Uruguay. Similarly, the WTO's first years overlapped with regional negotiations to convert Mercosur from a free trade area into a customs union. For many industries and firms, the impact of trade liberalization within Mercosur was more dramatic than the more gradual unilateral opening that the country had carried out. At the same time, regional negotiations included topics for which multilateral rules already existed but also issues for which new disciplines had to be established. In addition, even for those trade-related areas covered by the URAs (trade remedies, technical barriers to trade, standards, etc.) specific and deeper obligations were required at the regional level. Concurrently, preparatory work began for the FTAA in 1995. The technical work required time and efforts from governmental officials and the private sector and became more compelling to all. Building on the efforts derived from regional and multilateral negotiations, but on a broader scale, the FTAA working groups and the preparation of Vice-Ministerial and Ministerial meetings diverted attention from multilateral topics.

The year 1998 signaled a change in the relative importance of multilateral issues in Uruguay. On the one hand, the regional economic context deteriorated rapidly, shifting the attention to the multilateral forum. Uruguay began to feel the effects of the slowing down of neighboring economies amidst the international financial crisis. The 1999 Brazilian devaluation, and the differences of exchange rate regimes in Argentina and Brazil, highlighted the increasing difficulties faced by the Mercosur integration process. Furthermore, the technical preparatory work for the creation of a FTAA ended and the formal negotiations began, further drawing on the country's scarce diplomatic skills. On the other hand, new events were taking place in the post-1998 WTO. The Ministerial Conference held in Geneva in the beginning of 1998 marked the launching of the preparatory work for a new round of trade negotiations that would end in the Seattle debacle. Uruguay began to experience the effects of the international trading rules on its domestic policy as 1998 came to a close and the country was subjected to the periodic WTO Trade Policy Review.[20] Gradually, the general public became aware that international bureaucrats could act as external auditors of trade and trade-related policies and challenge domestic instruments, such as the Minimum Export Prices. Finally, Uruguayan officials were following the implementation of some commitments closely and with concern, particularly in agriculture. In their opinion they were falling short of the spirit of the URA on Agriculture. Consequently, the WTO as a multilateral forum became relevant to Uruguay from a market access perspective as well as a constraining system of rules that impacts the design and implementation of domestic trade and trade-related policies.

Later, Uruguayan delegates in the WTO were very effective in the preparatory work for the Doha Ministerial Conference of November 2001, particularly, in drafting a proposal to deal with developing country URA implementation problems. At Doha, Uruguay supported the launching of a new round of trade negotiations, indicating that its major objective would be the complete integration of agriculture into WTO rules and disciplines. In the same statement, authorities displayed frustration with the limited increase in trading opportunities derived from the multilateral trading system (see WTO, 2001a).

Key negotiating issues

Uruguay is presently involved in trade negotiations at sub-regional, hemispheric, interregional and multilateral levels. As a member of Mercosur the country is engaged in negotiations with the EU and the Andean Community, among other countries or groups of countries. Formally, Mercosur should have been fully operational as a free trade area since 2000. However, the Argentine and Brazilian crises imposed severe limitations to the functioning of the sub-regional scheme, leading Uruguay to threaten to search for alternative routes. Among other options, government officials were raising the possibility of direct bilateral negotiations for a FTA with the US as Chile had done, albeit at a rhetorical level, since a FTA with Uruguay has not been encouraged.

Agriculture and industry are not necessarily divided on trade issues. In effect, there is a large consensus on some trade issues. For instance, agricultural exporters and import-competing producers agree that the domestic AD legislation, while compatible with WTO norms, is not adequate to the contingency needs of a small developing country such as Uruguay. A small economy has much to loose from a lengthy process of investigation and determination of injury based on positive evidence such as the volume of imports, the dumped imports' effect on prices of domestic products and the impact of these imports on domestic producers. For a small economy, retaliation is seldom a credible threat. The damage is immediate whereas the legal procedure consumes time and money. Exporters would prefer to give more discretionary powers to the Executive to intervene more expeditiously in situations of unfair competition.

There is also agreement that Uruguay lacks the capacity to use WTO trade rules effectively to protect the domestic market. In this sense, entrepreneurs' experience with more effective *ad-hoc* discretionary measures runs against any innovation concerning trade relief measures. Furthermore, incentives are not in place for encouraging the private sector to take advantage of the new instruments for trade protection. It is striking that the situation is quite different regarding the use of new trade disciplines to attain better access to foreign markets. The fact that exports are highly concentrated in a relatively few sectors helps to explain these differences.

Agriculture is Uruguay's most important issue in the on-going negotiations. Expansion of its exports hinges upon a significant improvement in access to EU and US markets. In addition, subsidies to domestic production in industrial countries clearly affect international prices of major commodities as well as the competitive conditions in third markets. Therefore, agricultural subsidies result in unfair competition for otherwise highly competitive agricultural producers such as Uruguay. Uruguayan negotiators have been very active in the WTO agricultural negotiations, individually and as part of the Cairns Group and Mercosur.[21]

Some Uruguayan trade negotiators warn of possible roadblocks to achieving common ground among Mercosur members in agriculture and services negotiations. The prevailing idea is that Uruguay should not adopt Mercosur positions at the multilateral level because negotiating topics are country-specific. Uruguay has more in common with Argentina than with Brazil. Though Brazil is a member of the Cairns Group, its interests in a variety of agricultural goods may not coincide with those of countries with fewer temperate climate goods.[22] In the case of services, Uruguay has a rather liberal position in global terms, having taken part in the financial service agreement that Brazil did not join. In 1998, Uruguay consolidated an offer in the framework of the Financial Services Negotiations, which formed part of the General Agreements on Trade and Services (GATS) (see Abugattás and Stephenson, 2003).

Concluding remarks

The process of trade liberalization in Uruguay has brought institutional benefits but concrete costs to the nation. The elimination of jobs in inefficient import substitution industries was not matched by job creation in new export-oriented firms. Abundant natural resources have not helped the country to diversify its exports since major agricultural markets remain protected by tariffs and non-tariff barriers. Uruguay is a small and competitive exporter of a few agricultural and agroindustrial products. Its diplomats fought arduously to incorporate agriculture in the trade disciplines of the General Agreement on Tariff and Trade (GATT) during the Uruguay Round. Nevertheless, the Agreement on Agriculture brought very little to compensate competitive agricultural producers for market share losses derived from subsidized agriculture in industrial countries (see Diaz-Henderson, 2003). Developing countries had to make concessions in new markets such as services and in new trade-related topics such as investment measures and protection of intellectual property rights just to put agriculture on equal footing with other sectors under the GATT/WTO system. Notwithstanding this, benefits in terms of enlarged market access for agricultural products were less than expected as a result of practices such as tariff peaks in developed countries.

As stated recently by the Uruguayan delegate at the WTO, technical assistance, structural adjustment programs, training or longer implementation periods are relevant instruments to help developing countries, but they are not the real solutions to development problems. More relevant is unencumbered access to world markets in conditions of fair competition (see WTO, 2001b).

Yet, not all problems of market access for Uruguayan products have been related to the outcome of URAs as domestic factors also have played a role. Uruguay suffers from a rigid export mix that also restricts the diversification of destination markets. Despite the addition of several commodities to the export basket, it is still heavily dependent on beef, wool, rice, hides and leather, dairy products, and fish. Tariff and non-tariff barriers to trade affect the imports of these products in many countries. It should be recalled that even though average tariffs in industrial countries are low, tariff peaks and tariff escalation represent serious barriers to trade for specific products. Uruguay is heavily dependent on regional markets, and more directly on neighbors Argentina and Brazil. In spite of great advances in the liberalization of the internal market, Uruguayan rice and dairy products still face *ad-hoc* barriers to market access in Argentina and Brazil.

There is scant interest in the country for multilateral trade negotiations, since as a small economy Uruguay has little to offer in a system of reciprocal concessions. Nevertheless, as part of Mercosur, Uruguay is engaged in negotiations with its major markets, the EU and the US (FTAA). Negotiators believe that it is more likely that both the US and the EU will exchange bilateral concessions in agriculture at the WTO. In addition, more emphasis is put on agricultural interests at the multilateral level, as opposed to manufacturing interests at the regional level. With the exception of auto parts that is totally oriented to Mercosur markets, Uruguayan industry is concentrated on the processing of natural resources such as agroindustries, textiles and apparel. More than 32 per cent of Uruguayan employment is generated in resource-based manufacturing industries that also account for 35 per cent of Uruguayan exports (Hodara, 2000). The conditions of market access for those products will depend on the outcome of WTO negotiations.

Uruguay is in an ambiguous situation. It is a small economy with a high standard of living and one of the highest per capita incomes in Latin America. Public and private agents believe that they require institutional capacity to reap the benefits of the URAs. At the same time, the continuous leveling of the playing field implied in the harmonization of rules and institutions consolidated in the international trading system eliminated some of the flexibility that a small economy demands in order to defend its market from unfair trade practices.

Notes

1. In the second half of the 1970s, Uruguay eliminated all exchange-rate control and moved into full convertibility of the domestic currency.
2. A referendum blocked several articles of the Privatization Law of 1992 and therefore prevented the privatization of public telecommunications.
3. In the financial crisis of 2001–2002, the state had to intervene again to rescue the banking sector.
4. The evolution of trade openness coefficients at current and constant price describes different stories. In the 1990s the openness coefficient in current prices is virtually stable, while at constant prices it grows steadily. A specific feature of the Uruguayan openness process of the 1990s is that, contrary to other developing countries' experiences, the real exchange levels (p_T / p_{NT}) where p_T is the price of tradable goods and p_{NT} the price of non tradables, were low. The Uruguayan government pursued in the 1990s stabilization policies based in the management of the exchange rate, which produced a significant appreciation of the national currency (Vaillant, 2002). It can be shown that while trade policy caused the ratio of exports plus imports to tradable output to increase, this was counteracted by a reduction in the price ratio of tradables to non-tradables (exchange rate appreciation), which in turn was also accompanied by a shift of production from tradables to non-tradables. In the case of the trade openness index at constant prices, it increased sharply mainly reflecting the effect of greater trade openness on quantities.
5. Bilateral preferential agreements between Argentina and Uruguay and Brazil and Uruguay had existed since 1975 and 1976 respectively.
6. In 1997, two-thirds of tourists destined for Punta del Este, the biggest Uruguayan beach resort came from Argentina. Aggregate growth in tourism receipts between 1992 and 1996 reflected the region's improving economic condition as well as the diversification of Uruguay's tourism services.
7. The standard deviation of average customs duties was reduced from 14.4 per cent to 6 per cent from 1988 to 1994.
8. MEPs were created in 1983 by Decree n. 5/1983, to apply when reference prices proved insufficient to evidence the damage caused by unfair trade practices (Nattino, 1990). Rules were defined for the use of MEP in 1993–94. Changanaqui and Messerlin (1994) have shown that although reference

prices and MEP served their protection objective, they could not prevent a fall of more than 20 per cent in real average tariff.

9. Uruguay notified the WTO of three AD investigations between January 2000 and June 2001, against Argentina, Australia and Mexico respectively.
10. The General Directorate on Trade is the agency responsible for the implementation of competition policies.
11. Moreover, through Law 16.906 Uruguay granted the right to settle legal claims by investors of any changes in fiscal exemptions in independent courts.
12. The role of state-owned firms in the Uruguayan economy has been emphasized in the literature (Forteza *et al.*, 2002).
13. In the 1990s, the Uruguayan Congress ratified international trade treaties such as the Paraguay Treaty that created the Mercosur in 1991 and the Marrakech Act that created the WTO in 1994.
14. In accordance with the Uruguayan legal system, the set of agreements that make up the Final Act of the Uruguay Round form an integral part of national legislation with the status of law. Thus, any previous legal dispositions in conflict with or contradictory to the WTO Agreements are considered repealed under the principle of tacit derogation. Any amendments to trade agreements must be negotiated with treaty partners and then introduced into domestic law. To the extent that they have passed into domestic law, the WTO Agreements can be invoked in domestic courts.
15. Connolly and De-Melo (1994) pointed out that the key to understand the poor performance of the Uruguayan economy up to the first half of the 1970s was the role played by trade regulations and rent-seeking activities that it led to. See also Dixit (1996) for insights into the adjustments of legislation and institutions to purposes they were not originally created for.
16. National Directorate of Arts and Crafts (Dirección Nacional de Artesanias), Small and Medium Enterprises of the Ministry of Industry (Pequeñas y Medianas Empresas del Ministerio de Industria), Mercosur Sectoral Commission (Comisión Sectorial para el Mercosur – Comisec).
17. The literature on political contributions and lobby groups highlights the importance of organizing to defend particular interests with the government (see Vaillant, 2000 for a review of the literature).
18. There was a single federation known as the National Convention of Workers (Convención Nacional de Trabajadores – CNT) in 1964–73, which was declared illegal by the military. In 1983, a new labor federation called the Interunion Workers' Assembly (Plenario Intersindical de Trabajadores – PIT) was formed. The PIT was later converted into PIT–CNT to emphasize its historical links to the pre-military labor movement.
19. Uruguay adopted the Harmonized System and introduced changes in Customs Valuation.
20. The first Review of Uruguayan trade policy was conducted in 1992 under the GATT.
21. There are at least two different positions among the countries seeking agricultural liberalization (e.g. within the Cairns Group): agricultural exporters which are negatively affected by agricultural policies of industrialized countries and agricultural importers with their domestic markets affected by

the competition of imports with distorted prices resulting from agricultural policies in industrialized countries (Vaillant and Nin, 2002). Uruguay is clearly in the first group of countries who are the most actively involved in the agricultural liberalization.

22. Most of the negotiating positions at the Committee on Agriculture have been presented by Mercosur together with Chile and Bolivia.
23. A quite telling indication that multilateral negotiations are a second-order concern for both public authorities and the private sectors is the lack of any mention of them in the web site of the Ministry of Foreign Affairs – while it included specific pages for the FTAA and Mercosur (see http://www.mrree.gob.uy/mrree/cuadro2.htm).

Part III
The Andean Experience

7

Colombia and Venezuela: Trade Policy Reforms and Institutional Adjustments

Juan José Echavarría and Cristina Gamboa[1]

Introduction

Colombia and Venezuela, the two largest countries in the Andean Community of Nations (ACN), have pursued trade liberalization and reform unilaterally, regionally and multilaterally. Both countries have shown their commitment to World Trade Organization (WTO) rules and practices by introducing changes to their trade practices in response to the Uruguay Round Agreements (URAs). These modifications have implied challenges in many areas, especially in the common trade policy framework they share as the most active members of the ACN. In this sense, Colombia and Venezuela trade relations exhibit some particular characteristics within Latin America that have led to quite positive trade results and a considerable degree of private sector support.

This chapter discusses Colombia and Venezuela's trade policy reforms and institutional adjustments resulting from the Uruguay Round (UR), the ACN common trade policy, and sector-specific policies including agriculture and auto assembly. The next section provides an overview of the trade reforms undertaken at the unilateral and regional level and their trade results. Then current instruments of trade policy are analysed, accounting for WTO commitments and the role of business. The subsequent section describes government and business perceptions of the costs and benefits of WTO commitments. The penultimate section focuses on three issues: (i) the institutional framework governing public and private sector dialogue; (ii) the channels through which the private sector participates in trade negotiations; and (iii) the identification of active business groups in trade policy formulation. The final section presents the main conclusions.

Trade policy reforms and integration choices

During the first half of the 1990s, Colombia and Venezuela made considerable progress in economic and structural reforms through programs known as *apertura* (openness) and *el gran viraje* (the great turnaround) respectively. Resembling the 'Washington Consensus' design, trade regimes were opened, financial distortions were eased, currency controls were abolished, state-owned enterprises were privatized, and general deregulation took place. Complementary reforms were adopted in areas such as infrastructure and foreign investment.[2] Domestic economic and structural reforms, in general, and unilateral trade liberalization, in particular, made it easier for these countries to accept further trade reform commitments resulting from multilateral negotiations. Similarly, the revival of the Andean Group and the ensuing active regional integration agenda favored compliance with multilateral commitments.

Unilateral trade liberalization in Colombia (1990/91) and Venezuela (1989–91) was implemented as part of a broader package of structural reforms aimed at promoting macroeconomic stabilization and redefining the role of the state. These reforms included unilateral trade liberalization coupled with an active economic integration agenda of 'open regionalism'. Given the previous failures of inward-oriented import-substituting industrialization (ISI), the underlying trade policy objectives since the early 1990s have been to improve economic competitiveness and enhance growth prospects through export expansion, aided by an active economic integration strategy. However, export growth and diversification objectives have not yet been attained, with Colombia relying mainly on primary goods exports and Venezuela primarily on exporting oil. Exports of goods and services increased approximately 60 per cent in Colombia and Venezuela in the 1990s, less than in Latin America (90 per cent) or in East Asia and Pacific (160 per cent). Exports are also less diversified: manufactured exports account only for 32 per cent of merchandise exports in Colombia and 20 per cent in Venezuela, compared to 50 per cent for Latin America and 80 per cent for East Asia.

Though complex domestic macroeconomic and political situations have stalled export expansion, unilateral trade reforms in both countries have achieved rationalization in four main areas: reduction of trade restrictions and 'tariffication' of quantitative restrictions (QRs); rationalization of export incentives; institutional reform of trade policy agencies; and full participation in the multilateral trading system.

Tariff and non-tariff barriers

Trade reforms pursued neutrality of trade incentives, in parallel with a reduction of trade restrictions including elimination of import permits and import quotas, reduction of tariffs and the tariffication of QRs. The commitment to neutrality and efficiency at the initial stages of the reforms sought to level the playing field and eliminate special privileges for specific sectors. It was argued that this pledge to neutrality would also protect government officials and their policies from interest groups striving to retain the prerogatives they had enjoyed for decades (Naim, 1993).

Trade-weighted border taxes (tariffs and other non-quantitative border taxes) have fallen significantly in both countries, leveling out at the 12.8 per cent average for the Common External Tariff (CET) of the ACN. The ad-valorem tariffs of 1986 were much higher in Colombia (44 per cent) than in Venezuela (24 per cent); and were rather low in 1994 (11 per cent in Colombia and 13 per cent in Venezuela) compared to historical levels. Especially relevant, the average tariff level of the CET in 1995 was much lower than in the years previous to unilateral liberalization in both countries (1986–90), but slightly higher than in 1994. Other non-tariff border taxes, which represented 63 per cent of the official tariff in Colombia, were definitively removed in 1988.

QRs affected 73.8 per cent of trade in Colombia in 1988–90 and much less in Venezuela (11.9 per cent in 1988–90). They were virtually removed during the first part of the 1990s in both countries, covering only 1.7 per cent and 2.4 per cent, respectively, during 1991–93. Colombia eliminated the IDEMA, a state trading enterprise that monopolized agricultural imports, and the complex import-licensing regime. Venezuela also eliminated import licensing and some import prohibition practices.

Hence, after unilateral trade reforms, border protection relies mainly on tariffs which, in turn, decreased significantly. Tariff levels are now fixed at lower and less dispersed levels, providing appropriate signals to the private sector.

Export incentives

Many export incentives, designed mainly to offset ISI export biases, were in place before unilateral reforms. Colombia reduced the Certificate of Tax Reimbursement (CERT) from 8.4 per cent in 1989 to 7.6 per cent in 1991. Fiscal constraints and duty-drawback considerations accelerated its elimination. The country also nearly eliminated *Plan Vallejo* subsidies, associated with imported raw materials and capital goods used in the production of exports. Finally, Proexpo, the entity in charge of export promotion and export finance at that time, reduced its credit incentives from 0.7 to 0.3 per cent.

Venezuela granted direct export subsidies, input subsidies (especially oil-related), special lines of subsidized credit (through Finexpo), and matching funds for export development (Rajapatirana, 1999). As of 1989 a special fiscal credit program (*Programa de Incentivo Fiscal*) was applied to agricultural exports of 'vulnerable' products. The quite discretionary and non-neutral program's scope was reduced by two-thirds between 1989 and 1993, covering only 9.5 per cent of the FOB value of exports in the last year (WTO, 1996a). Since 1991 Venezuela has used a drawback system for manufactured exports. In theory, the system only returns to exporters indirect taxes on inputs used in the production of exportable goods, but in 1994 it also covered consumption and value-added taxes (VAT). Some pricing practices in the energy sector have translated into indirect subsidies. Refined domestic petroleum products have traditionally sold below world prices. Also, electricity prices have been fixed for certain products.

Some of these instruments have undergone only minor modifications to comply with URA obligations while others are being phased-out entirely. Colombia modified two of its fiscal incentive practices in response to URA obligations (CERT and special import-export program (SIEX) for capital goods). Venezuela reduced the number of export subsidies, but exporters of selected agricultural products receive a tax credit of 10 per cent of the export's FOB value under the special fiscal credit program. In the URA on Agriculture, Venezuela committed to limiting the budget of this program by 2005 (WTO, 1996a).

Trade-related institutional reforms

Colombian trade-related institutional reforms sought to centralize trade policy and reduce the influence of lobbying groups on policy making. Centralization took place in 1991 through the newly created Foreign Trade Ministry (Mincomex), a considerable undertaking as 53 uncoordinated government agencies were previously involved in the formulation and execution of trade policy. Proexpo, was split into two institutions, Proexport (1991) and Bancoldex (1992), a second-tier bank of mixed ownership. The former has focused on export promotion and marketing assistance while the latter addresses the financing needs of domestic exporters and foreign purchasers of Colombian exporters.

Venezuela followed a similar path, creating the Ministry of Industry and Trade (MIC) in late 1995, which merged the Foreign Trade Institute (*Instituto de Comercio Exterior*) and the Ministry of Promotion (*Ministerio de Fomento*). Export promotion activities were thus passed from the Foreign Trade Institute to the newly created Bancoex, a second-tier bank in charge of export promotion and marketing assistance. These institutional changes are considered highly supportive of trade policies' outward-oriented turn.

WTO participation

Institutional reforms and unilateral trade liberalization were reinforced and complemented by market access and transparency secured through participation in the multilateral trading system. The achievement of increased market access facilitated the building of political support for unilateral liberalization and free trade. Also, improved transparency strengthened commitments with rules of behavior. Once certain tariff rates are agreed to in the CET or multilateral commitments, they are bound not to increase except under very specific conditions.

When Colombia and Venezuela acceded to the GATT in 1981 and 1990, respectively, they followed quite different negotiation strategies. Not only did membership requirements on tariff ceilings become more demanding by the 1990s but, perhaps more importantly, their distinct product structures dictated different interests in accession. Venezuela is highly dependent on oil, with 'mining and quarrying' activities accounting for approximately 30 per cent of GDP, around 45 per cent of tax revenues and nearly 80 per cent of exports. Manufacturing represents around 19 per cent of GDP, and agriculture only 5 per cent. Key exports other than fuel are aluminum, motor vehicles (mainly to the Andean region), iron and steel products, coal, and agro-industrial goods, such as canned and preserved fish. In contrast, Colombia has a much larger agricultural sector (13 per cent of GDP) and a much less important 'mining and quarrying' sector. Manufacturing is more diversified, even though its share of GDP is smaller than in Venezuela, and therefore Colombia's export structure is less dependent on primary goods. Nearly 45 per cent of Colombian exports are non-traditional, including mainly agro-industrial products, flowers, textiles and clothing, refined sugar, synthetic and plastic fibers, printing and editorial products and motor vehicles. Manufactured exports represented 32 per cent of merchandise exports in Colombia and only 19 per cent in Venezuela. To protect its important agricultural sector, Colombia negotiated very high tariff ceilings in that sector; Venezuela agreed instead to bind agriculture tariffs at much lower levels. Table 7.1 shows the levels at which each country bound their tariffs, generally well over the applied levels. The existence of the four-tier CET and the commitment to the ACN

Table 7.1 Tariff bindings in Colombia and Venezuela

Product	*Colombia*	*Venezuela*
Manufactured	35% except motor vehicles, textiles (including hats) and parachutes (40%), and some chemicals, rubber and leather products (30%)	35% except motor vehicles (40%)
Agriculture	15–227% most are set at 70% except peas for consumption (15%), fresh apples (20%) and lentils (15%)	10–135% most are set at 30 and 40%

Source: WTO Tariff Schedules (www.wto.org).

integration process has prevented tariffs from rising to the maximum bound levels.

Integration

The Andean Group was established in 1969, when representatives of Bolivia, Colombia, Chile, Ecuador, and Peru signed the Cartagena Agreement. Venezuela joined the group in 1973 and Chile left in 1975. After a short-lived success, the agreement stagnated in the mid-1970s and was almost abandoned throughout the 1980s. A revival of the agreement began in 1989 when the Presidents of the Andean countries assumed the leadership of the integration process, setting up clear guidelines for the enactment of a free trade agreement and the adoption of a CET. The overall objectives of trade policy proved a divisive issue, as Bolivia and Peru advocated more aggressive free trade reforms, while Colombia and Venezuela held a more protectionist stance on 'industrialist grounds', arguing that higher tariffs would be still necessary to encourage the formation of a stronger industrial base.[3] These fundamental differences have made free trade and CET goals difficult to attain within the initial time frame. Nevertheless, stalled negotiations did not detain efforts to deepen the Andean integration. Because of their common trade policy objectives, Colombia and Venezuela started to negotiate a free trade area that began operating in March 1992, with a CET covering around 90 per cent of the tariff schedule. Ecuador rejoined the process and liberalized trade with its partners in January 1993. Because of the Colombian-Venezuelan initiative, and after intense and complex negotiations with the other members, agreements were also reached to eliminate administered trade (except in agriculture, autos and spare parts) and to establish a customs union.

Colombia and Venezuela signed bilateral free trade treaties with Chile in 1994 (see Silva Chapter 2) and with the Caribbean Common Market (CARICOM) in 1995. The two countries also signed a comprehensive free trade agreement with Mexico, known as the Group of Three (G-3), which became effective in 1995 (Ortiz Mena, Chapter 3). As a result of these agreements, bilateral tariffs will be reduced to zero with Chile in 2011 and with Mexico in 2004. Both countries jointly signed a framework agreement on free trade with the Central American Common Market (CACM) in 1994 and with Mercosur in 1998. A free trade agreement was signed between the ACN and Brazil in August 1999, built upon progress reached in the ACN-Mercosur framework agreement (Motta Veiga and Ventura-Dias, Chapter 5). The ACN-Brazil treaty was followed by an ACN–Argentina treaty signed in March 2000 (Tussie *etal.*, Chapter 4), underscoring the ACN's recent success in embracing trade negotiations as a bloc. Beyond the region, Colombia and Venezuela have signed General System of Preferences (GSP) agreements with the European Union (EU) as part of the latter's incentives to diversified crop production. Similarly, Colombia enjoys preferential access to the US market under the Andean Trade Preference Act (ATPA) as part of the US policy against drug trafficking and production.

Colombia and Venezuela have developed a common trade policy framework within the ACN covering some economic sectors and trade-related measures. The administered trade for auto assembly and agriculture, both highly sensitive sectors, are subject to special treatment and, therefore, are exemptions to the CET. Common rules and regulations are applied to other areas such as anti-dumping (AD) and countervailing duties (CVDs), foreign investment, intellectual property, and transportation.

Against this backdrop, trade flows within the ACN (intra-regional trade) were very dynamic during the 1990–2001 period, growing 29 per cent annually, falling in 1998 (–4 per cent) and 1999 (–27 per cent), and rebounding in 2000 and 2001 to surpass the previous record of US$ 5.628 billion intra-regional exports from 1997 with US$5.680 billion in 2001. Despite setbacks in 1999, due to economic growth slowdown and dismal domestic demand, intra-regional exports have continued to increase their share in the region's total exports, and in fact continue to grow in the face of declining extra-regional exports (Figure 7.1).

Colombia and Venezuela are the countries with the greatest participation in sub-regional exports (48 and 23 per cent respectively) followed by Ecuador (14 per cent), Peru (9 per cent) and Bolivia (6 per cent) (ACN, 2002). Colombia and Venezuela's dominance of nearly three-quarters

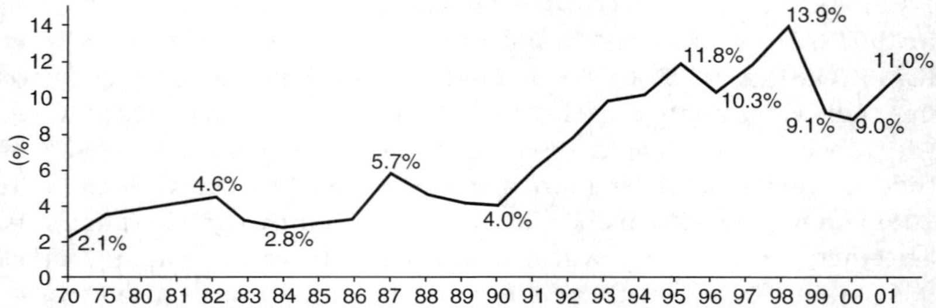

Figure 7.1 ACN intra-regional trade (exports to the region / total exports) 1970–2001

Source: Authors own figure using data provided by the Andean Community.

of total sub-regional exports explains their determination to move forward the integration process.

Colombia had a persistent trade deficit with Venezuela throughout the 1990s, though the beginning of the new century saw a trade surplus in favor of Colombia. From a low of US$563 million deficit in 1994 to a high of US$915 million surplus in 2001, Colombia overcame Venezuela's lead (DANE, 2002). The principal goods traded include food and beverages, motorcars and auto parts, chemicals, textiles and clothing, oil and oil products, and metallic products. All of these products are non-traditional exports except for oil.

Most intra-regional exports occur in manufacturing and are intra-industry. The participation of intra-industry trade in *total* intra-regional exports increased from 0.35 in 1990 to 0.41 in 1995, and in manufactured goods from 0.32 to 0.39. Moreover, the weight of intra-industry is much higher for intra-ACN trade than for trade between the region and Mercosur, US or Europe (Echavarría, 1998). Consequently, the agreement has had a high acceptance among local firms, as trade expansion takes places in both directions in each industrial sector, without apparent drawbacks. As an example, Colombia exports auto parts to Venezuela and Venezuela, in turn, exports assembled vehicles to Colombia.

Intra-regional trade does not differ much from trade with the US or EU in terms of capital intensity or revealed comparative advantage. In addition, trade creation effects outweigh trade diversion in almost all the industrial sectors at the end of the century, except for 'metal products and machinery' and 'non-metallic minerals' in the case of Venezuela. Trade creation was especially marked in 'textiles, footwear and clothing' and in 'wood products' for Colombia and Venezuela, and in 'iron and steel' for Venezuela (Echavarría, 1998). Thus intra-regional trade is relatively 'efficient', stimulated more by natural forces like vicinity than by regional preferences. Unilateral tariff reductions explain the largest part of the dynamism in ACN trade during the 1990s. In addition, important dynamic effects have also taken place. A survey of industrial firms in Colombia carried out by Fedesarrollo reveals that, in the process of exporting to the ACN market, many have learned how to export and compete in more challenging international markets (Echavarría *et al.*, 1999).

Current trade policy instruments

The reforms related to regional and multilateral integration and liberalization have spun a complex trade policy web in Colombia and Venezuela. Issues of concern include specially protected sectors that evade multilateral liberalization efforts, the effects of the CET, trade relief and bilateral disagreements, and the costs and benefits of WTO commitments. Analysis of these issues contributes to the conclusion that the URAs have not required significant changes in tariff structures or trade policies.

Special sectors

Though most of the ACN's sector-specific policies and industrial programs were dismantled during the 1990s, the automotive and agricultural sectors have continued to enjoy special treatment. These sectors generate significant distortions, which may be inimical for the development of a good trade policy. The extent to which these agreements violate URA commitments remains an open discussion. However, the General Secretariat of the ACN holds that the Common Automotive Policy (ACAP) conforms to WTO standards after the reforms introduced in 1999. Given that various business groups favor maintaining their special status, reversal of these counterproductive measures may prove difficult.

The auto assembly industry accounted for over 10 per cent of total intra-AC trade at the close of the century, becoming the most important industrial sector in intra-regional trade. It has received special treatment and protection in the ACN since 1993, when the ACAP was implemented by means of a six-year pact. Under this policy, Venezuela, Ecuador and Colombia jointly established tariff rates of 35 per cent for passenger vehicles, 15 per cent for mass transit and cargo vehicles and 3 per cent for completely-knocked-down (CKD) motor vehicle kits. Given the low domestic value-added tax (VAT) in auto assembly, the effective rates of protection (ERP) could go as high as 50 per cent for some products in the sector. However, the relative weight of those highly protected items under the auto program is low and thus the average effective rate for the whole sector is low.

The 1993 ACAP imposed regional content requirements in order to qualify for reduced duties on imports. This requirement for passenger cars was 32 per cent in 1997 and 33 per cent in 1998. Colombia, Ecuador and Venezuela jointly notified these local content requirements to the WTO and, because of their inconsistency with their obligations under the WTO Agreement on Trade-Related Investment Measures (TRIMs), agreement was reached to eliminate them by the end of 2000. To meet this deadline, a new auto pact was formalized in September 1999. It is considered WTO-compatible since it replaces local content requirements with rules of origin set at 60 per cent. The new pact establishes that firms fulfilling the rules of origin may request a government authorization to establish a free trade zone within their company (*Régimen Suspensivo*) and thereby defer payment of import tariffs on inputs and kits until the auto is duly nationalized.

However, some of the provisions established to meet WTO obligations have not been fully implemented. In December 1999 the ACN Automotive Policy Council decided not to eliminate all local content requirements, mainly in response to lobbying by auto assembly and auto parts business groups. These local content requirements are embedded in the complicated rules of origin, promoting import substitution of auto parts and integration among domestic providers of auto parts. This revised policy may be inconsistent with Colombia and Venezuela's WTO obligations under the TRIMs agreement. The situation is only likely to change if a third country denounces such inconsistencies and exerts bilateral pressure or asks for a WTO investigation.

Import QRs such as state trading enterprise monopoly on agricultural imports and import licensing were eliminated by the early 1990s, and almost all export restrictions were banned, but a new 'special' system of price bands for agriculture was introduced in 1991 in Colombia and in 1995 in the ACN. The Andean Price Band System (SAFP) was created to stabilize farm incomes and isolate agriculture from fluctuations in world prices (and from unfair trade practices by foreign countries) but in fact grants sizeable protection.

The SAFP operates as a system of variable import levies and covers 13 basic agricultural products called *markers* and their associated products, for a total of 149 tariff items (8-digit, harmonized system). The 'floor' and 'ceiling' of the price band are set every six months for the 13 product *markers*, based on the comparison of current domestic prices and the average international price during the last five years.[4] Official tariffs increase for all items included in each of the 13 groups when the international prices of the product *marker* are lower than the 'floor', and decrease when they go over the 'ceiling'. The system was created in 1991 in Colombia, and the number of products included increased steadily up to 1995. It was redefined in 1995 and extended to Ecuador, in the context of CET negotiations. The items included in the system still represent a small proportion of all harmonized items (2.3 per cent or 144 of 6,201 items) and of total trade (3.3 per cent in each country). However, their relative importance is high for some sub-sectors, representing more than 97 per cent of total trade for wheat, paddy rice, sugar, vegetable oils and fats, and oil seeds and more than 20 per cent for bovine cattle and sheep and meat products.

Colombia and Venezuela use several arguments to defend the band system, including claims that the resulting tariffs are not in violation of their tariff binding commitments and that the Agriculture Agreement does not clearly define variable levies, which are in theory prohibited by the WTO. Since customs valuation by means of minimum prices is generally prohibited under the WTO's implementation agreement (Article VII), both countries have justified their policies in terms of a special and differential (S&D) treatment clause contained under paragraph 2 of Annex III, which allows developing countries to use minimum prices for customs valuation on a temporary basis (Arguello, 1999). The SAFP's use of variable levies and minimum and reference prices should be looked at more closely by the WTO. Moreover, the countries' maintenance of the system should call into question the ambiguity of WTO norms.

Besides WTO non-compliance, the SAFP generates several problems. First, additional protection, both nominal and effective, has been generated beyond the CET rate in all but two of the marker products, instead of stabilizing prices as originally intended (Rajapatirana, 1998a,b). The five-year 'memory' of import or reference prices used to calculate the variable levy renders the bands unresponsive to price declines, creating significant distortions (Rajapatirana, 1998a). Secondly, the protection given to agricultural commodities within the bands has harmed the processed food industries that use them as inputs. In response, an increasing number of items have been included through time, trying not to affect the production of goods upstream in the production chain. Thirdly, the resulting high protection has caused friction with exporters from other countries. For example, under US pressure, Colombia issued Decree 2650 in December 1999 establishing a maximum tariff rate of 40 per cent for imports of soybeans and soybean products, down from the previous average tariff of 60 per cent that blocked US export competition. Fourthly, the system's high tariffs sometimes violate multilateral commitments of agriculture tariff bindings, which were negotiated at different levels by Colombia and Venezuela. This means that the SAFP only operates fully in Colombia (and with exceptions in Venezuela and Ecuador), creating substantial distortions to the sub-regional competition conditions for these commodities. The WTO expressed its concern during the Venezuelan trade policy review (TPR) of 1996, but the countries maintain that SAFP tariffs do not violate WTO tariff bindings.[5] Lastly, other measures could be more appropriate depending on the product involved. For example, mechanisms could be implemented that respond to product-specific problems and lessen the distortions caused by the high protection.

The ensuing high protection levels explain why Colombian business groups lobby in favor of the system. Agro-industrial producers that use sugar as the main raw material tend to oppose it, although some of them are quite satisfied with the modifications introduced in the early 1990s designed to include them under the protection scheme. Of course, this is a vicious cycle and opposition arises from those producers using agro-industrial goods as inputs. Venezuela's agriculture business groups have been much less outspoken in the mechanism's defense, as agricultural goods are produced on a smaller scale and imports represent a larger share of production than in Colombia.

Besides the price band system, both Colombia and Venezuela apply other restrictive measures such as procurement agreements and import licenses. Colombia has implemented procurement agreements (*convenios de absorción*) that require importers to purchase a government-specified quantity of domestically produced goods as a precondition for the granting of import licenses. These agreements have been used for some agricultural commodities (wheat barley, sorghum and palm oil) to improve prices for domestic producers by ensuring outlets for their output and controlling surpluses. The 1996 TPR on Colombia pointed out that this policy could have restrictive effects on imports but no accurate estimation has been made. What can be easily established is that purchases of these commodities take place at higher than world market prices (see Rajapatirana, 1998b). The domestic absorption contracts were notified to the WTO Committee on TRIMs when in fact it is an attempt at managed trade. This kind of notification is a clear example of a specific restrictive measure authorized by the WTO even though it does not technically fall under the agreement to which it is being notified. The use of this instrument was permitted until the year 2000 and, in response to pressure by domestic agricultural producers, the Colombian government requested authorization to continue using procurement requirements for agricultural commodities until 2006.

Similarly, Venezuela has used import licenses and sanitary considerations to limit influxes of sensitive products. In implementing an import licensing system in February 1997 to administer its WTO tariff-rate quota for sorghum and yellow corn, for example, the Ministry of Agriculture enforced procurement requirements for domestic sorghum so that feed manufacturers must purchase a government assigned amount of domestic sorghum at the high official price in order to obtain import licenses for yellow corn. Also, the Ministry of Agriculture has banned imports of some agricultural products; onions, potatoes and forage seeds from the US were prohibited in late 1998, and the import of citrus products is banned citing the danger of disease.

The Common External Tariff (CET) of the Andean community

One of the central instruments of current trade policy in Colombia, Venezuela and Ecuador is the ACN common external tariff (CET), established by Decision 370 of 1995. The average tariff of the 8-digit items is 12.8 per cent, guaranteeing historically low tariff levels for the coming decades. The CET was designed with four tariff levels (five, ten, 15 and 20 per cent) increasing from raw materials and intermediate goods to final goods in order to promote the creation of 'value added' goods. Bolivia is exempted from the CET in recognition of its lower stage of development and Peru has opted for observer status, apparently waiting for the CET to arrive at tariffs as low and uniform as its own (Fairlie Reynoso, Chapter 8). The tariff structures in Colombia, Ecuador and Venezuela were similar prior to the CET, which eased its adoption. Succinctly, the relevant differences are the following: Venezuela protects 'food and beverages' relatively more than Colombia and Ecuador, and 'transport equipment' relatively less. Not surprisingly, Venezuela tends to protect 'oil and lubricants' less than the other two countries, while Ecuador gives less protection to raw materials in general (Echavarría, 1998). The spread of the tariff schedule was reduced drastically. In 1986 there were 29 border-tax levels (26 tariff levels) in Colombia and 41 (41) in Venezuela, compared to only four tariff levels in the CET (Echavarría, 1998). The standard deviation also decreased considerably from 16.9 per cent in Colombia and 28.4 per cent in Venezuela to 4.8 per cent under the CET in 1995. The maximum tariff changed from 135 per cent and 113 per cent, respectively, to 35 per cent under the CET.

Exceptions to the CET are concentrated in raw materials, capital goods, agriculture (the SAFP) and the auto sector (the ACAP), making the resulting protection scheme much flatter than originally intended and effective protection lower than nominal protection for most sectors. Permanent exceptions include the SAFP, the ACAP, and the discretionary application of rates of zero or 5 per cent to goods that are not produced by or available from other ACN members (mainly raw materials and capital goods).[6] Temporary exceptions are contained in a set of lists with 230 products for Colombia and Venezuela and 400 for Ecuador. These exceptions were to be gradually eliminated over a four-year period, but the deadline was changed to June 2000. To meet this arrangement, Colombia and Venezuela withdrew 20 per cent of the products on the list in August 1999, but Ecuador broke its pledge to do the same. Venezuela and Colombia thus refused to withdraw an additional 40 per cent in January 2000, but surprisingly in April 2000 Venezuela complied with the schedule. The General Secretariat has therefore declared that Colombia and Ecuador are in violation of CET commitments. This situation will not lead to any type of sanctions until the Andean Justice Tribunal renders its judgment.

The ERP is lower than nominal tariffs for most sectors, and typically more heterogeneous with a standard deviation double that of nominal protection. The high rates of nominal protection in agriculture have led to low ERP rates in sectors that use these highly protected commodities as inputs. These distortions are key in explaining why aggregate ERP is lower than nominal protection for these products. Average ERP for 'transport equipment' is low, despite all of the protective measures considered by the ACAP, because the 28 tariff lines included in the program have a low weight.

Thus the ERP structure indicates that the tariff escalation sought by Decision 370 has been pre-empted by the significant exceptions, mainly through the agricultural price band mechanism. Contrary to initial expectations, the special treatment granted to vehicles and spare parts has not had a large impact.

The surge of contingent protection and domestic pressures

There has been a surge of contingent protection in response to pressures from lobbies suffering from import competition and drastic exchange rate revaluations during the 1990s. Private sector demands for AD duties rose significantly in the ACN during the 1990s, particularly between Colombia and Venezuela. Compared to AD claims, safeguard investigation petitions have been marginal, as have CVD cases. Hence the fine-tuning of AD policy according to WTO standards has not prevented a slippery slope towards protection.

Colombia introduced AD and CVD legislation in 1991 during the *Apertura* process and Venezuela did so in 1992, both motivated by desires to offset the reduction of protection. This provided a solution to the alleged deficiency in customs procedures (Rajapatirana, 1998a). Modifications were made to Colombia's domestic AD laws in 1995 to conform to WTO rules, which seems to have eroded the country's previously stringent test for AD (Guash and Rajapatirana, 1998). Venezuela also recently modified its legislation to conform to WTO rules and regulations. In Colombia, *Incomex* was the agency responsible for investigating these practices until May 2000 when it merged with the Ministry of Foreign Trade. The mirror institution in Venezuela is the Anti-dumping and Subsidies Commission (CASS), a decentralized agency of the Ministry of Industry and Trade (MIC).

In the case of dumping between the ACN nations, a supranational AD law (Decision 283 of 1991) applies, and the administering authority is the General Secretariat. This supranational law was replaced by Decisions 456 and 457 in May 1999 to comply with WTO rules and regulations. In addition, the General Secretariat decides on cases in which AD measures must be imposed in more than one country and when a foreign producer is causing material injury to the exports from one ACN member to another. With the adoption of Decision 452 in April 1999, the ACN established a safeguard mechanism for third country imports that threaten or cause harm to local production and intra-regional trade. The authorities claim that this regulation follows the spirit of the WTO Safeguard Agreement, but some authors argue that the new regulations are less stringent than before (Guash and Rajapatirana, 1998).

A total of 16 AD cases have been presented to the General Secretariat in the 1990s, mainly against Colombian products such as slide fasteners, crown corks and stoppers, polyester fibers, syringes, and flat-rolled iron or non-alloy steel. Venezuelan products that have been investigated include iron and steel products, stainless steel sinks and washbasins and electric motors. Nearly half of the cases led to the imposition of final duties and a similar percentage of provisional duties were denied. Between 1998 and 2000 there were a total of eight AD investigations, four of them involving Colombia and Venezuela, showing the recent rise of the use of this instrument at the ACN level.

There is a clear trend in Colombia to increasingly resort to AD. Between 1991 and late 1999 there were a total of 29 AD and CVD cases, initiated in response to private sector demands. The products were from the EU (6 cases), US (4), Russia (3), non-ACN Latin American countries and the Caribbean (3), China (1), South Korea (1), and Vietnam (1). Recent AD cases have involved tires (from South Korea), rice (Vietnam), polyvinyl chloride (US), and several steel products (Russia). The two subsidy cases investigated did not end in the imposition of duties, while 11 of 27 AD cases resulted in the imposition of final duties. There have only been three ACN investigations against alleged subsidies, none of which led to the imposition of CVDs. Two of these investigations took place in 1992, associated with Venezuelan exports of phenol alcohol and rice to Colombia. The third subsidy claim took place in 1999 against Indian exports of 'ampicillin and its salts' negatively affecting Peruvian exports to the ACN. Colombia has actively requested ACN authorization for the imposition of safeguards, accounting for eight of a total of 12 cases between 1991 and 1999. Interestingly, the General Secretariat has only authorized two demands, both made by Colombia against Ecuadorian exports of polypropylene sacks (1994) and veneer and plywood sheets (1996). The imposition of AD and CVD duties, as well as domestic legislation in defiance of WTO obligations, have created unresolved bilateral trade disagreements. Pressures from lobbies negatively affected by liberalization have emerged, and rather than resort to WTO mediation, both countries have opted for a cooperative dialogue between the trade ministers every three months.

Colombia has four main bilateral problems with Venezuela. One is the transportation restriction set on Colombian ground carriers, who have to transship Colombian cargo to Venezuelan trucks at the border. In June 2000, the ACN Tribunal of Justice ordered Venezuelan authorities to stop this practice, and the transport sector in Venezuela subsequently threatened to block all trade if the Venezuelan government complies. The second problem is the use of sanitary permits to restrict the entry of Colombian meat, eggs and potatoes, based on the competitiveness of these goods that would displace Venezuelan products. The third dispute is related to an additional 2 per cent customs tax that is costly to Colombian exporters and is prohibited according to ACN regulations. The last problem relates to a sugar import quota. The ACN General Secretariat should rule on the validity of this measure and the trade remedies that Colombia can employ. Venezuela has three essential trade problems with Colombia: (i) Colombian legislation on liquor trade; (ii) contraband cigarettes from Macao (a free port in Colombia); and (iii) delays in the expedition of import licenses for glassware and diapers. The last two are considered marginal problems in comparison to the liquor trade. Colombian liquor legislation in Article 336 of the

Constitution of 1991, which has been called into question by several countries but never by the WTO, establishes that the regions have monopoly power over liquor trade and can set up the conditions that govern the market. However, modification to enable competition from third countries in regional markets is unlikely due to the high monopoly revenue obtained by the regions and their strong lobbies in Congress.

WTO commitments: costs and benefits

The Colombian and Venezuelan private sectors have not been greatly pressured by the implementation of WTO commitments, largely due to loopholes left for crafty interpretation by the governments. Unilateral policies and regional developments are perceived as the major source of trade policy change, while the URAs have been seen as less costly. Increased market access and, to some extent, greater transparency in trading rules and procedures have been perceived as a major benefit gained from the URAs by Colombian and Venezuelan businessmen. Also of significant benefit to the international business community was the greater certainty, and to some extent insurance, that WTO member governments would not act arbitrarily in their trade policies.

Another benefit identified by the private sector is the improved dispute settlement procedures. These enhanced norms have enabled Colombia and Venezuela to participate on equal footing with developed and developing countries in the resolution of trade disputes. For example, Venezuela together with Brazil succeeded as claimant on the US discriminatory application of environmental regulations that affected import of refined gasoline (Standard for Reformulated and Conventional Gasoline). Colombia was one of the countries that established a panel against EU banana trade practices. Also, Colombia asked for a panel against Nicaragua because of its 35 per cent tariff on Colombian products due to a border dispute. Some private sector representatives approved of the handling of Colombia-Venezuela bilateral trade problems at the bilateral level usually using the ACN General Secretariat as a referee rather than in the WTO (Weston and Delich, 2003).

The private sector has also highlighted the agreement to phase-out the Multifiber Agreement (MFA) as a meaningful benefit offered by the URAs. Colombia's textile and apparel sector will most likely gain market share because of its relatively high level of competitiveness. Venezuela's textile and apparel sector will also benefit, but to a lesser extent.

Tariff bindings are understood by many as an important benefit of the URAs, but they have led to the use of other protectionist measures, such as AD duties. Moreover, bindings remain extremely high: 35 per cent for most industrial goods in both countries and 70 per cent and 30 per cent for most agricultural goods, in Colombia and Venezuela respectively. However, they serve government officials as a barrier against renewed protectionist pressures, both from interest groups and from within the administration itself, as occurred in Colombia because of fiscal strains and devaluation. They also work against potential rollback of actions carried out unilaterally, locking in trade liberalization.

The public and private sectors have somewhat different opinions on the inclusion of agriculture into the multilateral trading system. The public sector praises the URAs for the fortification of their opposition to domestic agricultural interests that seek revival of out-dated protection measures, such as non-tariff barriers, especially in periods of recession and devaluation. Domestic agricultural sectors, especially in Colombia, on the other hand, claim that their countries unnecessarily bound themselves to tight multilateral norms. The private sector cited the limitations on export incentives, particularly export subsidies, as one of the leading costs of the URAs. Oddly, export subsidies were already quite low before Colombia and Venezuela ascribed to the URAs. Though Colombian firms needed government subsidies to export successfully, particularly to the ACN, the subsidy component of these instruments was marginal. Another important cost identified by the private sector, chiefly by the auto assembly industry, is the restriction of local content requirements associated with the TRIMs agreement. As mentioned before, Colombia and Venezuela have protected the auto assembly and spare parts sector through the ACAP, under which local content requirements and geography have been instrumental in creating an intra-regional market for these goods. After intense lobbying by the auto assembly and parts industry, Colombia and Venezuela opted to keep local content requirements disguised as rules of origin. Hence, no real adaptation cost has been incurred by the auto industry.

The trade and integration agenda

Private sector involvement

Private sector participation in trade policy has been increasing since the early 1990s in Colombia, partly as a result of the new liberalization and integration strategy that compelled the public and private sectors to act together. Moreover, the Constitutional Reform of 1991 shifted the relationship between private agents and the government, replacing the concept of 'representative democracy' with a new principle of 'participatory democracy.' The Foreign Trade Ministry, created by the 7th Law of 1991, is to support and facilitate private initiatives and efforts of all economic agents in foreign trade operations. According to the law, trade-related entities (public entities and the business sector) must coordinate interactions in order to adequately exert their functions and formulate policy. The Comisión Mixta de Comercio Exterior (Joint Commission of Foreign Trade) was created to join the representatives of the Consejo Superior de Comercio Exterior (Foreign Trade Superior Council) and the private sector. This Superior Council is the advisory body to the national government on foreign trade topics, and is formed by the Ministers of Economic Development, Foreign Trade, Foreign Relations, Finance, Agriculture, Mining and Energy; the National Planning Department Chief; the Central Bank Manager and the President. The main objective of the Foreign Trade Commission is to analyze trade policy and to formulate recommendations for the national government. The Foreign Trade Ministry also relies on advisory committees with businessmen and private sector representatives at the national and regional levels.

Despite these institutionalized channels of participation, regular participation by the private sector in the design and implementation of trade policy only occurred on limited occasions during the 1990s. 'Informal' channels paralleled the formal avenues of participation, particularly with the Ministry of Foreign Trade. Based on experiences set forth in the ACN and NAFTA, a working system with trade and business associations was adopted in 1991 in order to maintain a permanent communication and coordination channel between the Ministry of Foreign Trade and the private sector. This working system was actively used in G-3 negotiations, ACN–Mercosur negotiations, and WTO negotiations on agriculture and textiles. This 'linking strategy' with the private sector worked well through preparatory meetings, which are intended as a discussion ground for the definition of negotiating positions. The private sector is continuously informed about the state of the negotiations through the 'next door room'. Technical aspects of the negotiation are discussed, as the government has relied on private sector inputs in negotiations regarding textile contingents in the Multifiber Agreement (MFA), preferences granted under the GSP, intellectual property rights and regional trade agreements. Nevertheless, the key issues are tackled at the highest political level (ministerial or even presidential), with the private sector excluded from negotiations when deemed necessary by the government. Cases in point include decisions adopted within the Andean Group in Galapagos in December of 1989 that later were included in the Act of Barahona in 1991 and resulted in the consolidation of the Andean free trade area, and decisions adopted by the Presidents in the Declaration of Port Spain in 1993 during G-3 negotiations. WTO negotiations have not been an exception, with the private sector excluded on issues such as tariff bindings and financial services negotiations in the early 1990s. Business groups consequently use the press to voice their opinions when they lack political leverage, forcing the government to counter through the media instead of relying on the next door room.

Amendment of the 7th Law in 1999 clarified some issues and formalized others including the Colombian Ministry's working system with the private sector. The structure and functions of the Foreign Trade Ministry were modified, particularly through the creation of separate negotiation divisions, one devoted to multilateral negotiations and the other to bilateral negotiations and international organizations. Both divisions must seek to establish mechanisms that promote private sector participation in trade negotiations. The Bilateral Negotiation Division is compelled to maintain thorough coordination with public and private entities on WTO negotiation issues, especially intellectual property rights, investments, services, environment and labor standards. These institutional changes have, no doubt, served to make interactions between public officials and private actors more democratic, opening-up a space for all business groups to voice their interests. In practice, nevertheless, participation has not translated into increased influence. Indeed, 'informal' mechanisms such as bilateral meetings, press articles and conferences continue to be the main platform from which the private sector makes known its views. To a large extent, this reliance on informal participation has its root in the diversity and fragmentation of the power structure. This is particularly so in the manufacturing sector where, while a few business associations and groups gather major interests, a unified front fails to coalesce due to the lack of shared objectives and criteria.[7]

The agenda for future trade negotiations

Coordination between Colombia and Venezuela was very active in G-3 negotiations and in negotiations with Brazil and Argentina. However, more thought and discussion will be needed for the important decisions that lie ahead, like the convergence upon a common agenda in multiple fora. While it was relatively easy to design an integration strategy with partners of similar size when the potential impact of the partner country was relatively small, stakes in negotiations like the Free Trade Area of the Americas (FTAA) will be considerably higher. Moreover, new negotiations will necessarily complicate old market access agendas with complex issues such as intellectual property rights, services, investment and the environment.

Colombian and Venezuelan administrations seek to maintain an active participation in both regional and hemispheric negotiations. At the regional level, the main task is to consolidate the Andean Common Market by December 2005 in order to correct distortions derived from the CET and strengthen areas such as physical integration, technical and sanitary rules, government procurement and customs regulations. However, the auto and agriculture exceptions have eluded discussion.

As a direct consequence of the importance that ACN trade has to Colombia and Venezuela, efforts have been stepped-up to maintain consensus on negotiations with other blocs and countries. Economic and trade relations are to be intensified with Mercosur and trade negotiations that began with the CACM at the beginning of the 1990s are still underway. Finally, the ACN has begun negotiating a common agreement with Panama.

At the hemispheric level, Colombia and Venezuela have maintained an active participation in the preparatory meetings of FTAA negotiations, with a clear conviction that the delay and possible demise of hemispheric trade negotiations would deprive them of improved access to their most important export market the US. Efforts to consolidate an agreement at the hemispheric level has run in the opposite direction of Peru and Mexico where preferential trade arrangements with the US deter efforts of extending such preferences to the entire hemisphere (Fairlie Reynoso, Chapter 8; Ortiz Mena, Chapter 3). Venezuela has been unsuccessful at edging its way into the ATPA under which the US allots preferential trade to all other ACN members (Fairlie Reynoso, Chapter 8).

Finally, Colombian and Venezuelan economic authorities have established an agenda to improve trade relations with the EU, focusing on three key aspects. First, they seek to promote use of preferences obtained through the Special Regime of Trade Preferences, an anti-narcotrafficking regime extended to Andean countries through the GSP. Secondly, Colombia hopes to defend its position on the Banana Regime that was approved in January 1999, establishing a larger quota for banana exports. Thirdly, joint ventures and strategic alliances will be encouraged.

Conclusions

Most of trade policy and institutional reform designed to embrace an outward-oriented economic development model took place unilaterally during the 1990s. Thus the URAs played a marginal role with regard to liberal trade policy changes in Colombia and Venezuela. Moreover, URA loopholes have allowed Colombia and Venezuela to keep trade practices that are quite contrary to WTO standards. For example, minimum prices continue to be applied in agriculture, and the auto sector still applies local content requirements. Similarly, the adoption of improved WTO anti-dumping rules and procedures has not prevented a slippage into sector-specific protection.

Nevertheless, the URAs will strengthen multilateral discipline in world trade, and promote the further inclusion of good trade policy in Colombia and Venezuela's development strategy. Certainly they have improved export promotion practices in Colombia and Venezuela. Export subsidies are being phased-out and the use of other export promotion instruments is more transparent. Important discussions will continue on those issues, especially since Colombian and Venezuelan private sectors perceive export subsidy cuts as one of the main costs of joining the WTO.

The ACN regional integration process has played a leading role in redefining the countries' trade policy. In particular, the CET guarantees stable tariffs at historically low levels. Exceptions to the CET introduced by the ACN price band mechanism (SAFP) has produced a flatter tariff structure than originally intended. A more transparent and efficient way to flatten the tariff structure would be to consolidate the four-level tariff structure to two levels, thereby facilitating deeper integration with Peru and Bolivia.

Several bilateral trade disputes riddle the Colombian–Venezuelan relationship, none of which have been taken to the WTO for resolution. Nevertheless, Colombia and Venezuela have increased their coordination in trade negotiations, progressing in the definition of a common position regarding WTO-related negotiations. Because of its comprehensive coverage of trade disciplines, the future of Colombian and Venezuelan trade policy is intimately linked to the future nature of the ACN and its other members. The private sector perceives that the URAs have not implied considerable costs or benefits, maintaining that unilateral trade policy and ACN integration have had much larger impacts.

The real challenge for Colombia and Venezuela is to address the remaining integration agenda, particularly that of the ACN integration process, while not neglecting their WTO obligations. Past integration agreements between similar partners were easy to manage, but the new integration agenda could inflict large costs if not handed correctly. Potential benefits are of course much larger. The political tensions emerging in the early 2000s added to the economic difficulties for a closer cooperation between the two Andean nations.

Notes

1. Pilar Esguerra made helpful comments to a previous draft. Sandra Zuluaga significantly assisted in writing the section of the chapter entitled 'The trade and integration agenda.'
2. Reforms were initiated in Colombia under stable and positive economic conditions (see Hommes *et al.*, 1994 and Echavarría, 2000). In sharp contrast, Venezuela faced a serious crisis when the reforms were launched, with an increasingly isolated and grossly inefficient economy on the brink of hyper-inflation and socioeconomic collapse (Naim, 1993).
3. For example, as part of the general Peruvian policy aimed at imposing a lower CET, in May 1992 Peru unilaterally suspended the preferential treatment granted to imports from within the Andean Group (Edwards, 1995). Peru decided in 1995 to apply a low and uniform tariff of 12 per cent with some exceptions in agriculture and textiles and clothing, which increase the average tariff to 13.2 per cent.
4. The 13 product markers are powdered milk, wheat, malting barley, yellow and white corn, crude palm and soybean oils, white rice, soybeans, white and raw sugars, chicken and turkey pieces, and pork meat.
5. Interestingly, during the TPRs of 1996, Venezuela was directly questioned about the SAFP and Colombia was not, and the mechanism was not fully expounded upon or criticized in either country's TPR text (WTO, 1996a, 1997b).
6. A list of those goods is produced periodically by the AC General Secretariat, and each country can choose between the tariff rate of Decision 370 or the special tariffs of zero or five per cent. There are 2,200 8-digit tariff lines included in this type of exception category, mostly used by Colombia (85 per cent of the 2,200 products), followed by Venezuela (75 per cent) and Ecuador (67 per cent).
7. Notwithstanding this, business groups have advantages with respect to other civil organizations, particularly in terms of organizational development and access to decision-making centers. As noted, this access can be formal or informal but, in any case, trade negotiations represent a quite successful instance of public-private cooperative interaction.

8

Peru: Trade Policy and International Negotiations

Alan Fairlie Reynoso[1]

Introduction

Peru revamped institutions and practices that had been in place for more than three decades during the 1990s, in one of the most radical processes of economic liberalization in Latin America. Yet the reform was neither new nor unique in the region, having been largely crafted according to 'Washington Consensus' doctrines of privatization of public assets, state deregulation, trade liberalization, and elimination of price controls and subsidies in goods. Unlike the short-term stabilization policies of previous decades, based on draconian monetary and fiscal measures aimed at curbing inflation, the policies of the 1990s sought to overcome economic crises over the long term. Underlying this shift was evidence that policies of import-substituting industrialization, protectionism and state intervention during the 1960s and 1970s had failed to generate a sustained process of development. Macroeconomic indicators hailed the successes of the new model until the late 1990s, as it occurred in other Latin American countries following a similar policy path. The Asian financial crisis called into question the shift's growth effect *vis-à-vis* the foreign capital that flooded the economy until 1997. Furthermore, questions have arisen concerning the long-term sustainability of such policies in a context of severe external financial restrictions and increasing rates of unemployment and poverty.

This chapter focuses on one of the central components of the Peruvian economic reform: trade policy. In particular, policy changes during and following the Uruguay Round (UR) are examined, including implications for regional integration agreements, sector-specific costs and benefits and the private sector involvement. The following section depicts major trade flow trends in order to provide a backdrop to Peru's insertion into world markets. The next section 3 traces the evolution of Peruvian trade policy during the 1990s, analyzing its goals, the changes in policy instruments, and the relationship between the reform process and adherence to WTO disciplines. Subsequently, integration initiatives undertaken during the past decade are considered. The penultimate section explores the costs and benefits felt in various sectors and the private sector's participation in the process. The final section discusses the complexities posed by simultaneous negotiation fora for Peru's future trade strategy.

Trade performance

Trade patterns have been quite erratic in terms of export growth, trade partners and trade balances. Between 1990 and 1993 exports virtually stagnated, but grew between 1994 and 1997, thanks to increased prices for primary goods and growth in non-traditional exports like textiles and agricultural products. This diversification was largely an unexpected benefit of liberalization as it served to mitigate negative effects of the currency overvaluation and to lower resilient costs that impinged upon export competitiveness (Vega, 1997).

Furthering a process that began in the early 1980s, Peru diversified export markets post-1990 (see Table 8.1). Prior to 1980, the US was the most important export market, followed by Europe and countries in the Latin American Integration Association (LAIA). In the 1990s the EU grew to be the most important export market, and again fell to be on par with the US. In turn, LAIA gained importance as an export market through the decade of the 1990s, with a slight dip in 1998–99 due to financial crises. Increases in imports from Latin America and Asia have been the most significant variation in Peruvian import structure. By 2001 LAIA countries contributed the largest share of Peruvian imports, no doubt the result of the region's economic opening and trade liberalization in the 1990s. The increase in imports from LAIA, especially Mercosur and the Andean Community of Nations (ACN), drove Peru into a persistent trade deficit throughout the 1990s. However, from a US$2.4 billion deficit in 1998 the trade balance rebounded to positive territory by 2001. Table 8.1 shows the evolution of Peruvian foreign trade over the last decade.

The composition of Peruvian exports has gone largely unchanged, despite some diversification in non-traditional products. As in previous decades, shipments abroad are largely comprised of primary and semi-processed products from mining and fishing activities. Traditional

Table 8.1 Export destinations, import sources and trade balances

	1980	*1990*	*1994*	*1998*	*1999*	*2000*	*2001*
Export participation							
LAIA	17.3%	12.9%	17.8%	17.0%	15.1%	16.7%	17.1%
US	33.5%	23.5%	16.6%	32.9%	29.6%	27.5%	24.9%
EU	29.4%	36.6%	34.4%	22.0%	25.4%	21.1%	26.5%
ASIA	13.6%	20.7%	25.0%	12.8%	13.2%	19.8%	18.7%
Total exports (in US$ billion)	3.6	3.3	4.6	5.7	6.0	6.7	6.9
Import participation							
LAIA	14.5%	35.4%	31.8%	31.4%	37.9%	35.2%	36.9%
US	39.7%	28.5%	26.8%	32.5%	31.7%	29.7%	23.0%
EU	28.2%	23.1%	18.7%	16.1%	15.5%	13.6%	13.9%
ASIA	12.8%	7.6%	17.9%	15.2%	9.8%	15.4%	18.5%
Total imports (in US$ billion)	2.5	2.9	5.6	8.1	6.7	7.4	6.7
Trade balance (in US$ billion)	1.1	0.4	–1.0	–2.4	–0.8	–0.7	0.2

Source: Banco Central de la República de Perú (BCRP) (1998, 1999, 2000) and customs statistics available at www.aduanet.gob.pe

exports continued to account for nearly 70 per cent of total exports throughout the 1990s and into 2000 and 2001.

Thus a primary product export-oriented model based on higher-productivity sectors seems to have maintained its hold in Peru. These sectors have been the traditional target of foreign direct investment (FDI) and the areas of most interest in the privatization process. However, in the hostile international economic environment of the late 1990s, arguments about the vulnerability of this model were fueled by the drop in metal prices produced by the Asian crises and the drastic decrease in capital investment flows towards South America caused by the Brazilian crisis.

Peru's trade policy

Reform in Peru, not unlike reforms described in the other case studies, was propelled by initiatives at the unilateral, regional and multilateral levels. The reforms sought to replace a closed trade regime, which contributed economic distortions and inefficiencies, with a system of liberalized trade and fair competition. The end goal was a virtuous insertion in the world economy via specialization in international markets. Reform began in 1990 as a unilateral process, and was later anchored by UR commitments.[2] Liberalization measures included tariff reductions and elimination of export taxes and quantitative restrictions, encompassing virtually all-existing trade policy instruments on goods, services and intellectual property.

Trade in goods

A first phase of tariff changes beginning in 1990 consisted of a gradual tariff reduction. The average tariff was 66 per cent, while applied rates ranged from 0 per cent to 110 per cent with a standard deviation of 25 per cent. Of the total tariff items 22 per cent were covered by tariffs of 40–50 per cent. In September 1990, the restructuring of the Common External Tariff (CET) in the ACN set three levels of tariffs at 5 per cent 25 per cent and 50 per cent. All waivers, tariff reductions, special benefits and prohibitions, except for special considerations, were eliminated. Furthermore, the number of selective consumption taxes was reduced from eight to three.

A second phase coincided with commitments made at the Uruguay Round. UR commitments established tariff ceilings of 30 per cent, except for 20 tariff lines subject to variable specific duties and certain agricultural products for which final rates were set at 68 per cent (WTO, 2000). This phase of the reform set tariffs below bound CET levels, lowering the average tariff from 26 to 17 per cent and thus stepping-up the trade opening. Per UR commitments, the average tariff had decreased to 16 per cent by 1993, with a standard deviation of 3 per cent and 87 per cent of the tariff items paying 15 per cent. The 854 remaining tariff items were textiles, garments, footwear, food, and machinery. Effective rates of protection (ERP) initially fell from 74.6 to 41.9 per cent (Rossini, 1991), with agriculture as one of the most favored sectors. ERP for industry further decreased from 44 to 24 per cent by the mid-1990s, with higher protection on goods like clothing and footwear. Rates were again cut in 1997, when the average tariff rate fell 3 percentage points to 13.2 per cent with a standard deviation of 3 per cent. Also in 1997, a 5 per cent temporary additional duty was instated for agricultural products including meat, dairy products, grains and alcoholic products. The average ERP by 1997 was estimated to be about 15 per cent and around 84 per cent of all tariff lines were subject to tariff rates of 12 per cent by 2000. The ample margin between bound and effective tariff rates undermines the regime's predictability given that as many as 330 tariff lines receive additional protection through a tariff surcharge of 5 per cent or 10 per cent.

In addition to these measures, special regimes have also been temporarily established. Other temporary regimes grant the exemption of taxes or duties in the cases of temporary import for re-exportation (acquisition of merchandise to be later exported without any transformation), temporary admission (acquisition of merchandise to be later exported after some value adding), and merchandise replenishment (import of inputs for manufacturing export products).

By the time the reform was launched it was estimated that about 20 per cent of the tariff universe was subject to NTBs. Trade liberalization efforts thus targeted a drastic curtailment of their use: exchange controls and import prohibitions were eliminated, import licenses were suspended, and other NTBs were terminated, including license requirements and import registries (except sanitary ones).

Local content norms and rules of origin have been eased or eliminated. More significantly, exports are no longer restricted by previous requirements that goods first be supplied to the local market, that they contain a minimum percentage of national components, and that they be partially assembled domestically.

In customs valuation, the goal has been to ensure that the tax basis used to calculate tariff duties corresponds to the real value of the concerned goods. Thus Peru implemented a pre-inspection system in 1992, which seeks to avoid under-invoicing through pre-customs valuation inspection of the merchandise by a contracted supervising firm. Peru was exempted from applying the Agreement on the Implementation of Article VII of GATT (customs valuation) from April 1999 to April 2000. Since early 2000, disciplines agreed to in the Agreement on Customs Valuation of the Tokyo Round have been applied to all imported merchandise (WTO, 2000).

Trade relief measures were also shaken-up by reform winds. Anti-dumping regulations were adopted in 1991 in accordance with ACN disciplines (Tortora and Tussie, 2003) and a national institute for the defense of competition and intellectual property rights (INDECOPI) was created with a Commission of Dumping and Subsidies Control. In April 1997, domestic legislation was brought into compliance with the Agreement on Implementation of Article VI of GATT 1994 (anti-dumping) and the Agreement on Subsidies and Countervailing Measures (ASCM). Anti-dumping measures have not been grossly over-used since then. Only nine measures were in effect at the beginning of 2000, the majority of which affected non-WTO member countries (WTO, 2000).

In December 1998 regulations were adopted to incorporate the Agreement of Safeguards and the ATC. Peru did not choose to retain the 'right to use' the transitional safeguards included in Article 6 of the Agreement on Textiles and Clothing (ATC). However, Peru does apply safeguards on agricultural products from LAIA. For example, 65 per cent of the preferential margin was applied for certain products coming from Argentina, Chile and Uruguay in 1994–96. Nevertheless, no safeguards were imposed on ACN members between 1994 and 2000. In general, Peru has not applied import limitations that restrict the value or amount of products imported from other countries and, tellingly, has not restricted imports for trade balance motives since 1991 (WTO, 2000).

Export restrictions were eliminated in 1991, except in the case of protecting flora, fauna and cultural patrimony. Neither export licenses, voluntary export limitations nor specific export subsidy legislation are applied. The government has used the Commission for the Promotion of Exports (PROMPEX) to promote exports since 1996. In 1990 the government eliminated the Certificate of Tax Reimbursement to Exports, which granted an export subsidy of 15 per cent. Drawback mechanisms were established in March 1991, authorizing the return of the General Sales Tax, the National Housing Fund tax, and the ad-valorem import taxes paid by nontraditional exporters. Additionally, all export taxes were removed in 1992. The new Customs Law includes drawback as a special reimbursement regime that becomes effective once the merchandise to export has been deposited in a Customs warehouse.

The Export Processing Zone (EPZ) of Ilo and the trade zone of Tacna were the only active special fiscal zones in 1996. New zones were created under the name of Centers for Export, Transformation, Industry, Commercialization and Services, which exempts the firms established there before 2004 from all national, regional and local taxes until 2012. Nevertheless, this tax exemption is subject to exportation of 92 per cent of total annual sales and has therefore had a minimal effect except in used auto exportation (WTO, 2000).

Trade in services

Liberalization of trade in services was undertaken through horizontal and specific commitments made within the framework of the General Agreement on Trade in Services (GATS) (Abugattás and Stephenson, 2003). Although commitments only apply to the sectors included in Peru's list of commitments annexed to GATS, the country offers equal treatment (national treatment) to both foreign and domestic suppliers and grants equal access to its market (Most Favored Nation treatment, MFN) in most services. MFN exemptions favor trade partners of the ACN and other Latin American countries.

There are no limits to foreign participation in financial services and financial entities can function via an authorized representative without actual local presence. Despite the large presence of foreign capital in the telecommunications privatization process, there are limitations to national treatment and market access in broadcasting services, where foreign participation cannot account for a majority in the sector. In the case of maritime transport services, it is no longer mandatory that Peruvian firms provide the service to at least half of imported or exported goods.

Intellectual property rights

Peru is part of most international treaties on intellectual property and it signed the Agreement on Trade-Related Intellectual Property Rights (TRIPs) in 1995. Accordingly, industrial property rights and copyright laws were passed at the domestic level in 1996 to implement the agreement. However, Article 65 of the Agreement on TRIPs allows developing countries to postpone the patentability of pharmaceutical products until 2005, which Peru has chosen to do. A key government objective has been to extend the TRIPs provisions to protect indigenous traditions and knowledge. Newly obtained vegetables are protected by a unique ACN system – *sui generis* – to protect industrial propriety, though Peru is not a part of the International Union for the Protection of New Vegetable Varieties (UPOV).

Open regionalism

In addition to unilateral measures and a stronger commitment to multilateral disciplines, Peru's quest for a more liberal trade regime in the 1990s included a deliberate search for 'open regionalism' (ECLAC, 1994). Attempts to make integration policies compatible with and complementary to multilateralism have unfolded hand-in-hand with efforts to spin out integration schemes of varying depth and breadth. This problematic and complex situation is compounded by Peru's participation in negotiations both unilaterally and as a bloc with the ACN. The following paragraphs offer a disaggregate picture of the integration initiatives in which Peru is involved.

Andean Community of Nations (ACN)

Liberalization unilaterally pursued in the early 1990s distanced Peru from sub-regional integration processes. In August 1992, Peru was relegated to an observer status in Andean Free Trade Area (AFTA) negotiations for having suspended its obligations in the liberalization program; it was not until December 1996 that member countries invited Peru to become a member of AFTA. After high-level political negotiations, Peru began its reintegration to AFTA in July 1997 via Decision 414 that established a tariff reduction schedule beginning 1 August 1997. AFTA is to be fully functioning by 31 December 2005, but Article 3 of Decision 414 allows for an earlier completion date. Several steps towards the completion of the integration process have been taken:

- the ACN adopted a framework of principles and norms to liberalize trade in services by 2005 in Decision 439 of June 1998;
- Ecuador and Peru signed an Acceleration and Deepening Agreement and its corresponding implementation instrument in October 1998, liberalizing many ACN tariff items in August 1999;
- the ACN Commission approved Support to the Ecuador–Peru Acceleration and Deepening Agreement in Decision 451 of April 1999; and
- Peru granted complete MFN status to ACN countries in October 1999.

Changes continued into the 2000s with progress towards common positions and negotiations as a bloc, especially with Mercosur; inclusion of a social agenda; and adoption of WTO-compliant disciplines on industrial property. Some progress has also been made in sector-specific policies, though difficulties persist in sensitive products that are highly protected by member countries, like agriculture.

Peru grants significant tariff preferences to ACN countries, and imports from Bolivia were almost completely liberalized by July 1999. Although these preferences include an ample variety of products, Peru's imports from ACN partners continue to be concentrated in relatively few products, with fuel and mineral oils accounting for about 45 per cent of total imports. Peruvian exports to the bloc increased to US$450 million in 2000, after falling to US$350 million the previous year. Colombia and Venezuela are Peru's largest trade partners in the bloc.

Mercosur

The ACN and Mercosur initiated negotiations to form a free trade zone between the blocs in 1995. Negotiations are still underway, stalled by disagreement over issues such as tariff reduction schedules, sensitive product lists, and the agricultural sector. After the failure of bloc-to-bloc negotiations, Peru began bilateral negotiations with individual Mercosur countries. An agreement was reached with Brazil that took effect in Peru in August 1999, granting preferential treatment to nearly 98 per cent of

Table 8.2 Phases of ACN–Mercosur negotiations

Period	*Issues*	*Participants*	*Results*
February 1995 First meeting	Formation of a FTA	– ACN – Mercosur	Stagnation caused by the project's ambitiousness.
1995–96	Adoption of the LAIA 'historical patrimony' negotiation scheme	– Mercosur – Individual ACN countries	No progress achieved.
1997	Formation of a FTA including only tariff issues	– ACN – Mercosur	Stagnation caused by sensitive sectors, rules of origin, and safeguards.
1998	Change to negotiations of historical patrimony. FTA creation by 2000, prior to tariff reductions.	– ACN – Mercosur	Problems arose over preferential tariffs. The ACN sought complete tariff reduction while Mercosur would only offer between 30 per cent and 50 per cent. Disagreement on the list of 'historical patrimony' products.
1999–2000	Proposal by Brazil to negotiate a FTA separately. The ACN and Argentina propose restarting negotiations in the framework of those advanced with Mercosur as a bloc. Uruguay and Paraguay prepare for a similar process with the ACN.	– Various	ACN–Brazil: ECA signed August 1999. ACN–Argentina: agreement signed June 2000.

Source: Author's own data.

Peru's exports to Brazil and 44 per cent of Peru's imports from Brazil. An agreement was signed with Argentina in June 2000, leaving negotiations with Paraguay and Uruguay pending.

Free Trade Area of the Americas (FTAA)

Peru's strategy in FTAA negotiations has focused on facilitating foreign investments in both goods and services. This strategy has relied, in turn, on increasing the competitiveness of the economy in order to take full advantage of the capital inflow. FTAA integration is quite appealing for Peru and could prove very beneficial, given the weight of the country's trade relationships with major FTAA markets. Indeed, Peru's largest trade partners are members of NAFTA; approximately 30 per cent of total Peruvian exports went to NAFTA countries during 2000 and 2001. Nevertheless, similar to Mexico's position, Peru, together with other Andean countries, may resist the idea of an FTAA because it would end its preferential relationship with the US. Special trade preferences were conceded by the US to Peru in the Andean Trade Preferences Act (ATPA). The ATPA, approved by the US Congress in December 1991, supported the fight against drugs through preferential tariffs for the majority of imports from ACN members (except Venezuela) until December 2001. The renewing of this special treatment in July 2002 was contingent upon support of the US's antiterrorism missions, but also expanded preferential treatment for key 'alternative' products. Preferential treatment will be withdrawn with the conclusion of FTAA negotiations, turning the stepping-up of tariff and NTB liberalization in the ACN and other regional agreements a priority. Further sub-regional liberalization would foster participation in FTAA and multilateral negotiations with a single voice and thereby increase the ACN's negotiating leverage.

After several years of preparatory activities, the FTAA negotiation process gained momentum following the Ministerial Meeting held in Buenos Aires in April 2001. A schedule for the meetings of Groups and Committees was established and drafts of the Agreement chapters are on the table. Therefore, the definition of an adequate negotiating strategy has become a pivotal issue in the Peruvian foreign trade agenda.

Asia-Pacific Economic Cooperation (APEC)

Peru joined Asia-Pacific Economic Cooperation (APEC) in November 1998. The country is not only the sole ACN member involved in the agreement but, with 20 per cent of its exports directed to Asia, it is also the largest ACN exporter to that region. Given these trade ties and its strategic

Pacific location, Peru could play a key role in the creation of a bi-oceanic corridor for the projection of Brazil and other neighboring countries towards Asia. The ACN integration process is compatible with progress already made within APEC and would allow Peru to act as a link between the two regions. Such an arrangement would depend on the dynamics of relationships between Peru and Asian countries and the scope for regional agreements within the framework of APEC. The first meeting between the ACN and the Association of Southeast Asian Nations (ASEAN) held in May 2000 fostered the relationship between the two regions. Moreover, the ACN and China have begun to work together to increase trade flows and strengthen scientific and technological cooperation. Peru is well positioned to benefit from expanded trade, as its exports to China account for 80 per cent of ACN exports to China.

European Union (EU)

Similar to ATPA provisions, the EU grants duty-free access for different ACN agricultural and industrial exports, in theory aiding the fight against drug production and trafficking through promotion of export diversification. The Special Regime of Trade Preferences, which forms part of the Generalized System of Preferences (GSP) of the EU, gathers together initiatives in Colombia (Special Program for Cooperation in the Fight Against Drugs), Bolivia (Alternative Development Strategy and Coca Cultivation Substitution Program), Ecuador (Cooperation in the Fight Against Drugs), Peru, and Venezuela. The regime began in 1990, and Venezuela was incorporated in 1995. Special tariffs have been extended until 2004. The main products to enter the EU duty-free are industrial, textile, and agricultural products like coffee, cocoa, fish products and cut flowers. The agricultural sector has been the main beneficiary of GSP with 85 per cent of exports covered, though greater utilization of these preferences has been accompanied by export diversification. Nevertheless, ACN relations are not a priority for the EU, so efforts have concentrated on cooperation and preferential measures to support the fight against drugs, rather than on the creation of a more encompassing trade agreement between the two regions.

Peru–Chile Economic Cooperation Agreement (ECA)

After three years of bilateral negotiations, Peru signed an ECA with Chile in 1998, with the end goal of forming a free trade area within 18 years. Tariff reductions affected 2600 products in the first two years alone. Unilateral reduction schedules have been set for 5 and 10 years, with up to 18 years for sensitive products. According to schedule, products with a five-year reduction timetable, mostly food products, reached 40 per cent tariff preferences in July 2000. There is a petition for accelerating the reductions on products with more than ten-year reduction schedules. Frozen chicken, wheat, wheat flour, wine, paper, oil, chocolate, fish flour, medicine, starches, and plastic products are among the sensitive products that would be affected by an acceleration of the process.

The ECA has positively affected Peruvian trade. While bilateral trade rose nearly 70 per cent from 1998 to 2001, Peruvian exports to Chile increased by over 100 per cent and Chilean exports to Peru rose by only 50 per cent. The traditional Peruvian trade deficit with Chile fell drastically at the agreement's outset, but in 2000 and 2001 was on the upswing again (Silva, Chapter 2).

The impact of trade reform and private sector involvement

Ten years of trade reform revolutionized economic activities across the board, but the costs and benefits of trade opening and the reduction of government support varied among sectors. There is consensus among scholars and policy-makers that commitments at the multilateral level have helped to 'lock-in' unilateral reforms. But it is also generally conceded that benefits have fallen short of expectations, especially in terms of improved market access and disciplined use of anti-dumping. As in other Latin American countries, those sectors traditionally shielded from international competition have been particularly hit by the reform while more outward-oriented sectors have benefited (Silva, Chapter 2; Tussie *et al.*, Chapter 4; Motta Veiga and Ventura-Dias, Chapter 5). It is therefore not surprising that the Peruvian private sector, like its peers in other countries of the region, does not hold a monolithic position on trade policy reform. Differences have arisen among business groups according to their trading interests, the scope and nature of policy changes, and the costs and benefits associated with negotiations in different fora. These differences are, in turn, largely rooted in the sectors of economic activity in which they operate.[3]

Traditional exports: mining and fishery

The mining sector forms the bedrock of Peruvian exports, averaging a total of 45 per cent of exports and constituting nearly 10 per cent of GDP over the past decade. Copper, ore, refined silver and tin production have been on the rise. The General Mining Law of 1992 imposed environmental standards on the sector, including requirements that companies adjust their contamination levels to international standards by 2002, with some extensions until 2007. Specific government support policies have been kept in place with some adaptations to fulfill multilateral commitments.

Fishery is a far second to mining in its export contribution, constituting less than 15 per cent of traditional exports and less than 5 per cent of non-traditional exports during the 1990s. The sector began to recuperate losses suffered in 1998, and by 2001 constituted 20 per cent of traditional exports and nearly 15 per cent of total exports. Peru ranks as one of the leading world producers of fish products, especially in fish flour and fish oil. Domestic firms are protected from an onslaught of foreign products and negative side effects of the economic opening, because of the large variety of products, their nearly exclusive exportation, and little domestic demand. The majority of the processing industry has adjusted to quality standards adopted in 1991, such as the Hazard Analysis Critical Control Points (HACCP) program in the production process. As a consequence of the adoption of these quality control systems, Peruvian fish (hake) has taken a firm hold in nearly 40 world markets. The General Fishery Law of 1994 introduced environmental protection measures to the sector. Similarly, the fishery industry has adopted the Environmental Management and Adjustment Program.

Because of their outward orientation and considerable competitiveness in regional and international markets, both mining and fisheries benefited from trade reform and multilateral commitments undertaken by Peru in the 1990s. On one hand, since the domestic market is only a secondary market for their products and local firms enjoy a relatively strong position from which to withstand foreign competition, trade opening and policy adjustments have had only minimally detrimental effects. On the other, new windows of opportunity have emerged in regional and international markets as a result of gains obtained from negotiations, although non-trade factors (mainly the over-valued currency) have impaired firms from taking full advantage of them.

Non-traditional exports: textiles, agro-industry, industrial manufacturing, and services

Non-traditional exports are products that were not part of the traditional Peruvian export basket but that, in the last ten years, have refocused on exporting the bulk of their produced volume, given limited domestic demand. They represented only 32 per cent of total exports in 2001, reflecting the limited progress made in diversifying the primary-export model that has prevailed throughout Peruvian history. Textiles, especially clothing, stand out as the main non-traditional export, followed by agriculture, chemicals, and the non-traditional fishery sector. The agriculture sector experienced 34 per cent growth in 1999, followed by 22 per cent growth in textiles in 2000 and 66 per cent growth in mechanical metals in 2001, powering an 11 per cent growth in non-traditional exports for the period 1999–2001. Non-traditional exports directed to ACN countries, including textiles, pharmachemicals, paper and boxes, copper cables and wires, ceramics, coffee, and cement may deepen trade among industries in the bloc by incorporating higher added value production and engendering a stronger connection within sectors.

Textiles, which include yarns, fabrics and clothing, are the non-traditional products most exported from Peru, representing approximately 10 per cent of total exports. Nearly three-quarters of textiles produced are exported, accounting for 30 per cent of non-traditional exports in 2001. The market structure continues to be essentially export-oriented because, unlike other textile producing countries, Peru is not blessed with a sufficiently large domestic market to complement export markets. The textile sector's benefits as a result of trade opening included new market opportunities through increased trade flows with Chile and Ecuador. Similarly, the EU prolonged its GSP with the ACN so that nearly 90 per cent of exports continue to enter the EU tariff free. Chile, Ecuador, Colombia, Cuba and Brazil offer Peru tariff preferences, and concessions with the US are in sight. The agreement between the ACN and Brazil will open access to the Brazilian market with a range of preferences of between 40 and 80 per cent, facilitating trade in cotton fabrics. However, risks stemming from a weakening of credit flows and a deepening of the Brazilian crisis may now jeopardize these opportunities. The building-up of protectionist measures in partner countries, such as Venezuelan restrictions on textile trade, could also jeopardize the export drive. Costs of the liberalization process and multilateral commitments affected the textile sector through the elimination of production and export incentives. Consequently, firms with very low productivity levels, especially the large group of small and micro enterprises focused on the internal market, suffered a shock treatment. Without resources to invest in plant upgrading and new technologies, many of these firms were forced out of the market. In response, demands have emerged for cuts in taxes on incorporating technology, reductions of excessive labor costs and changes in the currency exchange rate to enhance the competitiveness of the sector, particularly *vis-à-vis* Asian products. Similarly, complaints have been raised against the precarious and short-term nature of remaining promotional mechanisms and the bias of new rules against exports of high value-added products.

Agro-industry, also predominantly an export sector, accounted for 9 per cent of total Peruvian exports in 2000 and 2001 through the export of traditional products like coffee, sugar and cotton and non-traditional products like asparagus, cochineal, fruits, olives, mandarins, oranges, dessert grapes, dried vegetables and mangoes. Exports of these products increased, despite difficulties faced in penetrating foreign markets and developing efficient distribution chains. In fact, since 1999 export growth has gone hand-in-hand with falling world prices and meager profitability. According to the National Asparagus Census of 1998, asparagus leads agriculture exports, although threatened by competition from Chinese and Mexican products. Trade reform has implied a complex mix of costs and benefits. Unlike textiles, the agriculture sector continues to benefit from higher tariffs than industrial products. Additional tariff protection is offered to a limited number of basic crops (corn, rice, sorghum and sugar) while dairy products receive protection through specific variable duties. On the other hand, the government now taxes agricultural exports and multilateral commitments have failed to relieve tariff and phytosanitary restrictions in export markets. Japan and the EU present high levels of tariff barriers, while the North American market has more lenient tariff levels but considerable sanitary restrictions. These costs and benefits have given rise to two distinct trade policy demands. First, the agriculture sector calls for consistent support policies that help the sector confront high tariff and NTB barriers in developed countries. Second, the sector calls for more substantial progress in the elimination of NTBs affecting Peruvian exports, particularly in the FTAA given the relevance of North American markets as export destinations.

Industrial manufacturing was largely inward-oriented prior to the process of trade reform. During the past decade, the sector's export performance has shown only modest gains and has varied across industries. Sales abroad of mechanical metal have grown, but account for only 2 per cent of total exports. Iron and steel have had minimal export growth rates while non-metallic minerals suffered losses in 2000 but experienced significant growth in 2001. Export growth for year 2000 reached 12 per cent, powered by textile, clothing and steel metallurgy shipments abroad. Industrial manufacturing has been the sector hardest hit by trade reform. The combined effect of drastic tariff reductions and the dismantling of non-tariff protection and export incentives have forced firms, for the first time in many years, to face the rigors of international competition. The impact has varied across industries, but there is little doubt that the industrial sector as a whole lost its status as a policy priority and pillar of growth during the 1990s. Consequences have been particularly hard for household appliances, radios, televisions, fertilizers, frozen food, distillery and beverage manufacturing, which have suffered negative growth and increasing idle capacity. The reform wreaked less havoc with industries like intermediate goods for construction (cement, ceramic, and porcelain goods, iron and steel, paint and plastics), processing of raw materials for exportation, textiles and cotton clothing, and food-processing. Industries in which large firms predominate fared better that those in which small and micro enterprises have a significant participation, as large firms were better prepared to undertake the reorganization and upgrading required to increase efficiency and productivity in the face of mounting competitive pressures. The locking-in of reform measures affecting manufacturing industries with UR commitments does not preclude the adoption of alternative policy instruments to support those industries (Tussie and Lengyel, 1998).

Trade in services accounted for an average of 52 per cent of GDP in 1999–2001 and has been in deficit since the mid-1970s. This negative trade balance was accentuated by market restrictions and a stringent debt payment policy established after the financial crisis of the 1980s (Cáceres, 1989). During the 1990s, the activities defined as 'non-financial services' showed different trade balance results. The sector with the largest deficit has been transportation, reaching a deficit of US$517 billion in year 2000. Quite to the contrary, tourism and communications have registered positive trade balances with increasing earnings and growth since 1994. Although the insurance and reinsurance sectors have usually registered trade deficits, they exhibited a positive balance in 1998 mainly due to increasing demand caused by the El Niño threat.

Judging by FDI figures, the reforms' goal of attracting foreign investment seems to have been met. Disaggregated, however, the statistics show that firms lost and benefited according to their positioning in the economy. Gains were obtained by the mainly foreign 'new entrants', as state participation was reduced through privatization and market access was eased. On the other hand, costs have been born by previously established services providers, which were not used to tough competitive conditions or were implicitly discriminated against, and by domestic producers of goods and equipment, as foreign operators have tended to resort to external sources of supply.

Private sector perceptions

The private sector expressed a spectrum of assessments on the reforms, largely based upon the nuanced situation of and consequences for individual economic areas. For example, primary sectors grouped in the National Society of Mining and Petroleum or the Society of Foreign Trade (COMEX) support the reform policies, advocating full market liberalization and flat tariffs while opposing differential or promotion policies. Similarly, since they favor markets outside the region, these sectors focus on negotiations in the WTO and FTAA and with APEC and the EU, while downplaying the importance of regional integration agreements. The mix of preferences is slightly different for the agro-industrial sector, which emerged during the 1990s with competitive advantages in regional agreements as well as in other regions. While less enthusiastic about trade reform and the lack of consistent export promotion policies, agro-industry prioritizes adoption of strong negotiation positions at the multilateral and regional level to attain greater market access and elimination or reduction of sanitary, phytosanitary and standard barriers. The export industries grouped in the Association of Exporters (ADEX) are not entirely opposed to the overall orientation of trade reform, though they stress the need to complement the process with appropriate pro-competitiveness policies. Moreover, given their presence in Latin American markets, they favor strengthening integration agreements with the ACN and Mercosur rather than with the FTAA, APEC or the EU. Furthermore, export industries perceive multilateral negotiations as a remote and less accessible forum in which it is more difficult to disentangle the negotiations' likely costs and benefits. Table 8.3 presents a detailed account of the main costs and benefits of major bilateral and regional agreements as perceived by the Peruvian private sector.

Rifts in private sector positions suggest that the government's task of 'speaking with one voice' on trade policy is increasingly difficult. Indeed, the official position must articulate interests and demands that are varied, even contradictory, not only across sectors but also within them. Moreover, the multiplicity of fora compounds the problem, especially since Peru coordinates positions with ACN partners in some fora.

Institutional underpinnings

Trade policy is managed by many areas of the state apparatus, creating a demanding task of coordination and consensus-building. The Ministry of Economy and Finances (MEF) establishes the general economic policy and works with other government agencies on related policy areas.

Table 8.3 Peruvian private sector costs and benefits

Bilateral agreements		
Country	*Benefits*	*Costs*
Chile	• Chile's geographical closeness and economic conditions • Potential volume of trade to be developed • Significant number of tariff lines to be effected by reductions	• Different tariff structures • Trade deficit with Chile • Minimal bilateral exchange developed
Brazil	• Take advantage of Brazilian market • Potential niche markets for Peruvian products • Entrance of Brazilian investment flows • The majority of products exported to Brazil receive preferences, though Brazilian products imported to Peru do not	• Limited export portfolio dominated by traditional products • Brazilian demand reduced by the recession
Regional agreements		
Agreement	*Benefits*	*Costs*
ACN	• Increased exports to the ACN market • Export structure dominated by manufactured products • Negotiations on services, support programs, customs valuation, etc.	• Growing trade deficit with ACN countries
APEC	• Agreement's flexibility and gradualism. • Trade facilitation, economic and technical cooperation. • Reduced tariffs to allow reduced costs. • Inflow of Asian investments.	• Reduced exportable supply • Minimal value-added products • Sectors that compete with Asian products will be effected
FTAA	• Trade volume growth due to tariff and NTB reductions • Costs reductions for firms. • Increase in investment volume expected • Improved negotiating position in the WTO and other fora	• Trade structure: traditional products • Differences in sectors to undergo tariff reductions that are sensitive for some countries and not for others such as textiles

Source: author's own data.

For example, the MEF sets tariff policy together with the Ministry of Industry, Tourism, Integration and International Trade Negotiations (MITINCI), tax policy together with Customs, and foreign trade policy together with the MITINCI and the Ministry of Foreign Relations. Customs administers, applies and collects central government tariffs and other taxes, and the National Institute for Defense of Competition and Intellectual Property (INDECOPI) protects the market from monopolistic practices and unfair competition and is responsible for intellectual property rights. Additional agencies were created by the reform so that the public sector could better manage trade policy issues. PROMPEX was established in 1996 with the task of promoting and facilitating the development of exports. It has crafted various export promotion programs, including market investigation, organization of business fairs, and export promotion missions. Similarly, PROMPEX sponsors a series of programs and roundtables to increase the quality of the export supply, offering technical and technological assistance in the production process. Courses on export management are offered to foster the emergence of new exporters and a database of trade information and basic advice is also provided. Progress was also made in customs through tariff simplification, reduction in clearance time (from 10 days in 1990 to 2 hours in 1998) and increases in tariff collections (from US$626 million in 1990 to US$2.84 billion in 1998). Table 8.4 presents the issues attended to by each of these agencies.

Public-private cooperation has progressed in trade policy issues, though there is still a long way to go. Certainly, negotiation of issues like tariff preferences, dumping and subsidies call for a high degree of coordination between both sectors in order to achieve an agenda that incorporates the positions of stakeholders. Involvement of private sector representatives is limited in multilateral negotiations. Some business leaders do actively participate on an ad-hoc basis, though attempts to endow this involvement with more systematic institutional channels have failed. Such initiatives are impinged upon by the business community's perception of the WTO as a relatively remote, less accessible forum. To the contrary, the Peru-Pacific Economic Cooperation Council and the Peru-FTAA Commission are two examples of joint initiatives achieved between the government and the private sector at the regional level. The Pacific Economic Cooperation Council (PECC) is a non-governmental organization that promotes economic cooperation in the Pacific region. Working Groups focus on particular policy issues at periodic seminars, followed by the publication of studies on financial and capital markets, development and cooperation, human development, science

Table 8.4 Key agenda issues and corresponding agencies

Issue	*Agency*
Foreign Trade policy	MEF, MITINCI and Ministry of Foreign Relations
Tariff policy	MEF and MITINCI
Customs Valuation	Customs
Import Prohibition	MITINCI and INDECOPI
Government Procurement	MEF and MITINCI
Rules and Requirements of Origin	MITINCI and INDECOPI
Sanitary and Phytosanitary Rules and Requirements	MITINCI, INDECOPI, Ministry of Health, and Ministry of Agriculture
Safeguard Clauses	MITINCI
Tax Refunds	MEF and Customs
Monopoly, Competition Policy and Anti-dumping Measures	MITINCI and INDECOPI
Market Access Polices	MITINCI and Ministry of Foreign Relations
Services	MITINCI and INDECOPI

Source: author's own data.

and technology, transportation, telecommunications, tourism, and trade issues like NTBs and competition. The Peru–PECC commission played a decisive role in Peru's incorporation in APEC. The Peru–FTAA Commission contributes proposals that bring together perspectives from diverse private sectors on FTAA agenda issues. The Lima Chamber of Commerce opened an institutional space for public-private interaction through 11 Working Groups, which was immediately supported by academics and the most important unions in the country. The Commission's mirroring of the FTAA Working Group structure allowed, for the first time in history, Peruvian representation and coordination in all of the Working Groups at the FTAA Business Forums in Toronto in 1999 and in Buenos Aires in 2001.

Complexities of the Peruvian trade agenda

The revamping of trade policies, instruments and practices over more than a decade in Peru has only partially paid-off, falling short of expectations on efficiency gains and export and economic growth. Not only has export growth been moderate, but Peru also continues to be an essentially primary-product exporting country with minimal export diversification. Greater involvement in multilateral negotiations has served, as in other Latin American countries, to anchor unilateral trade reforms and deepen them in areas such as NTBs and TRIPs by requiring harmonization of domestic trade policies and instruments with WTO disciplines. Yet hindsight reveals that benefits accruing from multilateral negotiations have been significantly meager compared with Peru's expectations, especially in key areas of market access and trade-relief measures. Gains were obtained from integration initiatives at the regional, sub-regional and bilateral levels, particularly in market access, with potentially larger benefits should the dynamics of recent years maintain momentum.

The challenge ahead is how to fully reap the benefits of growth and development that trade liberalization promises to deliver. Sound domestic policies to promote exports and investments must be designed within the existing maneuvering room (Tussie and Lengyel, 1998; Agosin and French Davis, 2002). Furthermore, international trade negotiations must be taken advantage of with greater agility, which will prove exceedingly difficult in the multiplicity and complexity of fora at the multilateral, hemispheric, extra-regional, regional, sub-regional and bilateral level. Faced with an uneven playing field in nearly all fora, Peru will have to search for allies from which stronger leverage may be attained. ACN members were unable to come together as a bloc during the Uruguay Round, because Peru and Columbia, who were already GATT members, focused on new commitments while the other ACN members discussed their accession to the WTO. To the contrary, the Ministerial Meeting of Seattle offered an opportunity for the ACN countries to coordinate joint action, given common interests in issues like investment and competition policy. However, even in the only common initiative among ACN countries -intellectual property- countries acted separately. On one hand, Bolivia, Colombia, Ecuador, Peru and Nicaragua proposed to research the most appropriate vehicle to recognize and protect traditional knowledge and to set up a normative system to protect its expression and demonstration (WTO, 1999a). On the other hand, Venezuela proposed the establishment of a system to protect such knowledge (WTO, 1999b). The Doha work program opened new opportunities for ACN countries to work out joint proposals. In this context, Peru will pursue key points of its multilateral trade agenda, as summarized in Table 8.5, together with other ACN countries. Many of these Peruvian interests coincide with those of other ACN countries, particularly in agriculture, market access and special and differential (S&D) treatment (SELA, 2000). This shared turf could lay the groundwork for common negotiation positions.

Table 8.5 Peru's agenda in the WTO

Issue	*Position*
Agriculture	• Eliminate distortions from export subsidies. • Avoid use of sanitary and phytosanitary barriers to market access.
Textiles	• Step-up S&D treatment for developing countries. • Review ATC, sanitary and phytosanitary aspects, and the Dispute Settlement Understanding (DSU).
Fishery	• Eliminate subsidies offered by many countries, because their generation of fishery float damages marine populations and causes trade distortions.
Industry	• Continue liberalization, if industrialized nations do so in basic industrial sectors.
Services	• Seek a greater trade opening and development of multilateral disciplines. • Include liberalization of ocean and air transport in GATS.
Intellectual Property	• Create a multilateral system of notification and registration of geographical indications for wines and liquors.
Investments	• Include the following in the negotiations: investment's effect on productivity, rights and responsibilities of the investors and the receiving government, technological transfer, transfer of management skills, and promotion and incentives to the investors. • Form a Working Group to implement a Multilateral Agreement on Investments.
Preferential treatment	• Define S&D provisions in favor of developing countries. • Facilitate integrity of commitments without hurting trade.

Source: WTO (2001c).

At other negotiation levels, positions must be defined and coordinated across the entangled web of liberalization commitments. The multiplicity of fora presents Peru with the difficult challenge of coordinating participation in simultaneous processes, but also offers opportunities for reaping benefits in more fruitful environs. As illustrated in Table 8.6, by 2005 Peru will have lowered tariffs in multiple fora, shuffling multilateral, extra-regional, regional, sub-regional, and bilateral commitments to come out with a winning hand. Peru must pursue a strategy of adding a bonus beyond other initiatives at each level. APEC must be a WTO-plus agreement, the FTAA must be APEC-plus, the free trade area of South America must be FTAA-plus, and the ACN must be 'free trade area of South America'-plus. Without achieving distinct levels of integration, formal maintenance of sub-regional agreements is fruitless.

Table 8.6 Peruvian negotiation participation timetable

Agreement	*Maximum term for tariff reductions*		
	2005	*2005–2010*	*2010–2020*
ECA with Chile	List I of Export Products (agro, fish, and mineral and chemical manufacturing)	List II of National Industry (malt, chemical inputs and rolled paper)	List III of Sensitive Products (wheat and wines)
ACN	Common Market		
ACN–Mercosur 2000	Free Trade Area		
FTAA	Free Trade Area		
EU	GSP		
APEC			Trade Liberalization
WTO	Program of the end of the Millenium Round – 2003		

Source: author's own data.

Peru's political transition since the early months of 2000 has left economic policy decisions on stand-by, and until domestic problems are brought under control little attention and resources will be devoted to trade negotiations.

Notes

1. Translated by Brita Siepker.
2. Prior to the UR, Peru had about 500 tariff lines negotiated in the GATT within a tariff universe of nearly 6000 items, largely because of bilateral agreements with major trade partners like the US, the EU, Japan, New Zealand and Australia. In the UR virtually all tariff lines were bound.
3. Private sector perspectives were attained through a series of interviews and surveys with sector representatives in Lima in April 1999, including the Association of Exporters, the National Industry Society, the Office of Agrarian Imports, and the Chamber of Commerce.

Conclusions: The Latin American Countries and the World Trading System – Addressing Institutional Barriers to Development

Miguel F. Lengyel

Introduction

As in the 1950s and 1980s, the birth of the 21st century shows Latin American countries struggling again to find a sustainable path to development. The sequence of events is already well known: decreasing returns from and even fatigue with the state-led, inward-looking model of industrialization – embracing, with almost blind faith in the ability of public sector bureaucrats to drive the process – paved the way in the 1980s for an across-the-board U-turn. Either out of pragmatism or conviction, but with similar determination, countries adopted development policy prescriptions coined by international organisms stressing the role of markets and deeper integration in the world economy. Privatization of public assets, de-regulation and greater exposure to international competition became the thrust of the standard policy package.

Although contrasting in terms of policy scripts, both experiences share some striking weaknesses. First, they rely on development views that, on one hand, assume that the road to progress has clear and predefined contours so that it mainly involves adapting policies and institutions to a given series of blueprints; and, on the other, they endorse what some authors have called *dirigisme*, i.e.'... the assumption that ... there is an expert agent that already sees the future of development and can, therefore, issue instructions for arriving there. Whether through celebration of the developmental state or by adulation of a cosmopolitan, technical elite, this dirigisme has led to unholy alliances with the powerful and the exclusion of the weak' (Reddy and Sabel, 2002: 1). Secondly, both experiences ended in deep financial crises – with their corresponding episodes of debt default – that in turn underscored serious macroeconomic imbalances and fiscal accounts on the verge of collapse. What gives tragic dimensions to the experience of the past two decades are the unprecedented rates of unemployment, poverty and immiseration.

Trade policy was an essential component of the package of policy reform in Latin America. First through unilateral liberalization of trade regimes and later by anchoring and expanding it through the fully fledged commitments made at the Uruguay Round (UR), most countries of the region clearly showed their willingness to come out of the fringes and play by the new rules. This was a sea change with regards to previous positions; indeed, in former rounds, countries that had already joined the General Agreement on Trade and Tariffs (GATT) had either remained quite by-standers or concentrated their efforts in expanding their rights to free themselves from prevailing rules (Tussie and Lengyel, 2002). Hopes that such a move would contribute to bring tangible benefits in terms of market access for their products and of development as well were as large as disenchantment is today. It is not surprising, therefore, that increasingly critical appraisals of those reforms have emerged in many Latin American countries. Moreover, the organization that epitomizes the drive towards trade liberalization the world over, the World Trade Organization (WTO), is also under harsh criticisms from a wide variety of sources.

The chapters in this book provide a balanced and rich account of key aspects of the process of trade policy reform in selected Latin American countries over the last 20 years. They explore with a common methodology and an empirical orientation the main costs and benefits of the Uruguay Round Agreements (URAs) and the public–private pattern of interaction framing those countries' negotiating positions at the multilateral level. All the chapters are very generous in detail, allowing the reader to grasp the scope and micro-aspects of the policy changes unleashed by reforms as well as key economic, political and institutional intricacies of those processes. Furthermore, because of their focused analysis at the country level (and within it, at the sectoral level), they highlight the relevance of national case studies to understand the peculiarities and nuances of the national experiences of trade policy change within an overall, quite uniform trend of reform. At the same time, the eight countries selected for study vary to some extent in terms of size, economic structure, per capita GDP, 'openness', export profile and other characteristics; this variety substantiates the strength of any generalizations the studies may generate (although such a variety also makes it more difficult to derive them). Finally, the chapters adequately complement the companion edited by Diana Tussie on trade negotiations in Latin America, where the main issues of the Uruguay Round agenda are the point of entry to analyse the involvement of the region's countries in the multilateral trade regime.

These concluding remarks follow the structure of the chapters, building upon their major insights to put forward some ideas that dovetail with the redesign of trade institutions at the global, regional and national levels. Rather than an exhaustive review of those findings, these remarks thus seek to use them as a platform to present an argument, still incipient and exploratory, on how the rules and practices governing trade could be turned more supportive of development – a matter that became the subject of a heated debate after the fiasco of Seattle and that ranks high in Doha's discourse.[1] In line with the above critical comments on standard views, this argument will draw from an alternative development approach that focuses on individual and collective learning, and stresses institutional diversity and innovation instead of convergence and adaptation or outright 'clonation'.[2]

In keeping with this goal, the chapter is organized as follows. The next section looks at the evidence brought by the case studies on the gains and losses of the URAs, linking them to the processes of rule-making at the WTO. The subsequent section moves from the multilateral to the national level, reviewing the chapters' findings on the public–private dynamics in Latin America regarding trade policy and underlying some flawed institutional traits. The final section addresses the main problems identified in the previous sections. It does so by discussing first some changes in the configuration and functions of the WTO whose rationale is to relax the constraints they place on developing countries to device their own solutions to major development bottlenecks. It then moves to discuss some novel institutional arrangements and mechanisms that may foster local knowledge for crafting development-promoting policies in a wide range of (in the WTO's jargon) 'trade-related' policy fields; and, finally, it suggests a new role for subregional integration initiatives as intermediate level instances of coordination where national solutions could be rendered compatible and linked, in turn, to the global trade regime.

The outcome of the UR: some critical issues at stake

Following the conclusion of the UR and as countries gradually got into the implementation of commitments, scholars and policy makers increasingly agreed that the net gains accruing to developing countries were extremely lean, if not negligible. Moreover, such a consensus still holds, no matter whether the yardstick for assessment is market access payoffs (the traditional GATT's purview) or the suitability of the domestic regulatory/institutional reforms unleashed by the URAs in several 'trade-related' policy fields now under the reach of the WTO (intellectual property rights, investments, sanitary and phytosanitary measures and technical barriers to trade) (Rodrik, 2001; Finger and Nogués, 2002; Hoekman, 2002). Complaints of an unbalanced or asymmetrical exchange of concessions and claims to redress it were thus voiced by a growing number of developing countries in the run-ups to the 1999 Ministerial Meeting in Seattle and the 2001 Ministerial Conference at Doha (World Bank, 2001).

To be sure, it is well known today that developing countries did not leave the UR negotiation table with their pockets empty. The inclusion of agriculture, the commitment to phase out the restrictions on textiles and the strengthening of the dispute settlement system can be deemed as important returns. In exchange, however, those countries made concessions that largely compensated for such gains, including a more restrictive S&D approach, the binding of all tariffs on goods and more stringent disciplines on subsidies and custom valuation. The expansion of the multilateral agenda in areas such as intellectual property and services further loaded their package of concessions.

Furthermore, a more careful assessment of the outcome underscores that many of the alleged gains has yet to materialize or has been largely diluted during the implementation of the agreements. Just to illustrate, that is the case with two agreements – Agriculture (AA) and Textiles and Clothing (ATC) – that particularly matter to developing countries. In the first case, although the agreement contemplates several provisions aimed at increasing market access (reduction of tariffs, export subsidies and domestic supports, replacement of non-tariff measures with tariffs), it has not inhibited the proliferation of tariff peaks (well over 100 per cent in some cases) in many OECD countries that affect export products particularly sensitive for developing countries (Josling, Tangermann and Warley, 1996; Olarreaga and NG, 2002). Similarly, the progressive phasing out of quotas committed in the ATC has not meant that significant trade liberalization is to be achieved before the end of the 10-year transition period in 2005 (Panagariya, 2001; Kheir-El-Din, 2002). Equally relevant, while the new dispute settlement mechanism is an asset, the need it imposes on developing countries to generate new expertise on international trade law to take full advantage of it has raised questions about their capacity to bring cases efficiently as complainants and to protect their interests as defendants (Weston and Delich, 2003). Last but not least, full adherence to some WTO agreements (e.g. SPS, TRIPS, custom valuation) required domestic institution building, which has proved not only costly because of the investments at stake but also not always fully consistent with the development needs and priorities of many developing countries (Finger and Schuler, 2000).[3]

The evidence from Latin America

The experience of Latin America easily fits into the above general picture of the UR results regarding developing countries' interests and largely contributes to substantiate it. Yet, a more disaggregated analysis, as the one provided by the chapters in this volume, is necessary to better grasp the mix of costs and benefits resulting from the agreements, its complexities and nuances. In particular, two aspects on which the chapters shed light are worth discussing with some detail, namely, the interplay between unilateral reforms and multilateral disciplines on one hand, and the distributional game the agreements entailed, on the other.

As for the first aspect, a quite common reading made in the aftermath of the UR emphasized that the WTO Agreements were economically and politically functional to the processes of trade reform most Latin American countries had already chosen to carry on. To put it shortly, they greatly helped to 'lock-in' those reforms by both anchoring the policy move towards more open trade regimes through enforceable commitments and helping to contain domestic pressures to roll back or mitigate trade liberalization. The agreements thus should be deemed as largely beneficial by contributing to endow trade policy regimes with greater transparency and predictability, and to undermine the rent-seeking practices that had plagued the period of import substitution industrialization.

While these assessments are right when taken at a broad level of generalization, they fall short of capturing the full picture; therefore, some refinements and qualifications are in order. First, by the UR closing phase, the stage and scope of the process of unilateral trade reform across Latin American countries were not uniform. That is, in terms of granting access to their own markets, most countries had already made considerable progress by the early 1990s[4] and cemented it in the UR by binding virtually all their tariff lines;[5] yet, the situation is not as straightforward in other policy areas such as export promotion and investments. In those areas, rather than just 'locking in' ongoing reforms, the UR catalyzed deeper policy changes than the ones many

Latin American countries were ready to make. For instance, with the only exception of Mexico – which had revamped its export promotion regime within the framework of NAFTA (Ortiz Mena, Chapter 3) –, the Agreement on Subsidies and Countervailing Measures (ASCM) implied the redefinition or abandonment of policy instruments untouched by unilateral reform. Even Chile, a front-runner within the region regarding trade reform, faced the need to dismantle or reconvert some of its programs to make them fully consistent with multilateral disciplines (Silva, Chapter 2).[6] The picture in the field of investments policies is quite similar, with the caveat that countries such as Mexico, Brazil and Argentina (under the umbrella of the MERCOSUR Automotive Regime), and Colombia and Venezuela (within the framework of the Andean Common Automotive Policy) resorted to the waivers allowed in the TRIMs Agreement to postpone the adjustment of domestic legislation to multilateral disciplines (Ortiz Mena, Chapter 3; Tussie *et al.*, Chapter 4; Motta Veiga and Ventura-Dias, Chapter 5; Echavarría and Gamboa, Chapter 7).

Secondly, even in those policy areas in which unilateral reform was well underway, the actual impact of the 'lock-in' effect should not be overestimated, as countries attempted and were able to keep some margin of maneuver to deal with the new rules. The case of tariffs stands out, as all countries bound tariffs at the WTO well above the applied levels.[7] Actually, some countries have further taken advantage of this remaining maneuvering room. Mexico, for instance, raised tariffs by 3 per cent and 10 per cent in 2001, moving the average applied rate from 14 per cent to 16.5 per cent (Ortiz Mena, Chapter 3). Similarly, Brazil managed to keep higher levels of protection to industrial sectors such as motorcars, electric and electronic goods, and capital goods, which had been the major targets of former decades' industrial and export promotion policies (Motta Veiga and Ventura-Dias, Chapter 5). A similar argument may be extended to other policy areas such as trade relief measures (Tórtora and Tussie, 2003) and export subsidies (Tussie and Lengyel, 1998). Against this backdrop, it is fair to say that the lock-in effect of URAs was not to reduce Latin American countries to bare role-players since it left some room for them to use loopholes or interstices in the rules craftily.

However, the picture is quite different when the analysis move from the above policy areas to several of the so-called 'new issues' of the UR agenda. These issues involve 'non-border' policies and domestic regulatory regimes that were beyond the boundaries of most Latin American countries' unilateral reform programs but on which they had, nonetheless, to take on significant commitments.[8] Moreover, the outcome in these cases was the adoption of specific rules that usually reflected 'best practices' as defined by developed countries or plainly transplanted standards prevalent there. The case of TRIPs is paradigmatic of this kind of UR 'induced' reforms.[9] This agreement's commitments can easily be singled out as a United States' key demand for a successful conclusion of the negotiation round. Except again for Mexico – which by the early 1990s had already brought its intellectual property regime in line with the standards prevailing in high income economies (Ortiz Mena, Chapter3) – Latin American countries had to pass new laws and to set up new institutions in order to fulfill those commitments (Silva, Chapter 2; Tussie *et al.*, Chapter 4; Vaillant and Ventura-Dias, Chapter 6; Echavaría and Gamboa, Chapter 7; Fairlie, Chapter 8). The case of the Agreements on SPS, TBT and Custom Valuation closely mirror developments in TRIPs.

The former discussion about the impact of UR Agreements for Latin American countries raises concerns about the manner in which the WTO works as a platform for their integration in the world trading system. Some of these concerns, such as the challenges those countries face to manage the increasingly complex WTO agenda and how they may enhance the effectiveness of their participation in multilateral negotiations, has been largely addressed elsewhere (see, for instance, Tussie and Glover, 1993; UNCTAD, 2000; Oyejide, 2002; Tussie and Lengyel, 2002). Yet, the discussion also raises concerns over the rule-making process of the WTO, particularly when the issue is addressed from a development rather than just an integration perspective. To put it neatly, the rationale of that process was, on one hand, the expansion of market access and, on the other, the harmonization of a broad range of developing countries' 'behind-the-border' regulatory policies and institutions with the practices existing in their developed counterparts. In this last sense, there was an inherent bias in the WTO process of rule-making towards a particular set of institutional arrangements, with disregard for any careful pondering of the actual development needs in different national settings (Rodrik, 2001; Hoekman, 2002). Of course, the other side of the coin is that developing countries were left with minimal, if any policy autonomy in many 'trade-related' areas to search for and devise home grown rules and institutions to address those needs. This trait of the WTO rule-making process may be challenged on conceptual grounds as it relies on various highly questionable assumptions. The first, which might be called the 'monopoly of knowledge' assumption, is that knowledge about the best policies in critical areas for the working of market economies lies in a few countries, the developed ones, out of the 145 that are members of the WTO. The second, 'universal fitness' assumption is that the policy prescriptions therein established are deemed to work appropriately in every context, no matter local economic, political and social peculiarities. The third assumption, which logically derives from the former two, is that a division of labor exists between countries that are 'thinkers,' and are thus in charge of coining the policy solutions, and those that are merely 'doers,' whose task is to apply the scripts crafted elsewhere. Yet, as the following paragraphs highlight, the WTO rule making may be also challenged on grounds of the distribution of tangible gains and losses it has brought about.

Considering Latin American countries as a whole, the chapters in this book suggest a continuum in which the Agreement on Agriculture (AA) leans towards the positive side, TRIPS clearly falls on the extreme of costs and a more mixed picture prevails in the rest of the agreements. The AA had gathered the greatest expectations regarding gains in market access, although these were only partially realized.[10] The relative success achieved in tariffication of non-tariff barriers and identification of export subsidies is definitely an asset in that it lays the ground for further reform of international trade on agricultural goods. This particularly holds for countries such as Argentina, Uruguay, Brazil, Chile and Colombia, which are highly competitive in world markets for several farm products.[11] Yet, as for developing countries in general, actual gains in market access shrank during the implementation of the agreement as the flexibility and 'dirty tariffication' it allowed enabled countries to get away with minimal tariff reductions (Finger and Schuknetch, 1999). Moreover, because of tariff and subsidy reductions sharply varied across products, benefits were uneven among countries depending largely on their specific export profile. For instance, while market access gains for some of Mexico's largest agricultural exports (e.g. fruits, vegetables and tropical products) were overshadowed by export subsidies, some agricultural products (honey, fresh flowers, avocados, mangos, lemons, coffee, oranges, papayas, onions and cantaloupes) benefited from the AA (Ortiz Mena, Chapter 3).

On the side of costs, nearly absolute consensus exists that the TRIPs agreement left Latin American countries empty-handed.[12] To begin with, gains to be reaped through the overhaul of the domestic normative and institutional architecture governing IPRs – i.e. greater technology transfer and local innovation and increased inflows of FDI – never materialized.[13] Further, anecdotal evidence indicates that post-reform prices rose substantially, particularly in the case of the pharmaceutical sector. This had largely to do with the fact that the new legislation endowed patent rights holders with an overly dominant position in particular market segments while Latin American countries lacked strong competition laws or enforcement capacity. Of course, this also meant that a significant transfer of rents occurred from royalty payers (domestic firms) to patent right holders (international companies).[14] Finally, the TRIPs Agreement has not lessened pressures from the United States over IPRs protection and enforcement in Latin America. Under different allegations (broad compulsory license provisions, omission of data protection requirements, weak enforcement against piracy and counterfeiting of copy right laws) the United States Trade Representative (USTR), following Special 301, has put Argentina and Uruguay in the Priority Watch List and Chile, Peru, Colombia and Venezuela in the Watch List. Particularly in the case of Argentina and Chile, the United States ask for the speeding up of pending patent applications. Given these results, it is hard not to coincide with *The Economist* when in 1851 stated that 'The public will learn that patents are artificial stimuli to improvident exertions; that they cheat people by promising what they cannot perform; that they rarely give security to really good inventions, and elevate into importance a number of trifles ... no possible good can ever come of a Patent Law, however admirably it may be framed' (2002: 13). The Agreement on Subsidies and Countervailing Duties is also deemed costly, even for countries such as Chile and Mexico where export promotion policies and instruments were more attune with WTO disciplines. As stated by Silva (Chapter 2), the impact of the policy changes required by the agreement should not be underestimated in that '... the few instruments that had to be revised were deemed vital for export development, such as the Simplified Export Drawback System [and] the Deferred Payment System for Imports of Capital Goods ...'.

The balance of gains and losses in other policy areas is much more complex, making it difficult to identify clear-cut patterns not only across countries but also across sectors within countries and even across products within the same sector. The distinction between 'export-oriented' *vis-à-vis* 'import-competing' activities provides a fair proxy to individualize the distribution of costs and benefits at the sectoral level. For instance, commitments on market access for manufactured goods benefited, even if modestly, some outward oriented sectors (e.g. beer and spirits, pharmaceuticals and chemicals, computers, furniture and glass in Mexico, textiles in Peru and Colombia, orange juice in Brazil); at the same time, they brought huge adjustment costs to many other sectors formerly sheltered from international competition. On the other hand, the meager improvements resulting from the Antidumping Agreement (AD) to restrict the discretionary use of contingent protection by large importers is a liability for exporting sectors (e.g. steel and orange juice in Brazil, steel, lemons and honey in Argentina, salmon in Chile, cut flowers in Colombia) while an asset for those exposed to heightened competition at home (industrial goods producers, in general).[15] In other cases, however, it is necessary to go beyond the exporter-importer axis to better disentangle the actual distribution of gains and losses. In several production chains – say manufactured leather products –, the so-called 'tariff escalation' resulting from commitments on market access skews gains against final products and in favor of raw materials or low-processed goods (UNCTAD, 2002). Similarly, as is the case in Brazil's and Argentina's automobile production chains, losses for one segment of the production chain (auto parts producers) stemming from tariff reductions or lower local content requirements may be an asset for the following segment (car makers) bidding to have access to inputs at lower international prices. Analysis at a product- or production chain-level, which due to space constrains cannot be taken here, is thus required to get a more accurate and refined picture of the UR gains and losses in these policy areas.

In any case, the former discussion strongly suggests, as many authors stress for developing countries in general (Finger, 2001; Panagariya, 2001; Rodrik, 2001; Hoekman, 2002), that the UR exchange of concessions shortchanged Latin American countries. This is particularly so when results are opened up into market access and 'trade-related' issues (or non-border policies), the two grand negotiation areas addressed in that round. Paraphrasing one author, on their a priori *gain* dimension, market access – where multilateral disciplines essentially accompanied domestic reforms already in course – Latin American countries did not achieve a mercantilist surplus; on the other hand, their concessions in most of the new areas – where domestic reforms were not their choice – have been unrequited (Finger, 2001). Moreover, it should be borne in mind that what they gave in these new areas is qualitatively different as WTO disciplines on IPRs and standards concern the structure of the economy and its institutional underpinnings. These facts make concerns over the rationale of WTO rule making even stronger, helping to explain why such dimension has become under stiffer scrutiny and calls for some sort of redefinition.

At the same time, the discussion also underscores that an intricate and not necessarily equitable distributional game of gains and losses took place within each country, in which the interests of many actors were at stake. In this sense, 'trade policy is inherently a redistributive instrument whereby interests among sectors and between winners and losers within a sector will be at odds. The trade-offs must be clarified and negotiated so that compromises are allowed to emerge during rather than after the process when compliance is socially and politically costly and lack of compliance leads to international disputes which bear financial as well as credibility costs' (Tussie, 2003b, p. 9). This squarely places on the spotlight the domestic process through which commitments are decided, particularly its fairness in terms of interest representation and its capacity to device development-sensitive negotiating proposals.

The public–private framework of trade policy decisions: feeble bridges and institutional lags

The interaction between the public sector and socio-economic actors in Latin American countries around multilateral trade negotiations shows common trends with some national peculiarities.[16] A first striking trait of that interaction is its rather low level of institutionalization. That is, no particular formal instances of exchange and collaboration have been created either through legal means or under the initiative of public authorities or private actors. The only mild exceptions to this trend are the cases of Chile and Colombia; there, the Committee of Private Sector Participation (created in the late 1980s to foster the interplay between the government and business organizations on bilateral trade negotiations) and Technical Committees were respectively designated to provide a permanent channel of public-private exchange of information and discussion on multilateral trade issues (Silva, Chapter 2; Echavarría and Gamboa, Chapter 7). Both cases, however, lacked clear-cut working principles and rules of engagement and fell short of fueling an effective involvement of socio-economic actors and generating an institutional space for meaningful deliberation.

It is noteworthy that this poor record of formal institutional innovations contrasts to a large extent with the experience around other recent international trade negotiations, particularly the Free Trade Agreement of the Americas (FTAA). Indeed, these negotiations have triggered several institutional experiments at the national level, more strikingly in Peru and Brazil. In the former, the Chamber of Commerce created the FTAA–Peru Commission as an open forum gathering businessmen, academics and the most important unions. Its structure mirrors the FTAA, being thus organized along similar working groups (Fairlie Reynoso, Chapter 8). In Brazil, the Brazilian Business Coalition was born, bringing together business associations from manufacturing, resource based and services industries (Motta Veiga and Ventura-Dias, Chapter 5). These novel institutional spaces have been quite successful to coordinate and consolidate business positions on different issues of the FTAA agenda, and to generate a quite effective avenue for economic actors to voice their interests and opinions. In any case, two caveats are in order regarding these experiences. On one hand, those institutional channels of participation were not the result of any concrete opening of domestic avenues by governments but a by-product of the incorporation of 'civil society' into the hemispheric forum.[17] On the other hand, none of these experiments were born with the specific aim of developing new, more fruitful institutional channels of public–private interaction but of articulating private sector interests and priorities; therefore, the fact that they actually helped to open those channels has occurred rather by default than by design.

Now, the paucity of institutionalized patterns of participation does not mean the absence of interaction at all. To the contrary, as documented by all the chapters in this book, the active engagement of Latin American countries in the UR spurred the emergence of informal channels for civil society involvement in the process to define negotiating positions. Of course, the particular configuration, scope and dynamics of those channels in each national setting varied. Just to mention two examples, in Colombia the government adopted in 1991 a 'working system' or 'linking strategy' with business sectors that focused on the establishment of permanent communications and coordination on multilateral trade issues. The system provided a discussion ground for the crafting of negotiating positions that even included the treatment of technical aspects (Echavarría and Gamboa, Chapter 7). In contrast with this quasi-formal mechanism of interaction, informal channels of involvement in Argentina rarely went beyond discontinued and case by case exchanges fueled to some extent by interpersonal knowledge. Further, those exchanges fluctuated depending on the phase (presentation of proposals, elaboration of lists of commitments, etc.) of the negotiation process (Tussie *et al.*, Chapter 4).

Yet, even in the cases in which informal mechanisms were stronger and more systematic, they were not an appropriate substitute for institutionalized modes of interaction. Their usual lack of principles of ample participation, clear rules of engagement and effective procedural criteria was a fertile ground for the development of quite opaque, biased and discretion-prone patterns of interaction. Indeed, in virtually all Latin American countries, the strongest business associations – i.e. those more resourceful, better organized and endowed with professional cadres – became the preferential, if not exclusive interlocutor of government authorities (see, for instance, Silva, Chapter, 2; Ortiz Mena, Chapter 3; Tussie *et al.*, Chapter 4; and Motta Veiga and Ventura-Dias, Chapter 5). In other words, access to informal channels was to a greater or lesser extent contingent on the lobbying capacity of business interest representatives. Government capacity to 'fine tune' the involvement of socio-economic agents across issues or moments of the negotiations is also part of the same picture, even in cases where informal mechanisms were relatively more developed and consolidated (Echavarría and Gamboa, Chapter 7). It is not surprising, therefore, that the lack of participation of other stakeholders, such as unions, consumers and the Congress, has usually been the rule.

Although the issue cannot be examined at length here, it is worth mentioning some of the complex blend of factors, both institutional and conjunctural, underlying the above picture. There are, to begin with, organizational and functional traits of the public sector that create disincentives for the development of thicker and more stable public–private links; among these, the excessive rotation of bureaucratic cadres, the lack of coordination among public agencies and even jurisdictional struggles among them over the control of the negotiating process have been highly consequential. On the other side, the lower priority many sectors of the business community gave to the WTO *vis-à-vis* other negotiation fora (e.g. subregional agreements), different evaluation across sectors of the issues at stake, the atomization of interest representation and the growing number of foreign actors on scene (particularly multinational companies in public services and manufacturing) have also had a significant weight (Silva, Chapter 2; Ortiz Mena, Chapter 3; Tussie *et al.*, Chapter 4; Motta Veiga and Ventura-Dias, Chapter 5; Vaillant and Ventura-Dias, Chapter 6; Fairlie Reynoso, Chapter 8).[18] Finally, well-entrenched habits and rules of the game in the domestic political-institutional context have conspired against the emergence of more open and transparent patterns of participation in that they only tend to integrate that part of society structured along corporatist lines or patronage webs, condemning the rest to exclusion (Prats, 2000).

At least two critical and intertwined consequences for the fairness and efficacy of the decision-making process on multilateral trade issues stem from the above 'institutional deficit.' First, biased and opaque institutional arrangements for the involvement of socio-economic agents mean that both the entitlement and actual capacity to participate are at stake. Those agreements therefore run against the sense of 'ownership' stakeholders may achieve over the policy options there devised, obviously hampering the building of a minimally appropriate degree of consensus on decisions and undermining their legitimacy. This is particularly relevant in view that the weaving of negotiating positions has become a daunting political task, as decisions imply an important distributional game. That is, negotiating positions involve international trade-offs across a mounting number of trade issues as well as domestic trade-offs across and within sectors. From the standpoint of private sector's interests, who gets what is thus inseparable from engagement and leverage. In turn, from the standpoint of the public sector, the challenge of outlining the 'national interest' is enormous, as decision-making needs to aggregate a myriad of divergent interests. In this sense, prevailing patterns of public–private interaction in Latin American seem ill suited to build common grounds out of different, even antagonistic concerns.

Secondly, the dilemmas for national decision-making on multilateral trade issues are compounded by an increasingly complex and dynamic agenda, which turns the configuration of trade-offs fuzzy and highly volatile. In other words, decision-making has to deliver in the face of, to use a telling phrase, '...an open ended series of moments of choice which demand agile responses, less adept to the strategic planning world in which most policy-makers have been trained' (Tussie, 2003, p. 7). This casts additional doubts on the capability of prevailing patterns of public-private interaction in Latin America to help to produce adequate and timely responses. Indeed, as in many other macro and micro-level domains where similar challenges and needs for problem solving exist, those dilemmas put a premium on institutional arrangements suited to generate and stock knowledge on workable solutions (see for instance Sabel, 1994; Lengyel, 2000). In essence, as the existing evidence teaches and will be further discussed below, those arrangements build upon principles of democratic participation and operative rules (on information exchange, knowledge-sharing, etc.) that are not easily found throughout Latin America. They rest, in turn, on the assumption that the knowledge of actors is necessarily limited but, at the same time, can be substantially enriched through an open and collective sustained discussion.

As in the case of rule making in the WTO, the pattern of private- public interaction in the region also calls for improvement. In the spirit of avoiding pre-ordained and 'magic-bullet' solutions, moves in that direction will surely need to be sensitive to the institutional and political specificities of each country. To address these critical questions is the concern of the closing section.

Looking ahead: it is about rules!

The analysis conducted in this chapter has so far underscored some fundamental shortcomings in the WTO process of building the rules that govern the exchange of trade concessions at the multilateral level as well as in the national-level institutional practices through which negotiating positions are built in Latin America. In this section, both aspects are considered not in isolation but as integral parts of the multilevel institutional architecture governing trade relations. Moreover, the argument to be sketched here advances some ideas to reform that architecture in which changes in the multilateral and national dimensions are logically connected and bridged in practice by further institutional renewal in subregional trade agreements.

Reform at the top

Arguments stressing the need to introduce changes in the WTO rule making system are driven by the same concern, namely, how to make that system more development-consistent. Yet, the agreement barely goes beyond that, as positions about means considerably diverge.

On one side, sophisticated free traders propose what might be called a 'horizontal de-coupling.' This essentially involves re-focusing the WTO purview on a traditional market access agenda that includes all products – goods and services – while transferring the crafting of 'behind-the-border' regulatory polices to other international bodies (e.g. the International Organization for Standardization [ISO], the Codex Alimentarius Commission [CAC], the World Intellectual Property Organization [WIPO], the International Labor Organization [ILO] and so on). Developing countries would obtain a twofold gain through this move: a greater likelihood that 'good practices' are defined out of the high specialization of the agencies involved as well as, unlike in the WTO, the lack of enforcement to comply with the rules arrived at.[19]. The scheme is complemented by increased technical assistance to developing countries in order to reduce the resource and knowledge gaps impinging on their ability to meet the standards and norms agreed upon (Henson *et al.*, 2001; Wilson, 2001; Hoekman, 2002).[20] Countries' self-interest would be the driving force moving forward this more cooperative process.

Developmentalists propose, on the other side, a 'vertical de-coupling.' The central idea here is also to remove the discussion of 'trade-related' policies from the ambit of the WTO through mechanisms allowing developing countries to leak out from multilateral disciplines whenever their developmental needs required it and provided that such a move is a social choice, i.e. that broad support exists among all concerned parties after due deliberation.[21] The strengthening of the WTO monitoring and surveying role would ensure, in turn, that op-outs are made for the right reasons and in compliance with established procedures. The WTO would also carry out the fundamental task of rendering the resulting policy alternatives compatible. This reform would benefit developing countries by expanding their policy autonomy while providing enough reinsurance that the opt-out option is not abusively employed (Amsdem, 2000; Rodrik, 2001).

Both arguments go a long way to help developing countries to break the logjam in which the WTO grand bargain placed them, i.e. to give up policy autonomy in several pivotal development areas in exchange for increased market access in developed countries. They thus lay the ground for a greater institutional diversity that challenges, in one author's words, the 'one size fit all'[22]or the harmonization assumption informing the WTO rules. Yet, for different reasons, these arguments go halfway. The former still sees the task of consensus-building about rules as internationally centralized, even when moving it outside the boundaries of the WTO. Additionally, it may also be questioned whether the lack of enforcement in the process and top-down technical assistance are more relevant than domestic learning-enhancing institutional innovations for developing countries to fully take advantage of the more cooperative spirit. The developmentalist account, in turn, while stressing decentralization, only marginally addresses the issue of how the capacity of those countries to generate relevant indigenous knowledge may be harnessed. The unwanted result could be what Hirschman (1973) labeled a 'low equilibrium trap' – quite common in different Latin American policy fields – that aborts any attempt of reform favoring greater maneuvering room for developing countries on 'trade-related' issues. To put it shortly, those countries are unable to develop strong proposals of their own vintage – in the sense of addressing both their development needs and a deeper integration in the world trading system – as the existing rule-making system severely constrains their possibility to search for and experiment with new alternatives; developed countries, on the other hand, are reluctant to acquiesce to looser rules as they find that developing countries generally fail to advance such proposals. Therefore, in order to enhance its prospects to prosper, such a reform needs to simultaneously overcome the rigidities of the multilateral rule-making process and the domestic institutional barriers to knowledge accumulation.

A reform scheme along these lines would start where developmentalists do, but would also redefine some of their operational criteria. It would advocate a delegation 'downstream' to developing countries of the responsibility for devising proposals in the 'trade-related' fields now handled through the centralized and astringent rule-making process of the WTO. This could adopt the concrete form of a 'standstill' on new issues (such as environment) or on issues in which commitments have not still been made (e.g. the Singapore Agenda) or a 'roll-back' of some of the existing agreements deemed more detrimental for developing countries' interests (e.g. TRIPS and SCM Agreements). Of course, to become credible and thus more feasible, this relaxation of constraints at the top cannot be so lax as to give a carte blanche to those countries. Rather, it needs to be balanced with procedural reassurances that their enlarged policy autonomy will be geared to produce proposals in which development priorities are given due weight but not at the expense of integration efforts. This means that the enlarged room for experimentation it allows – which turns the 'monopoly of knowledge' and 'universal fitness' assumptions of existing rules upside down – needs to be somehow fenced by a new set of rules that include both inducements and enforcement. In practice this can be done by requiring, first, that decisions on stand-stills and roll-backs be duly informed both in terms of the potential or actual damage of the issue at stake for developing countries; secondly, that assessments to that end be subject to public discussion at the domestic level with the mandatory participation of all stakeholders, so that to avoid that deliberation be captured by sectoral interests, in particular those that would benefit from the decision in question; thirdly that developing countries establish a cooperative, workable mechanism of self-monitoring in which progress can be compared and pondered on the basis of both procedural and substantive benchmarks; finally, that a sunset clause be established by which the return to the status quo is automatic if developing countries fail to deliver the proposals in question after a given time-frame – say ten years.[23]

It could surely be argued that advanced countries would not be ready to accept a rule-based arrangement like this. To be sure, it means for them to move away from the largely beneficial traditional approach to make rules and nail commitments, and to accept a qualitatively different negotiation logic in which they have to concede today while eventual rewards are far in the future. Seen from this standpoint, the situation for developing countries would be just the opposite, i.e. they suspend disciplines that have been costly while committing themselves to distant and uncertain concessions. However, in the international mood surrounding current multilateral trade negotiations, such an arrangement could be also deemed as a win–win option. In this sense, negotiations launched at Doha are facing significant obstacles to move forward, in particular because it has been so far cumbersome to give concrete meaning to the discursive appeal of the name of the development round.[24] The prospects of fulfilling the 2005 deadline to conclude the round are thus highly uncertain, if not bleak. At the same time, this arrangement would be an opportunity, but also a challenge, for developing countries to build credit-deserving negotiating proposals that allow for divergent institutional practices, more suited to disentangle their development problems, without returning to past positions of detachment. Finally, from the perspective of the multilateral trading system as a whole, this provisory arrangement might lay the ground for a more enduring reform of the WTO rule-making by proving itself on the road to be able to deliver a more balanced and widespread distribution of benefits.

In any case, as noted before, this reform at the top is not going to have sustainable pay-off for Latin American countries if it does not go hand-in-hand with substantial institutional re-engineering at home. The key and challenging task in this sense is to introduce reforms in the decision-making process on multilateral trade issues that enhances its capacity to learn and to apply the new knowledge to the crafting of negotiating proposals that meet the development/integration yardstick.

Reform at the bottom

As shown in the section on 'the public–private framework of trade policy decisions', the record of institutional innovations in Latin American geared to make decision-making on multilateral trade negotiations more participatory is rather poor. On the other hand, the existing evidence strongly suggests that when they occurred, as in Peru and Brazil, results were largely positive, in that communications among private actors improved and new channels enabling them to voice their opinions emerged. Equally relevant, it should not be overlooked that these experiences worked to some extent as institutional learning spaces. As noted by Motta Veiga and Ventura-Dias (Chapter 5) in the case of Brazil, '...although at the beginning [the business position] was convergent with the defensive position of the Brazilian bureaucracy, it has gradually been evolving towards a more strategic position in which both defensive as well as assertive areas are identified.'

This outcome should not be surprising at all, as evidence from many other policy-fields (*World Development*, 1996; Sabel, 1996; Tendler, 1997; McDermott, 2000) highlights the high potential of those types of arrangements to generate synergies across the public–private divide that enhances the conditions for learning and improve performance. Scholarly analysis has also discussed at length the multiplicity of factors (economic, social, political, institutional) favoring or hindering their emergence and long-term sustainability (Evans, 1996, 1997). In any case, a key lesson this analysis brings about is that, even in contexts that are hostile to those arrangements, the rules governing public–private interactions are usually crucial to draw the line between success and failure.

As in the case of reform at the top, how such an arrangement could look like can only be addressed here in a sketchy way. The central idea in this regard is the construction of rule-based participatory instances for decision-making that bring together relevant public officials and socio-economic actors with the aim of enabling interactive and iterative learning and, therefore, nurturing the capacities for collective problem-solving. Rules of engagement and deliberation are an obvious building block in this task in that they structure the participation of actors, set the tone of their relations and define criteria for assessment and redefinition of positions.

In Latin America, as already noted, more than one state agency is usually involved in decisions on multilateral trade issues and civic participation is narrow and biased in favor of the more resourceful. Therefore, the rules of engagement would need to ensure, to begin with, that public officials' involvement cut across functional boundaries and that both the sectoral and geographical representation of private actors' interests is as encompassing as possible. Yet, as entitlement cannot be equated with actual participation, additional aspects may affect the effectiveness of those rules. In this sense, motivation needs not to be a crucial obstacle, even when WTO negotiations are in general a more remote concern for private actors than negotiations in other fora. This is so because the interest of an increasing number of economic agents (particularly those normally excluded from decisions) in those negotiations is on the rise as they are feeling the brunt of commitments made there and know that have to learn more about the issues at stake. Further, as the experience in the FTAA teaches, when business calls for greater participation, other actors such as unions and non-governmental organizations (NGOs) readily follow suit (Botto, forthcoming). Motivation, however, might well not be enough, as engagement could entail significant opportunity costs for some actors – especially those heavily burdened by the day-to-day management of their specific affairs. The government could thus help to level the playing field by making access to the relevant information more transparent and easier.

Public initiatives could, however, do more to stimulate active engagement and the disposition of actors to share their partial and complementary knowledge, so that to enable mutual and incremental learning and collective tackling of problems. Subsidization of participation and of the acquisition of lacking skills (through, for instance, training and support from external consultants) may be important, provided that it is tied – through adjustable rules of mutual oversight and assessment – to the disposition of actors to learn and make the new knowledge public. In such a way, the risk that those incentives lack transparency or are diverted to other ends, providing thus fertile ground for clientelism or capture by special interests, is substantially minimized (Reddy and Sabel, 2002).[25] Needless to say, this structure, well endowed to become the locus of a network of formerly scattered public and private actors, would be a masquerade if the principles and rules governing participation and interactions stop at the gate of final decisions. That is, whatever the specific mechanism adopted to make them (say, consensus or majority vote), those decisions have to be informed by open debate and meticulous review by all interested parties.

Ideally, the upshot of this process would be a negotiation proposal in a given area (e.g. TRIPS or SPS) that contains the main elements (even at the level of standards of behavior, criteria for performance assessment, etc.) to fill a domestic policy vacuum or to improve existing policy regimes. Indeed, the embededness of the process in a network of relevant state and social actors and its reliance on a open and systematic exchange of information and ideas substantially increases the likelihood that the resulting option both gives due attention to local circumstances and embodies the better alternatives discovered.

Again, skeptics may content that institutional innovations of this sort are an up-hill task in Latin American countries, where practices of patronage and even corruption are rampant and people suffers the lack of accountability of both public and private actions. In this context, how much room does exist for participatory governance structures that seek to tape on existing resources for more socially valuable uses by redefining patterns of public–private relations and allowing the 'disfranchised' a strong voice in the construction of policy proposals? After all, that kind of structures does not abound in the region. Some reasons for optimism however exist if those changes are seen against the backdrop of the reform of the WTO rule-making system above proposed. Indeed, such reform would require that developing countries carry out domestic institutional changes that expand stakeholders' participation in trade policy decisions in order to benefit from the greater latitude for policy-making it affords. In other words, even if the prospects of getting better results are not an incentive powerful enough as to trigger those institutional innovations, the 'conditionality' included in the new multilateral rules could be a good substitute to get the task in motion. A the same time, such conditionality is not as intrusive and constraining as to require that local institutional innovations follow a given specific design beyond basic principles of participation, let alone that the content of debate is confined to pre-ordained parameters.

Subregional agreements through new lenses

By the mid-1980s, analysis of the relationship between multilateralism and regionalism in academic and policy circles revolved around whether the latter would be a building or stumbling block for the former. The key question was if regional agreements would foster trade liberalization or would become the fortress' walls, as many claim it was the case in the 'first generation' of integration efforts in Latin America during the 1960s and 1970s. The question was settled a decade later, when it became clear that 'open regionalism,' in the sense of an outwardly oriented model of integration, was the dominant trend throughout the region (ECLAC, 1994).

A second, equally relevant question about that relationship was whether open regionalism would serve, as aimed and envisaged by most of its mentors, as a learning platform that allowed its members to better play in the 'mayor league,' the multilateral trade game. The answer in this case is that, at best, there is still a long road ahead, particularly when the assessment is narrowed down to the generation of policy alternatives in the trade-related areas that are thorny under WTO rules. This does not mean that some learning has not occurred, as Ventura (Chapter 1) rightly points out. Yet, this learning was piecemeal and rarely crystallized in consistent home-grown initiatives in those areas. The examples of Mercosur and the Andean Community of Nations (ACN) serve to illustrate the point, as they share this pitfall even when adopting different institutional designs – NAFTA-like in the case of Mercosur and EU-like in the case of the ACN. In Mercosur, for instance, Decisions on export subsidies, SPS and trade in services and the Protocols on IPRs virtually duplicate the templates established in the UR, while in the ACN the same happened in IPRs, SPS and support policies. In this sense, the enactment of the WTO agreements in those fields as domestic laws in the member-countries largely defined the boundaries for debate and negotiations within the subregional spaces.[26]

Within the framework of the former ideas to reform the WTO rule-making, subregional trade agreements not only would have an opportunity to remedy this situation but also their commitment to do so would be called for. On one hand, the new set of multilateral rules would require that countries establish mechanisms to monitor the proposals they craft as a result of their enlarged freedom of initiative. On the other, in order to properly work, the new rule-based system needs to avoid being paralyzed or subverted by an overload of proposals. Some intermediate instance of coordination and aggregation of national initiatives is, therefore, almost an imperative. Subregional trade agreements could well be fertile ground for that, provided that they are willing to undertake learning-encouraging institutional reforms.

How could this be made operative? Drawing from forceful arguments made with regards to particular policy fields (Sabel *et al.*, 1999; Charny, 2000), the first step would be to constitute independent entities within the subregional institutional structure in each of the policy areas subject to standstills or roll-backs at the multilateral level as coordinating and convening instances of the proposals devised in the member-countries. Independent experts from those countries as well as from regional (e.g. ECLAC, IADB, specialized networks) and international organizations (e.g. UNCTAD, World Bank) would integrate those agencies. Their programmatic criterion would be to foster development in the region and their mission would be to become the focal point of a process of collaborative and structured competition among national positions whose final result were a collective proposal that brings consistency among, and improves the individual ones. As in reform at the top and at the bottom, the rules governing this process would be essential for it to be workable and bring tangible achievements.

The starting point in that sense would be the development by the convening entity of a set of benchmarking criteria for the comparison and evaluation of national proposals along substantial and procedural performance dimensions. This benchmarking would provide initial standards by which participants could contrast and ponder local norms and practices without attempting to impose a unique formula on national institutional arrangements. If, for instance, TRIPs were the issue at stake, those benchmarking criteria could include dimensions such as medicine prices, market competition, technological transfer as well as mechanisms of monitoring of results and enforcement. Transparency would be, of course, a key precondition for the fairness of the process but, equally important, to turn it in a source of useful information and ideas for the improvement of national proposals. The convening entity should be thus in charge of building a data base on criteria for assessment, proposals submitted and results as well as of making that information fully accessible for the public.

The goal is that, over a certain span of time, several rounds of assessment and redefinition are set in motion, in which countries use the new knowledge acquired to enhance local arrangements and the proposals devised therein. In practice, this would imply that in each step of the process, a new phase of debate takes place at the national level – under the rules already set through reform at the bottom. This learning-encouraging local exchange could be reinforced by subregional instances of exchange among national authorities, in which the role of already existing institutional ambits (e.g. the *Grupo Mercado Común* in Mercosur or the General Secretariat in the ACN) could be fine-tuned to that end. In this sense, the risk that debates at this level be captured by special interest is not smaller than at national level. Therefore, the public disclosure of discussions should, at least, be established to avoid or minimize that risk.

It is crucial to note that assessment and redefinition not only takes place with regards to national proposals. If the process wishes to really elicit incremental but continuous improvement, the benchmarking criteria cannot be a fix target. Rather, they would also have to be upgraded *pari-passu* with changes in the national proposals so that they push for further improvements. This means that learning in this process is a two-way road: countries have at their disposal clear subregional yardsticks to assess where they stand and a stock of new knowledge to strengthen their standing; the convening entity, in turn, may draw on country proposals to gradually adjust criteria and standards. The expected final result is a collectively constructed set of rules and procedures that all member countries can make, to a large extent, their own.

The inevitable question is, again, whether the conditions for these institutional innovations are present or not within the space of the subregional trade agreements. In keeping with the optimistic position so far adopted, the answer is that some incentives exist to give them a shot. First, there is a feeling across Latin America that subregional agreements need to achieve a new impulse, if they are to play a more decisive role in the development of the region. This is particularly so in view that, among other challenges, considerable uncertainties stem not only from ongoing trade negotiations at the multilateral level but also from the determination of the United States to struck bilateral free trade agreements throughout the hemisphere. The 'more-of-the-same-approach' in these fronts is not likely to bring about different results than it has so far done. In addition, inasmuch as they sound workable, those innovations might also contribute to nurture the political meaning of subregional integration initiatives for their participants. As emphasized by Motta Veiga (2002), the value of Mercosur for Brazil is political and strategic as much as economic in that if the bloc can organize itself to negotiate collectively in trade negotiations its members stand a better chance of achieving more favorable terms, such as flexible scheduling for tariff reduction, regulatory leniency, and support for social and economic programs that assist less competitive industries and groups affected by economic transition. Not less important, the institutional innovations here proposed could well provide a way out to overcome the highly sensitive dilemma of reconciling national sovereignty with supranational instances of decision-making. Indeed, they would entail that the partial sacrifices of sovereignty implied by subregional convening may prevent a deeper erosion – at least in certain policy fields – resulting from the lack any coordination at all. Finally, countries may realize that the challenges of being exposed to the push and pull of the competition may be worth facing *vis-à-vis* the risks of forfeiting new sources for improvement and going along. The situation of the ACN countries during the 1999 Ministerial Meeting of Seattle is highly indicative of this last point: while they had an opportunity to coordinate joint action on several issues where their interests concurred (e.g. investments, competition policy), countries acted separately even in the unique policy field (TRIPs) in which they had been able to tentatively draw a common initiative (Fairlie Reynoso, Chapter 8).

The argument has come, thus, to full circle. It has attempted to put forward an alternative path to build the rules shaping trade negotiations at the multilateral level and their outcome. Each of its pieces make more sense when seen as constitutive and interconnected elements of a three-level process of reform, each one with its intricacies and challenges. In any case, it offers some hints to deal with the hard choices (integration vs. development, open vs. expeditious principles of decision making, national sovereignty vs. supranational coordination) to which Latin American countries, and probably many other developing economies, are supposedly doomed. Of course, the argument is just preliminary and needs refinement and expansion, but still offers some clues on how to move away from 'dirigism,' whatever its source, without falling into naïve voluntarism. In this light, it is an attempt to contribute from Latin America to the efforts of a crescent epistemic community to imagine workable and more equitable alternatives to global governance problems.

Notes

1. For an interesting account of the ambiguities concerning the Doha Declaration see 'The Doha Declaration's Meaning Depends on the Reader,' *Bridges*, Year 5; no. 9 (November/December 2001).
2. For extremely stimulating ideas about a learning centered approach to development see Reddy and Sabel (2002). For an account that places institutional diversity and innovation as crucial elements of a novel global trade regime see Rodrik (2001).
3. For a very interesting account that looks at the shortcomings of some of the WTO 'trade-related' agreements through the lenses of the Dispute Settlement Body Reports, see Drache and Froese (2002).
4. As generously documented by the chapters in this book, virtually all countries considered had by then drastically reduced both tariffs and non-tariff barriers. Tariff dispersion and escalation had also been reduced.
5. This sets apart Latin American countries from many other developing nations. As Michalopoulos (1999a) has pointed out, countries such as Hong Kong and Singapore, where applied tariff rates are low, have bound 38 per cent and 66 per cent of their tariff schedule. The proportion is even lower in other countries, e.g. India, Pakistan and Nigeria.
6. Additional information to the one provided by the chapters in this volume may be found in Integration and Trade Steering Committee (1998).
7. In the case of Argentina, Brazil and Uruguay the tariff ceiling consolidated was 35 per cent, with some minimal exceptions below and above, while the average applied tariffs were 14 per cent, 12 per cent and 12 per cent respectively (Tussie *et al.*, Chapter 4; Motta Veiga and Ventura-Dias, Chapter 5; Vaillant and Ventura-Dias, Chapter 6). In Mexico, the average applied tariff was 14 per cent while the weighted average bound rate under the URAs was 40.3 per cent (Ortiz Mena, Chapter 3). In turn, the values for Peru were 32 per cent and 19 per cent (except for 20 tariff lines subject to variable specific duties) and for Chile 25 per cent and 11 per cent. Finally, Colombia and Venezuela bound tariffs at 35 per cent whereas average applied tariffs were 13 per cent and 14 per cent respectively. For further analysis of this issue see also Michalopoulos (1999). It should be borne in mind that the margin between applied and bound tariffs is not applicable to partners in free trade zones.
8. Some authors have argued that the grand bargain between developed and developing countries at the UR actually was that the latter would take substantial commitments in the 'new areas' while the former, in exchange, would open up in areas of particular export interest to developing countries such as agriculture and textiles/clothing. See, for instance, Finger and Nogués, 2000; Rodrik, 2001)
9. See Maskus (2000) for a comprehensive review of analyses on the issue.
10. Obviously, these gains should be viewed as opportunities for a broader insertion which have to be seized in practice. This depends, in turn, on a mix of complex factors relating to both the working of markets (e.g. consumer preferences, distribution channels) and macro and microlevel factors shaping the competitive standing of goods (e.g., exchange rate, support policies, firm strategies and so on).

11. Not by coincidence, these countries are part of the Cairns Group, a coalition formed in the UR by agricultural exporters to bring the sector under GATT disciplines. The group proposed 'lines of negotiation' (for instance, over subsidies or export credits) that pushed for liberalization of agricultural trade while accommodating the key particular interests of its members.
12. This holds even when the relevance of TRIPs matters differs across these countries. For instance, while the protection of pharmaceutical patent rights is a common concern, the traditional knowledge debate is particular consequential for the Andean countries (See Fairlie Reynoso, Chapter 9).
13. As for FDI, the evidence so far points to that the opposite could be the case. In Chile, for example, most foreign subsidiaries in the pharmaceutical industry opted to leave the country and source from abroad after an 'upgraded' IPRs legislation was passed (Finger and Nogués, 2000).
14. Estimates for Argentina (Finger and Nogués, 2000) suggest that such transfer amounted to one-eighth of total expenditure on pharmaceuticals in 1999, i.e. about US$425 million in a market whose size amounted to about US$4 billion that year.
15. Actually, countries such as Mexico, Argentina, Brazil and Colombia have become heavy users of trade relief measures, and particular AD, to protect producers operating in their domestic markets. Further, this question goes far beyond the North–South dimension, as many of those measures have been applied against neighbors that, because of geographical proximity, are able to benefit most from trade liberalization. Of course, the 'gains' accruing from those measures require an active government intervention to materialize. It is not surprising therefore that the use of AD measures in such countries has been frequently subject to, and the result of, strong lobbying activities by different segments of the private sector (Ortiz Mena, Chapter 3; Tussie *et al.*, Chapter 4; Motta Veiga and Ventura-Dias, Chapter 5).
16. The focus of the analysis in this section refers to the public–private interaction in the process of the national agenda setting and definition of the negotiating strategy. It does not address the involvement of socio-economic actors during the implementation of the UR agreements as a result of provisions there contained making such participation legally necessary. This is mainly the case in the field of trade relief measures, where the URAs set up requirements concerning the representativeness of the applicants seeking protection or directly mandate the participation of some stakeholders in the mandatory process of investigation that precedes the application of one of those measures (e.g. representatives of consumer organizations in cases in which the product under investigation is sold at the retail level).
17. Particularly in the case of FTAA negotiations, entrepreneurs have nucleated in the American Business Forum, which was created in 1995 and meets two or three days before Ministers do and voice their opinion on every item under negotiation.
18. For interesting and comprehensive analyses of these issues see Jordana and Ramió (2002) and Aggarwal *et al.* (2002).
19. As one author has put it, '...cooperation is driven by the self-interest of countries, and implementation is gradual, depending on national circumstances and capacity,...There is generally no binding dispute settlement mechanism or threat of sanctions for non-implementation' (Hoekman, 2002,

p. 14). For an interesting discussion on enforcement vs. cooperation as mechanisms to get compliance, see Talberg (2002).

20. Perhaps the most important initiative to this end is the adoption by the High Level Meeting on Integrated Initiative for Least Developed Countries Trade Development of an Integrated Framework for trade-related technical assistance to support those countries. It is anchored on the assessment of needs by the countries themselves, which are them examined by the participating international agencies (IMF, UNCTAED, World Bank, ITC, UNDP and WTO) in order to design a comprehensive program of technical assistance. The WTO itself provides support, focused on training and the dissemination of information.
21. Rodrik (2001), for instance proposes an expanded 'safeguard clause' enabling an 'op-out' possibility.
22. See Hoekman (2002).
23. This time limit may look excessive and could, of course, be subject to discussion. It looks short, however, when compared with the one – the year 2020 – proposed by some free traders to get a Jubilee that eliminates protection on agricultural products. See, for instance, Bhagwati (2002).
24. To a large extent, these obstacles delve on how to redefine Special and Differential Treatment in a way that goes beyond the different time-frame to fulfil commitments granted to developed and developing countries in the UR. This, in turn, has to do with the rigidity of the WTO rules that are discussed in this chapter (See Tórtora, 2002; Botto *et al.*, 2003).
25. The availability of funds for these incentives should not be highly problematic, even in national economies plagued with severe budget constraints. Current soft loans from international organizations (such as the Inter-American Development Bank [IADB]) to many Latin American countries, directed to the institutional strengthening of their external trade policy, may be redirected at least in part to those ends.
26. The WTO rules had also a more subtle but equally relevant impact, namely, they set up the discursive parameters to conduct trade conversations in those spaces as GATT language (world trade's lingua franca) became the language to speak on trade matters.

Bibliography

Abuggatás, L. And S. Stephenson (2003) 'Liberalization of Trade in Services: Options and Implications' in D. Tussie (ed.), *Trade Negotiations in Latin America: Problems and Prospects* (New York: Palgrave Macmillan).

Abramovitz, M. (1986) 'Catching up, Forging Ahead, and Falling Behind', *Journal of Economic History*, Vol. 46, No, 2.

ACN (Andean Community of Nations) (2002) 'Exportaciones intercomunitarias 2001', available at http://www.comunidadandina.org/estadisticas/expint2001.htm, consulted 20 March 2002.

Aggarwal, V., R. Espach and J. Tulchin (eds)(forthcoming), *Regional and Transregional Trade Strategies in Latin America.*

Agosin, M. (1997) *Trade and Growth in Chile: Past Performance and Future Prospects* (Santiago de Chile: ECLAC International Trade Unit) LC/R. 1782.

——and R. Alvarez (2000) *Políticas Hacia la Inversión Extranjera Directa: Elementos para su Diseño. Informe Final* (Santiago de Chile: Economics Department of the University of Chile) July.

——and R. Ffrench-Davis (1998) 'La inserción internacional de Chile: Experiencias recientes y desafíos' in R. Cortázar y J. Vial (eds), *Construyendo Opciones: Propuestas Económicas y Sociales para el Cambio de Siglo* (Santiago de Chile: CIEPLAN-DOLMEN).

——and R. French Davis (2002) 'Trade Specialization and Economic Growth in Latin America', presented at ECLAC–World Bank Seminar on Globalization, Santiago de Chile, 6–8 March.

Alba Vega, C. (1996a) 'Los empresarios y el estado durante el salinismo', *Foro Internacional*, Vol. 36, Nos. 1–2, January–June.

——(1996b) 'La coordinadora de organizaciones empresariales de comercio exterior: Un caso de cooperación entre el sector público y el privado en México' in O. Muñoz (ed.), *Estado, Empresarios, Instituciones: Estrategias para la Transformación Productiva* (Santiago de Chile: CEPAL/CIEPLAN).

——(n.d.) 'Las empresas y el sector privado mexicano en el siglo XX' (Mexico, DF: El Colegio de México Centro de Estudios Internacionales), mimeo.

Alburquerque, M. (1994) 'Implicancias del factor laboral en un eventual tratado de libre comercio con Estados Unidos', *Programa de Estudios Prospectivos Working Paper*, Santiago.

Amsden, Alice (2000) 'Industrialization Under New WTO Law' presented at the High-Level Round Table on Trade and Development, UNCTAD, Bangkok, 12 February.

Anichini, J., J. Caumont and L. Sjaastad (1978) *La política Comercial y la Protección en Uruguay* (Montevideo: Banco Central de Uruguay).

Araujo Jr, José Tavares (1998) 'Os interesses brasileiros e a agenda da ALCA', *Revista Brasileira de Comércio Exterior*, No. 55, April–June, Funcex.

Arguello, R. (1999) 'Identification of Interests of the Andean Community and Its Member States in Preparation of the WTO Agricultural Negotiations: *Final Country Report*, Colombia' (Bogota: Universidad del Rosario-Institute of Development Studies), October.

Arriola, C. (1997) 'La ley de cámaras empresariales y sus confederaciones', *Foro Internacional*, Vol. 37, No. 4, October–December.
Banco Central (1997) 'Subsidios en el comercio internacional', *Indicadores de comercio exterior*, Febrero, Santiago de Chile.
Banco Central de la República del Peru (1998, 1999, 2000) *Memoria Annual* (Lima: BCRP).
Barbosa, Rubens A. and Luis F. Panelli César (1994) 'O Brasil como 'Global Trader' in Gelson Fonseca Júnior and Sergio H. Nabuco de Castro (eds), *Temas de Política Externa Brasileira II*, Vol. 1 (Sao Paulo: IPRI and Editora Paz e Terra).
Basco, C. *et al.* (2002) 'La Nueva Farm Bill: Ley de Seguridad Rural e Inversión de Estados Unidos, Un análisis de sus implicancias', *LATN Working Paper*, October, http://latn.org.ar
Bastos Tigre, Paulo (2003) 'The Interplay of Multilateral Agreements and Domestic Regulations in Telecommunications', in D. Tussie (ed.), *Trade/ Negotiations* in Latin America: Problems and Prospects (Basingstoke: Palgrave Macmillan).
Baumann, Renato (2001) 'Mercosul: orígenes, ganhos, desencontros e perspectivas' in Baumann, Renato (ed.), *Mercosul, Avanços e Desafios da Integração*, IPEA (Instituto de Pesquisa Econômica Aplicada), Brasilia.
——and Josefina Rivero and Yohana Zavattiero (1998) 'Tariffs and the Plano Real in Brazil' in *Cepal Review* No. 66, Santiago de Chile.
BCRP (Banco Central de Reserva del Peru) (1998, 1999, 2000, 2001) *Memoria Anual*, available at www.bcrp.gob.pe.
Bhagwati, J. (2002) 'The Poor's Best Hope', *The Economist*, 22–28 June.
Bittencourt, G. and R. Domingo (2001) 'El caso uruguayo' in D. Chudnosvsky (ed.), *El boom de Inversión Extranjera Directa en el Mercosur* (Buenos Aires: Siglo Veintiuno de Argentina Editores).
Blonigen, B. and T. Prusa (2001) 'Antidumping', *NBER Working Papers* 8398 (National Bureau of Economic Research, Inc).
——(1998) 'Para onde vai a estrutura industrial brasileira?', *Texto para Discussão* No. 540, IPEA), Rio de Janeiro, May.
——and Robson Gonçalves (1999) 'Padrões de desenvolvimento industrial no Brasil - 1980/95', *Texto para Discussão* No. 645, IPEA, Rio de Janeiro, May.
——(2000) *Ganhos de Produtividade na Economia Brasileira na Década de 1990: Um Retrato de Corpo Inteiro* (Sao Paulo: IPEA.).
Bonelli, Regis (2001) 'Políticas de competitividade industrial no Brasil–1995/2000', *Texto para Discussão* No. 810, IPEA, Rio de Janeiro, July (www.ipea.org)
Botto, M. (forthcoming) 'Conclusiones: La internacionalización del proceso de decisiones y el impacto en la agenda nacional' in D. Tussie and M. Botto (eds), *La Agenda de las Américas: ¿Una Nueva Dialéctica Público-Privado?* (Buenos Aires: FLACSO/Temas).
Botto, M., V. Delich and D. Tussie (2003) 'La lógica política de las negociaciones multilaterales: Implicaciones para la Argentina' in C. Bruno (ed.), *Argentina. Un Lugar en el Mundo* (Buenos Aires: Fondo de Cultura Económica).
Bouzas, R. and E. Avogadro (2001) 'The Private Sector and the Trade Policy-Making Process: The Case of Argentina', May. mimeo.
Brown, Jr, W. A. (1950) *The United States and the Restoration of World Trade (An Analysis and Appraisal of the ITO Charter and the General Agreement on Tariffs and Trade)*, (Washington, DC: The Brookings Institute).

Cáceres, A. (1989) 'Comercio internacional de servicios: una reflexión sobre la balanza de servicios no financieros del Perú: 1970–1988', *Grupo de Analasis para el Desarrollo (GRADE) Working Paper No.* 7 (Lima: GRADE) December.

Calderón, A. and S. Griffith-Jones (1995) 'Los flujos de capital extranjero en la economía chilena: renovado acceso y nuevos usos', ECLAC Working Paper, No. 37 (Santiago de Chile: ECLAC).

Cardoso, E. and A. Galal (2002) 'External Environment, Globalization and Reform', research proposal submitted to the Global Development Network, Project Understanding Reform, December (http://www.gdnet.org/).

Casacuberta, C. and M. Vaillant (2002) 'Trade and Wages in Uruguay in the Nineties', Working Paper 12, Economics Department, Facultdad de Ciencias Sociales, Montevideo, Uruguay, October.

CCS (Cámara de Comercio de Santiago) (1999) *Inversión Detectada de Empresas Chilenas en el Exterior 1990–1998*, (Santiago de Chile: CCS Editorial).

——(2000) *Estrategias Empresariales 2000–2001* (Santiago de Chile: CCS Editorial), available at www.ccs.cl

——(2002) *Comercio: Informe Económico Semanal – Análisis Sectorial*, Santiago, 28 February.

Centro de Economía Internacional (CEI) http://www.cei.gov.ar/html/estadistica.htm

Central Bank of Chile (1997) 'Subsidios en el comercio internacional', *Indicadores de comercio exterior* (Santiago de Chile: Banco Central), February.

Centro de Economía Internacional, Series estadísticas (2000) http://cei.mrecic.gov.ar

Changanaqui, F. and P. Messerlin (1994) *The Effects of Protectionism on a Small Country: The Case of Uruguay* (Washington, DC: World Bank).

Charny, David (2000) 'Regulatory Competition and the Global Coordination of Labor Standars', *Journal of International Economic Law*, Vol. III, Issue 2.

Chudnovsky, D., B. Kosakoff and A. López (1999) *Las Multinacionales Latinoamericanas: Sus Estrategias en un Mundo Globalizado* (Buenos Aires: Fondo de Cultura Económica).

——and A. López (2003) 'Policy Competition for Foreign Direct Investment' in D. Tussie (ed.), *Trade Negotiations in Latin America: Problems and Prospects* (New York: Palgrave Macmillan).

CIE (Comité de Inversiones Extranjeras) (2000) *Trayectoria de la Inversión Extranjera en Chile 1974–1999* (Santiago de Chile: CIE Vicepresidencia Ejecutiva).

CNCE (Comisión Nacional de Comercio Exterior) (1999, 2000) *Informe Anual* (Buenos Aires: CNCE).

Coeymans, J.E. and F. Larraín (1992) *Impacto de un acuerdo de Libre Comercio entre Chile y los Estados Unidos: Un Enfoque de Equilibrio General* (Santiago de Chile: PEPALC – Confederación de la Producción y el Comercio).

Connolly, M. and J. De-Melo (1994) *The Effects of Protectionism on a Small Country, the Case of Uruguay* (Washington, DC: World Bank Regional and Sectoral Studies).

DANE (Colombian National Administrative Department of Statistics) (2002) 'Colombia, balanza comercial según grupos económicos y principales países: 1994–2001', available at http://www.dane.gov.co/Informacion_Estadistica/Estadisticas/Comercio_Exterior/Balanza_Comercial/balanza_comercial.html consulted 20 February 2002.

David P. (1985) 'Clio and the Economics of QWERTY', *American Economic Review*, Vol. 75, No. 2 (Papers and Proceedings), pp. 332–7.

De Remes, A., T. Fitzpatrick and A. Ortiz Mena L. N. (1996), 'NAFTA and the Automotive Industry,' in V. Whiting, Jr. (ed.), *Regionalization in the World Economy: NAFTA, the Americas and Asia Pacific* (New Delhi: Macmillan Press).

Díaz, Alvaro (1995), *La industria Chilena entre 1970–94: De la Sustitución de Importación a la Segunda Fase Exportadora*, LC/R.1535. (Santiago de Chile: CEPAL/CIID (CAN)), June.

——and J. Ramos (1998), 'Apertura y competitividad,' in R. Cortázar y J. Vial (eds.), *Construyendo Opciones. Propuestas Económicas y Sociales para el Cambio de Siglo* (Santiago de Chile: CIEPLAN-DOLMEN).

Díaz-Henderson, M. (2003) 'The Negotiations on Agriculture: the Regional-Multilateral Relationship,' in D. Tussie (ed.), *Trade Negotiations in Latin America. Problems and Prospects* (New York: Palgrave Macmillan).

——(1998) *Relaciones Económicas Internacionales de Chile*, Estudio No. 1, (Santiago: Ministerio de Relaciones Exteriores), September.

——(1999) *Chile frente a la Ronda del Milenio* (Santiago de Chile: DIRECON) November.

Direcon (Dirección de Relaciones Económicas Internacionales) (2000) *Relaciones Económicas Internacionales de Chile 1994–2000* (Santiago de Chile: DIRECON Dirección de Estudios), February.

Dixit, A. K. (1996) *The Making of Economic Policy: A Transaction-Cost Politics Perspective* (Cambridge, Mass.: MIT Press).

Drache, D. and M. Froese (2002) 'One World, One System?.: The Diversity Deficits in Standard Setting, Development and Sovereignty at the WTO. A Report Card on Trade and the Social Deficit', Robarts Centre Research Papers (Toronto: York University).

Echavarría, J. J. (1998) 'Trade Flows in the Andean Countries: Unilateral Liberalization or Regional Preferences?' in S. J. Burki, G. Perry and S. Calvo (eds), *Trade: Towards Open Regionalism* (Washington, DC: IADB/World Bank).

——(2000) 'Colombia en la década de los 90s: neoliberalismo y reformas estructurales en el trópico', *Coyuntura Económica*, September.

——L. Zuleta and S. Zuluaga (1999) 'Impacto sectorial de la integración andina: el caso del sector textil-confección' (Bogota: Fedesarrollo), mimeo.

ECLAC (Economic Commission for Latin America and the Caribbean) (1994) *El Regionalismo Abierto en América Latina y El Caribe* (Santiago de Chile: ECLAC).

——(1998) 'Foreign investment in Latin America and the Caribbean 1998', LC/G.2042-P, United Nations Publication, Sales No. E.98.II.G.14 (Santiago de Chile: United Nations).

——(2000) 'Foreign investment in Latin America and the Caribbean 1999', LC/G. 2061-P, United Nations Publication, Sales No. E.00.II.G.4 (Santiago de Chile: United Nations).

——(2001a) 'Latin America and the Caribbean in the World Economy 1999–2000', LC/G.2085-P, United Nations Publication, Sales No. E.00.II.G.17 (Santiago de Chile: United Nations).

——(2001b) 'Foreign investment in Latin America and the Caribbean 2000', LC/G.2125-P, United Nations Publication, Sales No. E.01.II.G.12 (Santiago de Chile: United Nations).

——(2002a) 'The Chilean Strategy of Trade Liberalization and Market Access' (Santiago de Chile: ECLAC International Trade and Integration Division), March, Draft.

——(2002b) 'Latin America and the Caribbean in the World Economy 2000–2001', LC/G.2149-P, United Nations Publication, Sales No. E.02.II.G.6 (Santiago de Chile: United Nations).

Edwards, S. (1995) *Crisis and Reform in Latin America: From Despair to Hope* (New York, NY: Oxford University Press).

——and D. Lederman (1998) 'The Political Economy of Unilateral Trade Liberalization: The Case of Chile', *NBER Working Paper Series* No. 6510 (Cambridge, MA: NBER) April.

EU (European Union) (n.d.), 'Market Access and Trade Barriers Database', available at http://mkaccdb.eu.int, consulted 1 March 2002.

Evans, P., H. Jacobson and R. Putnam (1993) *Double-Edged Diplomacy: International Bargaining and Domestic Politics* (Berkeley, CA: University of California Press).

——(1996) 'Government Action, Social Capital and Development: Reviewing the Evidence on Synergy', *World Development,* Vol. 24, No. 6.

——(1997) 'Introduction: Development Strategies across the Public-Private Divide,' in P. Evans (ed.), *State-Society Sinergy: Government and Social Capital in Development* (Los Angeles: University of California Press).

Fanelli, J. (2000) 'Macroeconomic Regimes and the Trade Agenda in Latin America', *Latin American Trade Network (LATN) Working Paper,* No. 9 (Buenos Aires: LATN) July.

Feinberg, Ricahrd E. (1997) *Summitry in the Americas – A Progress Report,* (Washington, DC: Instittute for International Economics) April.

Ffrench-Davis, R. (1999) *Entre el Neoliberalismo y el Crecimiento con Equidad: Tres Décadas de Política Económica en Chile* (Santiago de Chile: Dolmen Ediciones).

——*et al.* (1992) 'Liberalización comercial y crecimiento: la experiencia de Chile 1973–1989', *Pensamiento Iberoamericano,* No. 21.

Finger, M., M. Ingco and U. Reincke (1996) 'The Uruguay Round: Statistics on Tariff Concessions Given and Received' (Washington, DC: The World Bank).

——and Julio Nogués (2000), 'WTO Negotiations and the Domestic Politics of Protection and Reform', presented at the CEPR/ECARES/World Bank Conference on The World Trading System Post-Seattle: Institutional Design, Governance and Ownership, Brussels, 14–15 July.

Finger, Michael (2001) 'Implementing the Uruguay Round Agreements: Problems for Developing Countries', World, 24(9), September.

——(2002) 'The Unbalanced Uruguay Round Outcome: The New Areas in Future WTO Negotiations', *The World Economy,* Vol. 25, No. 3, March.

——and Ludger Schuknecht (1999), 'Market Access Advances and Retreats since the Uruguay Round Agreement', presented at the Annual World Bank Conference on Development Economics, Washington, DC, 29–30 April.

——and Philipe Schuler (2000) 'Implementation of Uruguay Round Commitments: The Development Challenge', *The World Economy,* Vol. 23, No. 4, April.

Fischer, R. (ed.) (1997) *Las Nuevas Caras del Proteccionismo* (Santiago de Chile: Dolmen-CEA).

Fonseca, R., Carvalho Jr, M. and Pourchet, H. (1998) *A Orientação Externa da Indústria de Transformação Brasileira após a Liberalização Comercial* (Sao Paulo: Funcex (Fundação Centro de Estudos do Comércio Exterior)), April.

Forteza, A. (coordinator), D. Buquet, J. Lanzaro, A. Pereyra, E. Siandra and M. Vaillant (2003) 'Understanding Reform: the Uruguayan Case', research proposal submitted to 'Global Development Network, Project Understanding Reform, February (http://www.gdnet.org/).

Frieden, J. (1991) 'Invested Interests: The Politics of National Economic Policies in a World of Global Finance', *International Organization,* Vol. 45, No. 4, autumn.

Garrido, C. and W. Peres Núñez (1998) 'Grandes empresas y grupos industriales latinoamericanos', *Revista de la Cepal* No. 66 (Santiago de Chile: ECLAC), December.

Glover, David and Diana Tussie (1993) *The Developing Countries in World Trade: Policies and Bargaining Strategy* (Boulder: Lynne Reinner Publishers).

Goldstein, A. and S. M. McGuire (2002) 'The Political Economy of Strategic Trade Policy: Explaining the Brazil–Canada Export Subsidies Saga', mimeo.

Goldstein, J. and J. Gowa, (2002) 'US National Power and the Post-War Trading Regime', *World Trade Review*, Vol. 1(2).

——L. L. Martin (2000) 'Legalization, Trade Liberalization, and Domestic Politics: A Cautionary Note', *International Organization*, Vol. 54, No. 3.

——M. Kahler, R. O. Keohane and A.-M. Slaughter (2000) 'Introduction: Legalization and World Politics', *International Organization*, Vol. 54, No. 3.

Grey, Rodney de C. (1982) 'The General Agreement After the Tokyo Round', in Quiun, John and Philip Slaytou (eds), *Non-Tariff Barriers After the Tokyo Round*, Institute for Research on Public Policy, Montreal.

Guash, L. and S. Rajapatirana (1998) 'Total Strangers or Soul Mates?: Anti-dumping and Competition Policies in Latin America and the Caribbean', *World Bank Policy Research Working Paper*, No. 1958, August.

Hay, D. (1997) 'The post 1990 Brazilian trade liberalization and the performance of large manufacturing firms: productivity, market share and profits', *Texto de Discussão* No. 523, IPEA, Rio de Janeiro.

Henson, S., K. Preibisch and O. Masakure (2001) 'Review of Developing Countries Needs and Involvement in International Standards-Setting Bodies' (www.dfid.gov.uk).

Hirschman, A. (1970) *Exit, Voice and Loyalty: Responses to Decline in Firms, Organizations and States* (Cambridge, Mass.: Harvard University Press).

——(1973) Desar*rollo y América Latina: Obstinación por la Esperanza* (Mexico City: Fondo de Cultura Económica).

Hodara, I. (2000) 'Una nueva ronda en la OMC ¿Interesa a la industria uruguaya?', *Camara de Industrias de Uruguay, Interest Document*, available at http://www.ciu.com.uy

Hoekman, B. (1995) 'Trade Laws and Institutions: Good Practices and the World Trade Organization', presented at the Seminar on The Uruguay Round and the Developing Countries, World Bank (International Trade Division), Geneva, 26–27 January 1995.

——(2002) 'Strengthening the Global Architecture for Development' (Santiago de Chile: ECLAC/World Bank).

Hommes, R., A. Montenegro and P. Roda (1994) *Una Apertura hacia el Futuro: Balance Económico 1990–94* (Bogota: National Department of Planning), September.

Hufbauer, G. C. and J. Schott (1993) *NAFTA: An Assessment, Revised Edition* (Washington, DC: Institute for International Economics).

Hurrell, A. (1995) 'Explaining the Resurgence of Regionalism in World Politics', *Review of International Studies*, 21.

IEDI (Instituto de Estudos para o Desenvolvimento Industrial) (2000) 'Abertura, política cambial e comércio exterior – Lições dos anos 90 e pontos de uma agenda para a próxima década', August.

IERAL (Institute for Latin American Reality Studies) (2001) *La Inserción de la Argentina en la Economía Global* (Buenos Aires: IERAL).

IMF/The World Bank (2002) 'Market Access for Developing Country Exports – Selected Issues', Washington, DC, mimeo.

INDEC (Instituto Nacional de Estadísticas y Censos) (n.d.), various periodic publications.

Integration and Trade Steering Committee (1998) 'Export Promotion as a Key Element of Development Strategy', *Integration & Trade*, Vol. 2, No. 4/5, January/August.

Jordana, J. and C. Ramió (2002) 'Diseños institucionales y gestión de la política comercial exterior en América Latina', *INTAL-ITD-STA, Documento de Divulgación* 15, June.

Josling, Thimoty, Stefan Tangermann and T. Warley (1996) *Agriculture in the GATT* (New York: St Martin's Press).

Kahler, M. (1997) 'Liberalization as Foreign Policy Determinant and Goal' in M. Kahler (ed.), *Liberalization and Foreign Policy* (New York, NY: Columbia University Press).

Keohane, R. O. (1984) *After Hegemony (Cooperation and Discord in the World Political Economy)* (Princeton, NJ: Princeton University Press), 1984.

Krugman, P. (1992) 'Does the New Trade Theory Require a New Trade Policy?', *The World Economy*, Vol. 15, No. 4, July.

——(1997), 'What Should Trade Negotiators Negotiate About?', *Journal of Economic Literature*, Vol. XXXV, March.

Kheir-El-Din, H. (2002) 'Implementing the Agreement on Textiles and Clothing' in B. Hoekman, A, Mattoo and P. English (eds), *Development, Trade and the WTO: A Handbook* (Washington, DC: The World Bank).

Kume, Honorio (1996) 'A politica de importação no Plano Real e a estrutiva de proteção efetiva', *Texto para Discussão*, No. 423, IPEA, Rio de Janeiro, May.

Kupfer, D., J. Ferraz, L. Haguenauer, P. da Motta Veiga, J. N. Brito and M. Lootty (1998) 'Padrões de especialização, comportamento dos agentes e desenvolvimento de capacidades técnico-produtivas: avaliação dos efeitos da abertura na industrialização latino-americana. O caso brasileiro' (Rio de Janeiro: Instituto de Economia–Universidade Federal de Rio de Janeiro).

Krugman, P. (1992) 'Does the New Trade Theory Require a New Trade Policy?', *The World Economy*, Vol. 15, No. 4, July.

Laens, S. (1998) 'Apertura comercial e integración: Reflexiones a partir de la experiencia uruguaya' in D. Borda and F. Masi (eds), *Estabilización y Ajuste de las Economías del Mercosur* (Asunción: Centro de Análisis y Difusión de Economía Paraguaya (CADEP)).

Lacerda, A. Corrêa de (2000) 'Notas sobre a característica e o perfil do fluxo recente de investimentos directos estrangeiros na economia brasileira' in P. da Motta Veiga (ed.), *O Brasil e os Desafios da Globalização*, (Rio de Janeiro: SOBEET–Relume–Dumara).

Langebaek A. (2002) 'The Role of the Colombian Private Sector in Making External trade Policy' in S. Ostry (ed.), *The Trade Policy-Making Process: Level One of the Two Level Game: Country Studies in the Western Hemisphere*, Occasional Paper 13 (Buenos Aires: INTAL-ITD-STA).

Latin Focus (2002), 'Argentine Trade Balance, 1995–2002', available at http://www.latin-focus.com/countries/argentina/argentina.htm, consulted 20 March 2002.

Lengyel, M. (2000) *La Organización Moderna: Más Allá del Fordismo* (Buenos Aires: Mercado/Editorial Coyuntura).

——and D. Tussie (1998) 'Compromisos en la Organización Mundial de Comercio sobre promoción de Exportaciones', *Integración & Comercio*, Nos 4/5, January–August.

López Ayllon, S. (1997) *Las Transformaciones del Sistema Jurídico y los Significados Sociales del Derecho en México* (Mexico, DF: Universidad Nacional Autónoma de México).

Luna, M. (1995) 'Entrepreneurial interests and political action in Mexico: Facing the demands of economic modernization' in R. Roett (ed.), *The Challenge of Institutional Reform in Mexico* (Boulder, CO: Lynne Rienner).

Lustig, N. (1992) *Mexico: The Remaking of an Economy* (Washington, DC: Brookings Institute).

Maskus, K. (2000) *Intellectual Property Rights in the Global Economy* (Washington, DC: Institute for International Economics).

McDermott, G. (2000) 'Reinventing Federalism: Governing Decentralized Institutional Experiments in Latin America', policy paper for the Finance, Private Sector and Infrastructure Division, World Bank.

——(1993) 'Economía política de la apertura comercial chilena', *CEPAL Serie Reformas de Política Pública,* No. 5 (Santiago de Chile: ECLAC), April.

Meller, P. (ed.) (1996a) *Un siglo de Economía Política Chilena (1890–1990)* (Santiago de Chile: Editorial Andrés Bello), November.

——(1996b) 'La segunda fase exportadora chilena: elementos para el debate', Proyecto ECLAC/PNUD RLA/88/039, March.

Michalopoulos, C. (1999a), 'Trade Policy and Market Access Issues for Developing Countries', World Bank, mimeo.

——(1999b), 'The Developing Countries in the WTO', *The World Economy,* Vol. 22, No. 1, January.

Ministerio de Economía (1998) *Plan de Desarrollo de la Competitividad – Chile 1998–2003 (Propuesta)* (Santiago de Chile: Ministerio de Economía), January.

Miranda, J. C. (2001) 'Abertura comercial, reestruturação industrial e exportações brasileiras na década de 1990', *Texto para Discussão,* No. 829, IPEA, Brasilia, October.

Moguillansky, G. (1999) *La Inversión en Chile: ¿El Fin de un Ciclo en Expansión?* (Santiago de Chile: FCE-ECLAC).

Montero, C. (1997) 'Relaciones Estado – empresarios en una economía global: El caso de Chile', *Nueva Sociedad,* No. 151, September–October.

——and J. Federici (1997) 'La inserción comercial de Chile en el mundo: un caso de cooperación entre empresarios y gobierno', Santiago, August. Mimeo.

Moreira, Mauricio M. and Paulo Guilherme Correa (1997) 'Abertura comercial e indústria: o que se pode esperar e o que se vem obtendo', *Revista de Economia Política,* vol. 17, No. 2, April–June.

Mortimore, M. and W. Peres (2001) 'La competitividad empresarial en América Latina y el Caribe', *Revista de la CEPAL,* No. 74 (Santiago de Chile: ECLAC).

Motta Veiga, Pedro da (2000) 'As transformações na indústria nos anos 90 e o desempenho das exportações' in Motta Veiga, P. (ed.), *O Brasil e os Desafios da Globalização,* (Rio de Janeiro: Ed. Relume-Dumará).

——(2003) 'Unfolding Scenarios' in D. Tussie (ed.), *Trade Negotiations in Latin America. Problems and Prospects* (New York: Palgrave Macmillan).

——and Roberto M. Iglesias (2002) 'A institucionalidade da política brasileira de comércio exterior' (Preliminary report), FUNCEX, February.

——R. Marwald and F. Correia (1999) *Avaliação do Desempenho das Exportações Brasileiras para os EUA no Período 1990/1998,* prepared for INMETRO/MDIC, June.

——(1997) *Policy Competition and Foreign Direct Investment in Brazil* (Paris: OECD Development Center), December.

Naim, M. (1993) *Paper Tigers and Minotaurs: The Politics of Venezuela's Economic Reforms* (Washington, DC: Carnegie Endowment for International Peace).

Narlikar, A. and N. Woods (2003) 'Sectoral Coalitions: The Case of Services' in D. Tussie (ed.), *Trade Negotiations in Latin America. Problems and Prospects* (New York: Palgrave Macmillan).

Nattino, E. (1990) 'Política antidumping o aranceles diferenciales', *Uruguayan Ministry of Foreign Affairs Discussion Paper* (Montivedeo: Ministry of Foreign Affairs).

Nogués, J. (2002) 'Argentina and the WTO: Economic Consequences of Weak Negotiating Strategies', mimeo.

——(2003) 'Argentina and the WTO: Economic Consequences of Weak Negotiating Strategies', *Kluwer Handbook on the WTO*.

OECD (Organization for Economic Cooperation and Development) (1996) *Trade Liberalisation Policies in Mexico* (Paris: OECD).

——(2001) *OECD Economic Surveys, 2000–2001, Brazil* (Paris: OECD).

Olarrega, M. and F. NG (2002) 'Tariff Peaks and Preferences' in B. Hoekman, A, Mattoo and P. English (eds), *Development, Trade and the WTO: A Handbook* (Washington, DC: The World Bank).

Oppenheim, L. (1997) 'Chile's export-oriented development strategy in the new global order and the legacies of neoliberalism', presented at the International Political Science Association, Seoul, August.

Ostry, S. (1997) *The Post-Cold War Trading System (Who's on First?)* (Chicago: Chicago University Press).

Ostry, S. (2002) 'Preface', in S. Ostry (ed.), *The Trade Policy-Making Process: Level One of the Two Level Game: Country Studies in the Western Hemisphere* (Buenos Aires: INTAL–ITD–STA), pp. i–iv.

Ostry, Sylvia (ed.) (2002) *The Trade Policy-Making Process: Level One of the Two Level Game: Country Studies in the Western Hemisphere*, Occasional Paper 13, (Buenos Aires: INTAL–ITD–STA).

Oyejide, A. (2002) 'Special and Differential Treatment' in B. Hoekman, A, Mattoo and P. English (eds), *Development, Trade and the WTO: A Handbook* (Washington, DC: The World Bank).

Paiva Abreu, M. de (2003) 'Latin American and Caribbean Interests in the WTO' in D. Tussie (ed.), *Trade Negotiations in Latin America: Problems and Prospects* (New York: Palgrave Macmillan).

Panagariya, A. (2001) 'Developing Countries at Doha: A Political Economy Analysis', University of Maryland, mimeo.

Phillips, N. (2003) 'Hemispheric Integration and Subregionalism in the Americas', *International Affairs*, 79:2, March.

Pietrobelli, C. (1993) 'El proceso de diversificación de exportaciones en Chile', in *La Transformación de la Producción en Chile: Cuatro Ensayos de Interpretación* (Santiago de Chile: ECLAC).

Pizarro, R. (1994) *Contenido y Significación Económica de los Acuerdos de Complementación Económica de Libre Comercio* (Santiago de Chile: Dirección Económica del Ministerio de Relaciones Exteriores), February, mimeo.

Prats, J. (2000) 'Reforma del estado y desarrollo humano en América Latina', *Quórum: Revista de Pensamiento Iberoamericano*.

Prieto, F. (1999) *Chile y el GATS 2000, Hacia la Liberalización Efectiva del Comercio de Servicios: Propuestas para la Acción* (Santiago de Chile: DIRECON) December.

——(2000) 'Encuentro exportador 2000. Juntos en la nueva economía', presented at Encuentro Exportador 2000, Santiago, 28–9 August.

PROCHILE (2002) 'Análisis de las exportaciones chilenas', available at http://www.prochile.cl/documentos/anuaria_2001.pdf.

Putnam, R. (1988) 'Diplomacy and Domestic Politics: The Logic of Two-Level Games', *International Organization*, Vol. 42, Summer.

Putnam, Robert D. (1993) 'Diplomacy and Domestic Policies: The Logic of Two-Level Games', in P. Evans, H. K. Jacobson and R. D. Putnam (eds), *Double Edged Diplomacy: International Bargaining and Domestic Politics* (Berkeley and Los Angeles California: University of California Press).

Rajapatirana, S. (1998a) 'Colombia and the Andean Group: Choices and challenges', mimeo.

——(1998b) 'Colombian prade Policies and the 1996 WTO Trade Policy Review', mimeo.

——(1999) 'Venezuela: The evolving trade regime and integration choices', mimeo.

Reddy, S. and C. Sabel (2002) 'Learning to Learn: Undoing the Gordian Knot of Development Today', mimeo.

Robledo, M. (1997) 'Sector privado, política exterior y estrategia de inserción económica internacional' in P. Milet *et al.* (eds), *Chile – MERCOSUR: Una Alianza Estratégica* (Santiago de Chile: Ed. Los Andes – FLACSO).

Rodrick, D. (2001) 'The Global Governance of Trade as if Development Really Mattered' (Geneva: UNDP).

Rosales, O. (1993) 'Desafíos de la segunda fase exportadora', *Corporación Tiempo 2000/PEP Working Paper*, No. 21, Santiago, October.

Rossini, R. (1991) 'Liberalización comercial y estabilización económica', presented at Liberalización del Comercio Exterior en el Perú, Fundación Freidrich Ebert, 3rd Economic Forum, Lima.

Ruggie, J. G. (1982) 'International Regimes, Transactions, and Change: Embedded Liberalism in the Postwar Economic Order', *International Organization*, Vol. 36, No. 2.

Sabel, C. (1994) 'Learning by Monitoring: The Institutions of Economic Development' in J. Smelser and R. Swedberg (eds), *The Handbook of Economic Sociology* (Princeton: Princeton University Press).

——(1996) *Local Partnerships and Social innovation: Ireland* (Dublin: OECD).

——D. O'Rourke and A. Fung (1999) 'Open Labor Standards: Towards a System of Rolling Rule Regulation of Labor Practices', presented at the Annual Meetings of the World Bank Seminars on Labor Standards, Washington, DC, 28 September.

Sáez, S. (1999) *Estrategia y Negociación en el Sistema Multilateral: Economía Internacional Aplicada*; (Santiago de Chile: Dolmen Ediciones).

——and J. G. Valdés (1999) 'Chile y su política comercial "lateral"', *Revista de la CEPAL*, No. 67, April.

Schelling, T. C. (1960) *The Strategy of Conflict* (Oxford: Oxford University Press).

Schott, J. and J. Watal (2000) 'Decision-making in the WTO', *International Economics Policy Briefs*, 2 March.

——and J. Buurman (1994) *The Uruguay Round: An Assessment*, (Washington, DC: Institute for International Economics).

SECOFI (Secretaría de Comercio y Fomento Industrial) (1999) 'Reunión Ministerial de Seattle y la posibilidad de una nueva ronda de negociaciones', Powerpoint presentation.

SELA (Sistema Económico Latinoamericano) (2000) 'Intereses y opciones para América Latina y el Caribe en las negociaciones agrícolas de la Organización Mundial de Comercio', SP/CL/XXXVI.O/Di No 7–2000 (Caracas: SELA) October.

SFF (Sociedad de Fomento Fabril) (1998) *Memoria Anual 1997/98* (Santiago de Chile: SFF)

SHCP (Secretaría de Hacienda y Crédito Público) (n.d.), 'Balanza comercial acumulada', available at http://www.shcp.gob.mx consulted 15 March 2002.

Silva, V. (2001) 'Estrategia y agenda comercial chilena en los años noventa', *Serie Comercio Internacional*, No. 11, LC/L.1550-P (Santiago de Chile: ECLAC), June.

——(2000) 'Politica comercial y relación publico-privada en Chile durante los noventa', in O. Muñoz *et al.* (eds), *El Estado y el Sector Privado: Construyendo una Nueva Economía en los Años 90* (Santiago de Chile: DOLMEN-FLACSO) April.

Talberg, J. (2002) 'Paths to Compliance: Enforcement, Management, and the European Union', *International Organization*, Vol. 56, No. 3, Summer.

Tendler, J. (1997) *Good Governance in the Tropics* (Baltimore: John Hopkins University).

The Economist (2002) 'Intellectual Property and the Poor', 12 September.

Tórtora, M. (2002) 'Special and Differential Treatment in the Multilateral Trade Negotiations: The Skeleton in the Closet', presented at the Fourth Plenary Meeting of the Latin American Trade Network (LATN), Santiago de Chile, 12–13 December.

——and D. Tussie (2003) 'Commercial Defense Policy: Issues at Stake', in D. Tussie (ed.), *Trade Negotiations in Latin America. Problems and Prospects* (New York: Palgrave Macmillan).

——(1987) *The LDCs and the World Trading System: A Challenge to the GATT* (London: Frances Pinter and St Martin's Press).

Tussie, D. (1993a) 'Bargaining at a Crossroads: Argentina' in Tussie, D. and D. Glover (eds), *The Developing Countries in World Trade. Policies and Bargaining Strategies* (London, Lynne Rienner Publishers).

——(1993b) 'The Uruguay Round and the Trading System in the Balance: Dilemmas for Developing Countries' in M. Agosin and D. Tussie (eds), *Trade and Growth (New Dilemmas in Trade Policy)* (New York: St Martin's Press), pp. 69–88.

——(ed.) (2003) 'Introduction: On Shifting Ground – the Crossroads of Regional and Sectoral Associations' in D. Tussie (ed.), *Trade Negotiations in Latin America: Problems and Prospects* (New York: Palgrave).

——and D. Glover (1993) *The Developing Countries in World Trade: Policies and Bargaining Strategies* (Boulder, Col.: Lynne Rienner).

——and M. Lengyel (1998) 'WTO Commitments on Export Promotion', *Latin American Trade Network (LATN) Working Paper*, No. 1 (Buenos Aires: LATN), November.

——and M. Lengyel (2002) 'Developing Countries: Turning Participation into Influence' in B. Hoekman, A, Mattoo and P. English (eds), *Development, Trade and the WTO: A Handbook* (Washington, DC: The World Bank).

UNCTAD (2000) *Positive Agenda and Future Trade Negotiations*, (New York: UNCTAD).

——(2002) *Back to Basics: Market Access Issues in the Doha Agenda* (New York: UNCTAD).

Unidad de Prácticas Comerciales Internacionales, Annual Report, various years.

UPCI (Unidad de Prácticas Comerciales Internacionales) (n.d.) 'Resultados de la UPCI', available at http://www.upci.gob.mx, consulted 01 March 2002.

Vaillant, M. (1992) 'Inserción internacional, competitividad y tecnología', in *Proyecto Regional: Competitividad, Políticas Tecnológicas e Innovación Industrial* (Montevideo: ECLAC).

——(1995) 'El GATT 94 y la Organización Mundial del Comercio: una nueva agenda para el Uruguay', *ECLAC Discussion Paper* (Montevideo: ECLAC) LC/MVD/R. 125 Rev. 1.

——(2000) 'Limits to Trade Liberalisation: A Political Economy Approach', Ph.d. thesis (Belgium: University of Antwerpen (UFSIA)).

Vaillant M. and A. Nin (2002) 'International Coalitions for Agriculture Trade Liberalization', in Paolo Giordano (ed.), An Integrated Approach to the European Union – MERCOSUR Association, Chaire Mercosur de Sciences Po, Ed. Science Po, Paris.

Van Klaveren, A. (1998) 'Inserción Internacional de Chile' in C. Toloza and E. Lahera (eds), *Chile en los Noventa* (Santiago de Chile: Presidencia de la República–DOLMEN Ediciones).

Vega, J. (1997) 'Foreign Trade Policy and Economic Integration Policy in Peru: Analysis of a Dilemma' in A.J. Jatar and S. Weintraub (eds), *Integrating the Hemisphere: Perspectives from Latin America and the Caribbean* (Washington, DC: Inter American Dialogue).

Weston, A. and V. Delich (2003) 'Settling Disputes' in Diana Tussie (ed.), *Trade Negotiations in Latin America: Problems and Prospects* (New York: Palgrave).

Wilson, J. S.(2001) 'Bridging the Standards Divide: Recommendations for Reform from a Development Perspective', World Bank, mimeo.

Windham, G. R. (1986) *International Trade and the Tokyo Round Negotiation* (Princeton, N J: Priinceton University Press).

Wise, C. (2000) 'Introduction: Debates, Performance, and the Politics of Policy Choice' in C. Wise and R. Roett (eds), *Exchange Rate Politics in Latin America*, (Washington, DC: Brookings Institution Press).

Wonnacott, R. (1991) *The Economics of Overlapping Free Trade Areas and the Mexican Challenge* (Toronto and Washington, DC: Howe Institute and The National Planning Association).

Woods, N. (2000) *The Political Economy of Globalization* (Hampshire and London: Macmillan Press – now Palgrave Macmillan).

World Bank (2001) *Global Economic Prospects and the Developing Countries: Making Trade Work for the World's Poor* (Washington, DC: World Bank).

World Development, Special Issue, Vol. 24, No. 6 (1996).

WTO (2002) *Trade Policy Review: Mexico 2002* (Geneva: WTO).

WTO (1996a) *Trade Policy Review: Brazil* (Geneva: WTO).

WTO (1996b) *Trade Policy Review: Venezuela* (Geneva: WTO).

WTO (1997) *Trade Policy Review: Chile* (Geneva: WTO).

WTO (1998a) *Trade Policy Review: Mexico 1997* (Geneva: WTO).

WTO (1998b) *Trade Policy Review: Uruguay* (Geneva: WTO).

WTO (1999a), 'Preparations for the 1999 Ministerial Conference. Proposal on Protection of the Intellectual Property Rights Relating to the Traditional Knowledge of Local and Indigenous Communities', WT/GC/W/362 (Geneva: WTO), October.

WTO (1999b) 'Preparations for the 1999 Ministerial Conference. Proposals Regarding the TRIPS Agreement', WT/GC/W/282 (Geneva: WTO), August.

WTO (2000), *Trade Policy Review: Peru* (Geneva: WTO).

WTO (2001a) 'Statement by H. E. Mr Gonzalo Enrique Gonzalez Fernandez, Doha Ministerial Conference', WT/MIN (01)/ST/35 (Geneva: WTO), 10 November.

WTO (2001b) 'Statement by Uruguay, Seventh Special Session of the Committee on Agriculture', G/AG/NG/W/148 (Geneva: WTO), 4 April.

WTO (2001c) 'Peru: Statement at Doha Ministerial Conference', WT/MIN (01)/ST/130 (Geneva: WTO), 12 November.

Yarbrough, B. V. and R. M. Yarbrough (1992) *Cooperation and Governance in International Trade: The Strategic Organizational Approach* (Princeton, New Jersey: Princeton University Press).

Index